Praise for *There Shall Be No Needy: Pursuing Social Justice through Jewish Law and Tradition*

"What a pleasure to read Rabbi Jill Jacobs and to discover an exciting new voice addressing enduring and timely questions of Judaism and social justice. Jacobs brings a perspective honed through personal experience as an activist coupled with deep love and respect for traditional Jewish texts. Through her we hear an authentic American Jewish response to the challenges of poverty, inequality, and injustice."

—Deborah Dash Moore, editor, *American Jewish Identity Politics*

"A spectacular *tour de force*! Weaving her insightful reading of traditional Jewish texts with her real-world experience as an activist, Rabbi Jill Jacobs presents deeply felt recommendations to shape American public policy toward the crucial issues of the day: poverty, worker's rights, homelessness, health care, crime, and the environment. Must reading for every synagogue board member, communal leader, and community organizer in America, beginning with President Obama!"

—Dr. Ron Wolfson, president, Synagogue 3000;
Fingerhut Professor of Education, American Jewish University;
author, *God's To-Do List: 103 Ways to Be an Angel and Do God's Work on Earth*

"A wonderful resource for anyone seeking both breadth and depth of Jewish teachings on social and economic justice. Rabbi Jacobs brings a nuanced, honest appraisal of Jewish text and tradition to her subject, and in so doing provides new paradigms for wrestling with the most contentious issues facing American society today, from eradicating poverty to the health care crisis to the failures of the criminal justice system. *There Shall Be No Needy* marks a significant step forward in the formation of a uniquely Jewish contribution to American public policy debates."

—Rabbi Toba Spitzer, Congregation Dorshei Tzedek,
Newton, Massachusetts; former president,
Reconstructionist Rabbinical Association

"By using and explaining the mandates and definitions of Jewish law, historical analyses, the messages of *midrash*, and the stories of her own life, Rabbi Jacobs takes the reader on an honest journey through the Jewish pathways for dealing with some of the most important social justice issues of our time. One does not need to be a scholar to appreciate her book. This is a must-read for Jews and non-Jews seeking to understand the foundation of the Jewish drive to repair this broken world."

—Steve Gutow, executive director, Jewish Council for Public Affairs

"Jill Jacobs is a welcome new voice to the field of Jewish social justice. Her impressive knowledge of Jewish texts and her familiarity with social policy make her book an important contribution to the debate on what Judaism has to say about the most important public issues of our day."

—Rabbi Sidney Schwarz, author, *Judaism and Justice:*
The Jewish Passion to Repair the World; founder and president,
PANIM: The Institute for Jewish Leadership and Values

"Rabbi Jill Jacobs is one of the most gifted Jewish thinkers and activists of our generation. *There Shall Be No Needy* is a vital contribution to the burgeoning field of contemporary religious writings on issues of social justice and environmental responsibility. This book is a must-read for all concerned with the future of Judaism and its role in the healing of the world."

—Rabbi Or N. Rose, director, Interfaith &
Social Justice Initiatives, Hebrew College;
coeditor, *Righteous Indignation: A Jewish Call for Justice*

"What Jim Wallis, Tony Campolo, Ron Sider, Alexia Kelley, Chuck Collins, and others have done for Christian readers, Rabbi Jill Jacobs is doing for Jewish readers: helping them apply the rich resources of their faith tradition to today's issues of justice and compassion in our world. Christians, Muslims, and others will benefit as well from this beautifully written, solidly researched, and eminently accessible book. It models a humble yet passionate approach to anyone seeking to do justice and love kindness as they walk humbly with our Creator."

—Brian McLaren, author/speaker/activist (brianmclaren.net);
author, *Everything Must Change*

"A clear and courageous call to speak from our sources and bring an unabashedly Jewish voice to today's most critical issues of justice."

—Rabbi Jennie Rosenn, program director,
Jewish Life and Values, the Nathan Cummings Foundation

"Articulate and compelling, both clarion call and proof text, *There Shall Be No Needy* offers a nuanced, substantial look at Judaism's engagement with public life—one that is all too urgently needed. We're commanded to love our neighbor as ourselves, and this book helps us understand how to do that in a world whose complexity defies easy answers."

—Rabbi Danya Ruttenberg, author, *Surprised By God:*
How I Learned to Stop Worrying and Love Religion;
editor, *Yentl's Revenge: The Next Wave of Jewish Feminism*

There Shall Be No Needy

Pursuing Social Justice
through
Jewish Law & Tradition

RABBI JILL JACOBS

Foreword by Rabbi Elliot N. Dorff, PhD,
award–winning author of *The Way Into* Tikkun Olam (*Repairing the World*)
Preface by Simon Greer, president of Jewish Funds for Justice

JEWISH LIGHTS Publishing
Woodstock, Vermont

There Shall Be No Needy:
Pursuing Social Justice through Jewish Law and Tradition

2009 Hardcover Edition, First Printing
© 2009 by Jill Jacobs
Foreword © 2009 by Elliot N. Dorff
Preface © 2009 by Simon Greer

For information regarding permission to reprint material from this book, please mail or fax your request in writing to Jewish Lights Publishing, Permissions Department, at the address / fax number listed below or e-mail your request to permissions@jewishlights.com.

The author gratefully acknowledges the following for permission to use adaptations of previously published material: Pp. 9–23, "A Jewish Vision for Economic Justice," in *Righteous Indignation: A Jewish Call for Justice,* edited by Rabbi Or N. Rose, Jo Ellen Green Kaiser, and Margie Klein, published by Jewish Lights, Woodstock, VT, 2007, pp. 147–154; pp. 25–49, a version of "The History of *Tikkun Olam,*" in *Zeek* (www.zeek.net), June 2007; pp. 51–81, "Toward a Halakhic Definition of Poverty," reprinted with permission from *Conservative Judaism* 57:1 in Fall 2004: 3–20; pp. 83–100 © 2004 the Rabbinical Assembly, *Smart Tzedakah,* a publication of Jewish Funds for Justice, 2008; pp. 101–136, "The Living Wage: A Jewish Approach," reprinted with permission from *Conservative Judaism* 55:3 in Spring 2003: 38–51 © 2003 the Rabbinical Assembly; "Work, Workers, and the Jewish Owner," by Jill Jacobs © 2008 the Committee on Jewish Law and Standards.

Library of Congress Cataloging-in-Publication Data
Jacobs, Jill, 1975–
 There shall be no needy : pursuing social justice through Jewish law and tradition / by Jill Jacobs ; foreword by Elliot N. Dorff ; preface by Simon Greer.
  p. cm.
 Includes bibliographical references and index.
 ISBN-13: 978-1-58023-394-1 (hardcover)
 ISBN-10: 1-58023-394-5 (hardcover)
 1. Social justice—Religious aspects—Judaism. 2. Judaism and social problems—United States. 3. Judaism—20th century. 4. Rabbinical literature—History and criticism. 5. Jewish ethics. I. Title.
 BM645.J8J33 2009
 296.3'8—dc22

2008055280

10 9 8 7 6 5 4 3 2 1

Manufactured in the United States of America
✡ Printed on recycled paper.
Jacket Design: Jenny Buono

Published by Jewish Lights Publishing
A Division of LongHill Partners, Inc.
Sunset Farm Offices, Route 4, P.O. Box 237
Woodstock, VT 05091
Tel: (802) 457-4000   Fax: (802) 457-4004
www.jewishlights.com

For Guy

באהבתך אשגה תמיד

על פי משלי ה:יט

CONTENTS

ACKNOWLEDGMENTS

This book is the product of countless conversations with friends, teachers, colleagues, scholars, activists, and policy professionals. For fear of forgetting someone, I will not try to name everyone whose insights have contributed to my thinking about the intersection of Judaism, public policy, and life in America. I do, however, want to thank a few people who read and commented on individual chapters, previous incarnations of individual chapters, or the entire book: Rabbi Elliot Dorff, Simon Greer, Laura Jackson, Jeff Mandell, Sara Rostolder Mandell, Mik Moore, Rabbi Daniel Nevins, Dr. Robert Pollin, Dr. Mayer Rabinowitz, Rabbi Danya Ruttenberg, and Rabbi Larry Troster. Their contributions have certainly improved this work; mistakes, of course, remain my own. Thank you also to Debbie Mukamal and Sarah From, whose thinking very much shaped my explorations of criminal justice; Dr. Alyssa Gray for her thoughts and advice about *tzedakah*; and Rabbi David Ellenson and Rabbi Or Rose for their many suggestions and words of support along the way. Thank you also to my colleagues at Jewish Funds for Justice for their immeasurable enthusiasm and encouragement throughout the writing process. And a special thank you to Stuart M. Matlins, publisher of Jewish Lights, and Emily Wichland, vice president of Editorial and Production, for their extraordinary guidance through every step of the publishing process.

I also want to acknowledge my parents, Paula and David Jacobs; and my in-laws, Dan, Ziona, and Karen Austrian, for their support through the writing process.

The most important thank you goes to my life partner, Guy Austrian, who read and commented on every chapter of this book, but more importantly, who sustains me with his love every single day.

FOREWORD

Ever since the civil rights campaigns of the 1950s and 1960s, social justice has been the concern primarily of secular and Reform Jews. This book demonstrates beyond a shadow of a doubt, however, that social justice needs to be a focus of more traditional Jews as well. Those who take Jewish law seriously will find in this book not only references to general principles of the Torah and the ringing declarations of the prophets commonly cited to ground social justice activities in the Jewish tradition, but also ample citations from Jewish legal literature, including the Mishnah, Talmud, codes, *responsa* (rabbinic legal opinions), and medieval and modern commentaries. If nothing else, this deep rooting in Jewish legal sources should persuade traditional Jews that social justice must be a central concern of their Jewish commitment. Through citation, interpretation, and analysis, Rabbi Jill Jacobs leads the way in restoring Jewish civil law, *Choshen Mishpat,* to its rightful place in our tradition, as relevant and compelling to our day as the laws of daily ritual, prayer, diet, and Shabbat.

In addition to Jewish legal materials, a series of rabbinic statements and principles require us to go beyond the limits of the law in fulfilling God's moral mission for us as a people covenanted with God. To make that point, let me begin with a linguistic observation. The very word "religion" comes from the same Latin root that produces the English words "ligament" and "[tubal] ligation." The Latin verb *ligare* and the English words based upon it mean "connections or ties." Among other things, religions give us a broad picture of how we are connected to the other members of our family, our community, the larger human community, the environment, and the transcendent element of human experience, imaged in the Western traditions as God and in the Eastern traditions in other ways. Each of the religions of the world depicts in different ways who we are as individuals and as communities, as well as the kind of individuals and communities we should strive to create. The same is true for secular philosophies, such as Western liberalism, Marxism, and existentialism. Because every human being shares some things with every other human being, there is surely some overlap, but the differences among these various views of who we are and who we ought to be far outweigh the similarities.

American Jews inherit two such pictures: the Jewish and the American secular. For the latter, as the Declaration of Independence explicitly states, I am an individual with rights. I may and do see myself as attached to my family, and I may and do form other connections through the organizations that I join, but in the end all such connections are voluntary. I may abandon my family and leave any organization at will; so long as I have not committed a felony, I may even denounce my American citizenship.

The Jewish tradition portrays us in a radically different way. For Judaism, I am part of an organic community, and just as my foot cannot decide to leave me at will, so no Jew can give up his or her membership in the Jewish community. A Jew who converts to another religion becomes an apostate, and apostates lose the privileges of being Jewish (they may not be counted as part of a prayer quorum and may not be married or buried as Jews, for example), but they still have all the obligations that the Jewish tradition imposes on us. These laws may feel like another illustration of how Judaism instills guilt in us, but they also clearly manifest the strong, organic connections that we have to our family, our fellow Jews and, ultimately, to God's other human creatures.

It is this Jewish vision of who we are and should strive to be that is the ground of the Jewish moral vision. That is, when rabbis like me say that morality demands that we sometimes change Jewish law and that we must, in any case, strive to live beyond the minimal requirements of the law,[1] we are not importing a foreign set of moral ideas to the Jewish tradition. Much less are we simply adopting the current politically correct fad. We are instead applying the central vision of the Jewish tradition of who we are and ought to be—the same vision that has shaped Jewish law from its inception—to the moral demands that we must strive to fulfill beyond the minimal requirements of the law.

These moral demands, many of which are detailed in this book, are not "extra-legal" or somehow beyond the provenance of the law. They are instead what the law itself demands of us. Although Jewish law most commonly uses deontological terms—*assur* (forbidden), *muttar* (permitted), and *chayyav* (required)—there is a rich strain of Jewish law that speaks the language of virtue ethics, where actions are not clearly forbidden or permitted but rather are encouraged or discouraged. This is not the morality or the law of rules; it is rather the morality and law of aspiration. This is the ethic portrayed by the biblical prophets and the books of Psalms and Proverbs,[2] perhaps most famously in Isaiah's call for us to be "a light of nations."[3] Moreover, it is the ethic inherent in the Torah's overarching demand, "You shall be holy, for I, the Lord your God, am holy."[4]

The Rabbis of the Talmud expanded on this theme. So, for example, one of Hillel's favorite sayings was: "Where there are no men, strive to be a man."[5] This is a simple articulation of the concept of virtue ethics. We should do only that which we construe to be consistent with our moral ideals; we must all strive to attain the highest level of moral behavior.

Moreover, the rabbis insist that we behave morally *lifnim m'shurat ha-din* (beyond the strict requirements of the law). Indeed, Rabbi Yohanan asserted that Jerusalem was destroyed by the Romans in 70 CE because Jews "based their judgments solely on the law of the Torah and did not act beyond the requirements of the law."[6] Nahmanides attaches the requirement that we exhibit exemplary character to the verse, "Do what is right and good in the sight of the Lord" (Deut. 6:18), thus making it a demand of the Torah itself:

> This refers to compromise [rather than judgment according to strict law] and conduct beyond the limits of the law [*lifnim m'shurat ha-din*]. The intent of this verse is that initially [in Deut. 6:17] God has said that you should observe the laws

and statutes that God had commanded you. Now God says [in Deut. 6:18] that, with respect to what God has not commanded you, you should likewise take heed to do the right and the good in God's eyes, for God loves the good and the right. This is a great matter, for it is impossible to mention in the Torah all of a person's actions toward his neighbors and acquaintances, all of his commercial activity, and all social and political institutions. So, after God had mentioned many of them.... God later says generally that one should do the right and the good in all matters through compromise and conduct beyond the limit of the law.[7]

Other rabbinic concepts that, on the negative side, discourage us from immoral kinds of conduct include these: *kofin al middat s'dom* (we coerce a person not to act according to the trait of the people of Sodom, who cared only for themselves and not for others);[8] *mi-she-para* (cursing people publicly in court who renege on their agreements, even if those agreements have not reached the stage where they can be legally enforced);[9] and *ru'ach chakhamim einah nochah heimenu* ("the spirit of the Sages is not pleased with him"). The Rabbis apply this last disparaging remark to all of the following: those who do not fulfill their verbal agreements;[10] those who leave their children no inheritance, instead assigning it in their will to others;[11] those who accept repayment from someone who lends with interest, or from a repentant thief, lest people who commit such crimes in the future be discouraged from repenting;[12] those who kill snakes and scorpions on the Sabbath;[13] and those who return money loaned from a convert, who has since died, to his children—although a conflicting opinion asserts that that is an honorable thing to do, and the spirit of the Sages is pleased with him.[14] Other such derogatory categories include *minhag rama'ut* (the behavior of a cheat)[15] and *yesh bahem mishum mechusarai emunah* (they are untrustworthy, dishonest).[16] Later, Nahmanides introduced the category of *naval b'rshut ha-Torah* (a scoundrel within the bounds—or, a possible translation, "with the permission"—of the Torah).[17]

On the other hand, Rabbinic concepts that express pleasure at exemplary behavior include *ru'ach chakhamim einah heimenu* ("the spirit of the Sages is pleased with him");[18] *middat hassidut* (exemplifying the virtue of loyalty or, possibly, loving-kindness, in that he does not keep for himself another person's food that he saved from a fire on the Sabbath,[19] or that he pays the first poor man he sees for the produce he ate on the journey to Jerusalem from what was owing to the poor,[20] even though by law he needs to do neither of these things); *lifnim m'shurat ha-din* (going beyond the requirements of the law), as discussed above; and *derekh eretz* (a term sometimes used to mean a job,[21] but also to refer to decency and right living.

Finally, we should remember that the Rabbis explicitly assert that the whole point of the commandments is to purify us:

> Rav said: The commandments were given to Israel only in order that people should be purified through them. For what can it matter to God whether a beast is slain at the throat or at the neck?[22]

There is thus a plethora of terms that the Rabbis used to express approval and praise of conduct that the law did not require, as well as displeasure with acts that the law did not expressly forbid. They further saw a life of fulfilling the commandments as seeking to make us better, "purified" human beings.

Rabbi Jacobs demonstrates amply in this book that in many ways Jewish law itself demands that we act on behalf of others in need. Where the law does not explicitly require such conduct, moreover, the many biblical and rabbinic principles cited here should motivate us to serve the vulnerable in ways that God and the Jewish tradition would have us do in fulfillment of our mission to be "a kingdom of priests and a holy nation." May this book help its readers to see why and how we can bring this vision closer to reality.

−Rabbi Elliot N. Dorff, PhD

PREFACE

Imagine that you discovered a culture in which the laws and tradition required community members to treat the needy as siblings. A society that treated with respect those with fewer resources, where those with more honored the dignity of those with less. A civilization that placed into an ethical framework the relationships among its citizens.

What if this same culture spoke directly to your daily struggles. How should I relate to the homeless in Grand Central Station? Who is responsible to provide care to an elderly relative? What are my obligations to my nanny?

In each chapter of *There Shall Be No Needy*, Rabbi Jill Jacobs vividly illustrates that Judaism is this culture. She crafts an engaging dialogue among Jewish texts, public policy, and lived experience. Her book is a fascinating examination of how the essential principles of Judaism can inform our engagement with contemporary social and economic issues in the town square of American life.

For many years, I did not see a connection between my Jewish identity and my inclination to create a just world. The Jewish vision of justice, outlined in our foundational texts and scrutinized through exegesis over millennia, is not always obvious in secular communities. As I have studied our Jewish stories and teachings, my social change work has been deepened in profound ways.

After college, I became a union and community organizer. The years of tough organizing work took a toll, and I ached for a holistic way to address my growing anger and dejection at the intractable injustices I encountered day in and day out. In a long spiritual search, I studied Buddhism, Taoism, yoga, and eventually Judaism. In my work at Jobs with Justice, supporting workers' rights, I was often inspired by our slogan. But it was three years into my job that I encountered it in a Jewish context.

> "If I am not for myself, who will be for me? If I am for myself alone, what am I? And if not now, when?"
> —*Pirkei Avot [Ethics of Our Fathers]*

I had no idea these words came from a Jewish text; they certainly made a good labor solidarity slogan. After that, Jewish threads started coming alive to me. As I became increasingly attentive to them, they no longer existed as esoteric commandments with no bearing on my life. I discovered a rich, intellectual tradition that deepened and sustained my commitment to create a just and fair society. As Rabbi Jacobs eloquently demonstrates, our religious texts have direct relevance and application in our daily lives, and particular significance in our social justice work. Judaism and systems of justice are inextricably linked and mutually reinforcing.

In my current job with Jewish Funds for Justice, I continually turn to Jewish texts for perspective and guidance. Every day, we encounter struggling communities. Across our nation, millions lack access to affordable housing, good jobs, and economic opportunities. Great Jewish thinkers like Maimonides emphasize the obligation to lend money to the poor, arguing that a loan that helps an individual become economically self-sufficient is far more valuable than a one-time gift. For generations, Jewish communities have established free loan societies that provided interest-free loans to needy Jewish immigrants.

Guided by Rabbi Jacobs's work and inspired by my own experience, the diverse initiatives of Jewish Funds for Justice are each rooted in Jewish tradition and values. For example, our TZEDEC community development program uses education, organizing, and lending to increase Jewish investment and involvement in the work of revitalizing and rebuilding low-income communities. TZEDEC helps build healthier neighborhoods by pooling low- and no-interest loans from Jewish philanthropic investors to provide capital to communities often neglected by mainstream banks. Recognizing that each of us, not only the wealthy, has an obligation to the needy, we have expanded our TZEDEC program to include opportunities for investors at every giving level. We draw on centuries of Jewish teachings on obligations to the needy and integrate contemporary principles of social responsibility to guide the way we understand and use money. Through TZEDEC, we strive to implement the highest degree of *tzedakah*, defined by partnership and investment.

As individuals pursuing justice in our diverse society, and one of great extremes, we face numerous challenges. Ours is a land of contradictions, of wealth and poverty, of opportunities and dead ends, of greed and generosity. For those seeking solutions to complex problems, Judaism lends extensive insights honed through four thousand years of experience and debate. Rabbi Jacobs unearths Jewish wisdom from throughout these years, and demonstrates how it connects with our complicated societal struggles and political realities. Her book is an asset to religious and secular Jews alike.

In her introduction, Rabbi Jacobs uses the physical presence of her rabbinical school, with its back to Harlem, to demonstrate her dismay at those studying ancient text without living its directives. Jewish text, she asserts, cannot be wholly studied or understood in a protected environment. Yet there are many of us outside the walls, Jews passionate about helping neighborhoods like Harlem achieve a measure of justice, who wear a parallel set of blinders. We miss or ignore the school's resources, even though its library has much to offer us both in wisdom and sustenance. Far from closing minds, Jewish religious teachings offer a coherent framework that organizers of all backgrounds and faiths should exploit in our shared quest for social change.

At Jewish Funds for Justice, we strive to study in the library and work outside its walls. In that endeavor we are guided by the thesis Rabbi Jacobs presents in this book. I hope it can serve that purpose for you too, nourishing your work and illuminating your journey with new discoveries.

—SIMON GREER

INTRODUCTION

The Search for an Integrated Judaism

Until my early twenties, I vaguely knew that there was something Jewish about justice. I knew that many early leaders of the American labor movement were Jewish, and I had learned early in life from my parents never to cross a picket line. I had heard the Hebrew phrases *tikkun olam* (repairing the world) and *tzedek* (justice), but had never thought much about what these meant. And apart from a phrase or two and a general sense of Jewish involvement in historical social movements, I had little idea what Judaism in particular might have to say about contemporary social justice issues, nor did I find any need to reconcile my passions for justice work with my Jewish ritual practice.

Only when I began rabbinical school did my Jewish and my social justice commitments begin to seem at odds with one another. If you have ever visited The Jewish Theological Seminary of America in Manhattan, you know that the building is closed on three sides; the only entrance is on the side farthest from Harlem: the school literally has its back turned. As a young rabbinical student, I worried about the prospect of spending five years in a windowless *beit midrash* (study hall), physically and emotionally separated from the world around me.

Seeking a place for myself on the other side of the town-gown divide, I began volunteering with a tenant-organizing group in Harlem. From clients and staff, I heard horror stories about land-lords gone missing while water pipes burst, long-time tenants evicted from buildings in gentrifying areas, and elderly residents spending winters without reliable heat. Most painful for me were the many stories about absentee Jewish landlords who stopped pay-ing attention to the buildings they owned after their own families left Harlem.

The ten-minute journey back to JTS sent me back ten centuries or more. Joining my classmates in the *beit midrash*, I tried to immerse myself in the legal musings of the early Rabbis. I loved the intellectual challenge of studying difficult texts, but I didn't know how to reconcile my academic life with the education that the Harlem tenants were giving me. What could Judaism possibly have to say about the struggles of tenants in late twentieth-century Harlem?

And so I began to study. I delved into ancient chapters of Talmud and parts of medieval legal codes that I had never before explored. I saw again and again the words of the Rabbis coming to life in central Harlem. When I read in one chapter about the responsibilities of a landlord toward a tenant whose rental home has collapsed, I thought about the elderly woman whose hot water had stopped working weeks before. When I learned in another chapter about prohibitions against eviction without significant warning, I thought about the tenants I had just met who risked losing their apartments when developers purchased the buildings.

I soon learned that Judaism has much to say about dozens of areas of social policy—including worker-employer relations, health care, poverty relief, and more. While working for a labor union some time afterward, I often sensed the voices of the ancient and medieval Rabbis commenting on the day-to-day struggles of the janitors. The commentary ran in the other direction as well: I found that the texts were illuminated by my encounters with the people who were living out situations that the texts described. Later, working on a master's degree in urban affairs at Hunter College, I learned also to integrate current policy analyses into this conversation.

Jewish text is not meant to be studied in the protected environment of the *beit midrash*. Rather, the rich Jewish tradition of law and narrative must be lived in the world. Bringing sacred text into dialogue with real-life experience and political struggles has allowed me to wrestle with contemporary social and economic issues with greater nuance and complexity. Judaism does not dictate a clear-cut answer to every—or even any—social or economic issue. Throughout Jewish history, the most learned of rabbis have disagreed on virtually every interpretation of Torah and on virtually every law. As historical circumstances change, specific responses to societal problems change as well. And alongside particular rulings and debates, these ancient texts offer significant wisdom about human nature, economic cycles, the causes of inequality, and our obligations to each other. These insights can inform our own approaches to current issues, challenge our assumptions, and force us to consider alternative approaches. The conversation between our texts and our lives can enrich our experience of both.

For historical and cultural reasons, traditional Jewish education has de-emphasized civil law. Few Jewish communities throughout history have experienced significant political autonomy. Jews, therefore, have had little chance to create or enforce laws outside the realms of ritual practices and intracommunal relations. Rabbis could adapt Shabbat laws to changes in technology, offer opinions about the administration of communal *tzedakah* (support for the poor) funds, and rule on issues of marriage and divorce, but they could rarely determine the tax rate or enforce labor laws. The Talmudic principle of *dina d'malkhuta dina*—the law of the land is the law—has governed Jewish communities' interactions with the general society for centuries. Jewish religious and political leaders have generally refrained from interfering with the civil laws of the ruling nation. In many cases, it is unclear how or whether Jewish civil law was ever applied.

The founders of the state of Israel based the law of the new state on British common law, already the law of the land in the time of the British Mandate (1920–1948). Rather than attempt to revive and update centuries-old rabbinic civil law, the new state adopted a more modern and internationally recognized code of law for civil matters, while maintaining the authority of Jewish religious law for matters of personal status, such as marriage and conversion.[1] While the existence of the state has sparked an upswing in the number of *teshuvot* (rabbinic legal opinions) on issues of civil law, these *teshuvot* generally address individuals or private institutions and do not govern state practices.

In the United States, Jewish involvement in the public square has largely stood apart from the "religious" practice of Judaism.

There has certainly been no lack of Jews involved in American justice movements. From the time that Clara Lemlich stood on a podium at Cooper Union to inspire tens of thousands of garment workers to strike, to the busloads of Jewish college students who marched in civil rights demonstrations and registered African American Southerners to vote, to the continuing efforts by Jewish organizations to protect civil liberties and to promote antipoverty legislation, Jews have continuously challenged the United States to become a better place for all of its residents.

In private, many Jews involved in public life talk about the history of Jewish involvement in social movements or about the Passover narrative of liberation from slavery as a motivating force for their work. Sometimes rabbis and other communal leaders turn to texts to inspire Jewish communities to action, or to talk to general audiences about the Jewish commitment to justice. But in most cases, Jewish social justice leaders have kept their Judaism quiet, sometimes out of uncertainty about the relationship between Judaism and justice, sometimes as a reaction against the religious language of the right wing, and sometimes out of a belief that religion has no place in the public square. For the most part, there has been little effort to think seriously about American policy through the eyes of Jewish law and tradition.

I do not believe that the United States—or any other modern country, for that matter—should operate according to *halakhah* (Jewish law). I do, however, believe that Jews should openly bring Jewish text and experience into public policy discussions, both inside and outside of the Jewish community. Reducing the Jewish voice to a general call for justice or vague references to the past deprives the public debate of the texture that a more specific look at Jewish text and experience might contribute.

In this book I explore a number of current social and economic issues through the lenses of Jewish text, my own and others' lived experience, and contemporary public policy writings. In creating a dialogue between traditional text and current realities, I aim to develop a specifically Jewish approach to economic and social issues while offering perspectives that might not emerge out of an analysis either of text alone or of social policy alone. My examples come from the American context, as this is the world I know best and in which I operate. Given that no country is free from social and economic inequality, I hope that the principles outlined in this book can be translated to many other political contexts and brought into dialogue with a variety of realities.

Jewish law has evolved over the course of thousands of years, and comes down to us through numerous genres. The biblical text serves as the basis for much of Jewish law; I therefore often turn first to relevant biblical texts on the topic at hand. But Judaism has never been a literalist tradition; the words of the Bible are always understood as mediated through human interpretation. Thus, I often look to the major sources of biblical interpretation. The earliest among these are *midrashim*, collections of rabbinic elaborations on the biblical text. Some *midrashim* consist of stories or parables that explain or fill in gaps in the biblical text; other *midrashim* derive laws from the Bible, or explain biblical laws. Later, in the medieval era, a number of scholars took up the task of writing line-by-line commentaries on the biblical text. Some of the most famous of these commentators include Rabbi Shlomo Yitzchaki (known as Rashi; France, 1040–1105), Rabbi Moshe ben Nachman (known as Ramban or Nachmanides; Spain, 1194–1270), and Abraham Ibn Ezra (Spain, 1092–1167). I often look to these commentators and their peers for insight into the text at hand.

Much interpretation of biblical law is encoded in the Talmud, the record of the Oral Law traditionally understood to have been given along with the Torah on Mount Sinai. The Talmud consists of the Mishnah, codified around 200 CE in the land of Israel, and the Gemara, codified some four or five centuries later. The Mishnah consists primarily of case law, with little explanation or digression. The Gemara offers significantly more conversation about the laws included in the Mishnah, along with stories, hagiography, folk wisdom, and much argument. To make matters more complicated, there are actually two versions of the Talmud, each based on virtually the same version of the Mishnah. When people refer generically to "the Talmud," they are usually speaking of the *Talmud Bavli* (Babylonian Talmud), which is longer and considered the more complete and authoritative of the two versions. The Babylonian Talmud was codified in Babylonia (now Iraq), where the majority of the Jewish community fled after the expulsion from Jerusalem in 70 CE. The other version of the Talmud is the *Yerushalmi* (Palestinian or Jerusalem Talmud), which was composed in the land of Israel sometime earlier than the *Bavli*. In most cases, when I speak of the Talmud, I focus on the discussions in the *Bavli*, though I do occasionally turn to the *Yerushalmi* for elucidation of a point.

While the Talmud provides for fascinating reading and discussion, its discursive style makes looking for specific opinions or laws fairly difficult. To help Jews understand and follow the laws, later scholars distilled Talmudic precepts into legal codes that more concisely list and sometimes explain specific laws. Some of the major law codes include *Arba'ah Turim* (often known as the *Tur*), written by Jacob ben Asher in the thirteenth century; the *Mishneh Torah*, written by Rabbi Moshe ben Maimon (known as Maimonides or Rambam) in the twelfth century; and the *Shulchan Arukh*, written by Joseph Caro in the sixteenth century. Since the Talmud does not always offer a single clear opinion on every case, these law codes often differ in their interpretations of the law. Consequently, each law code has generated significant commentary on it.

A major feature of Jewish law is that each generation situates itself in an ongoing conversation about the content and interpretation of the law. In many cases, this conversation is visibly represented on the page: most editions of the Bible, the Talmud, and the law codes display the primary text surrounded by generations of commentators who explain and argue with the primary author and with each other. Each time a writer claims to have written the last word on Jewish law, multiple commentators chime in to remind us that the conversation never ends. Until the present day, rabbis continue to write *teshuvot* (legal opinions) that respond to specific incidents, and that interpret and reinterpret Jewish law for the current day. I look often to these *teshuvot*, and also place myself within this legal tradition by interpreting texts in relation to one another and in dialogue with the contemporary world.

One of the quirks of Jewish discourse is the common practice of calling many of the famous Rabbis either by acronyms (such as "Rambam" for Rabbi Moshe ben Maimon) or by the names of their most famous books (such as referring to Jacob ben Asher as "the Tur"). In this book, I have followed this convention so that those familiar with some of these Rabbis will easily recognize the references. When I introduce a Rabbi, I give his full name, along with the name by which he is most often known.

A guiding principle of my work is the belief that the traditional distinction in Jewish thought between *halakhah* (law) and *aggadah* (narrative) is an artificial one. From the Bible onward, narrative has influenced law and law has produced narrative. In the book of Numbers, for instance, the daughters of Tz'lof'chad approach Moses with a narrative that contradicts the existing law: Tz'lof'chad has died, leaving five daughters and no sons. The existing law denies these women any right to their father's estate. In response to the women's narrative, God adjusts the law to permit daughters to inherit land (Num. 27:1–8). Later, the Rabbis of the Talmud often use stories to prove, illustrate, or challenge laws. In a discussion about whether people with certain disabilities are obligated to bring sacrifices, the Rabbis refer to a story of a mute person who used to sit in the *beit midrash*. The Rabbis assume that this person did not understand what was happening, until one day the person begins to speak and reveals that he has learned all of Torah. The encounter with a single seemingly disabled person not only transforms the Rabbis' understanding of a particular disability, but also influences the laws of sacrifice (Talmud, *Chagigah* 3a).

Traditional methods of Jewish learning de-emphasized the importance of *aggadah*. In some *yeshivot* (academies), students studying Talmud even learned to skip the narrative sections. But narrative is an essential means of creating laws and of protecting against what the contemporary legal thinker Robert Cover has called the "violence of law"—the ability of legal interpretation to destroy or radically change human lives.[2] Martha Minow, another legal scholar, has commented:

Modes of analysis and argument that maintain their exclusive
hold on the truth are suspect. By casting doubts on alternative
modes, they shield themselves from challenge and suppress
alternative ways of understanding.... Stories disrupt these
rationalizing, generalizing modes of analysis with a reminder
of human beings and their feelings, quirky developments, and
textured vitality. Stories are weak against the imperializing
modes of analysis that seek general and universal applica-
tions, but their very weakness is a virtue to be emulated. A
story also invites more stories, stories that challenge the first
one, or embellish it, or recast it. This, too, is a virtue to be
copied.... the revival of stories in law is welcome, not as a
replacement of legal doctrine, economic analysis, or philo-
sophic theory but as a healthy disruption and challenge to
them.[3]

In accordance with this approach, I incorporate into my discussion
both texts ordinarily classified as *halakhah* and those generally understood to be *aggadah*. I also include what I call the *aggadah* of everyday
life—stories of individual people, whose life experience sometimes
challenges, confirms, or informs our reading of traditional texts. It is
not accidental that the Rabbis of the Talmud often choose to speak
about poverty through stories. These Rabbis realize that economic
laws must respond to the needs of real people, and not only to
abstract legal concepts. Similarly, our own interpretations of traditional text should respond to the real stories of the people and communities around us—not with backs turned, but with faces forward.

I hope you will join me in this dialogue between traditional
Jewish sources and contemporary American life, between law and
aggadah, and between study and action. I believe that both Jewish
life and American public life will be enriched by our conversation.

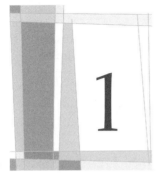

A Vision of Economic Justice

Our exploration of Jewish conceptions of justice should, quite naturally, begin in the beginning—that is, with the biblical vision of a just world. But which beginning? We might begin truly in the beginning of the Bible, with the Garden of Eden as our setting. There, the first human beings, Adam and Eve, dwell peacefully with animals, blissfully—if momentarily—unaware of the human potential for violence, hatred, or oppression.

But as readers of the Bible know, the idealism of the Garden of Eden cannot last. Upon disobeying the divine command by eating from the forbidden Tree of the Knowledge of Good and Evil, Adam and Eve understand, for the first time, the possibility of doing wrong (Gen. 3). Kicked out of paradise, human beings encounter a world in which brothers kill brothers (Gen. 4:1–16), a flood almost destroys humanity (Gen. 6–8), and people prioritize building a tower over developing a human community (Gen. 11:1–9).

A command simply to do no harm cannot keep us in the Garden of Eden. Rather, the development of a just society requires that human beings also assume positive obligations. Accordingly, as the Bible unfolds, God gives humanity in general, and the Jewish people in particular, a series of laws aimed at creating a functional civil society.

Many of the stories and laws of the biblical books of Genesis and Exodus offer the seeds of a vision for a just world. Among the most frequently cited of these precedents are the following:

- Abraham pleads with God to save the condemned cities of Sodom and Gomorrah. In these negotiations, Abraham embodies an obligation to protest injustice even in situations in which victory seems impossible, and in which the potential victims are mostly strangers.
- Joseph establishes a system for storing and rationing food so that the Egyptians will not starve to death during a time of famine. His example offers a lesson in using political authority to protect the lives of all members of society.
- The experience of slavery in Egypt teaches us the pain of oppression, and warns against inflicting such oppression on others.

While these stories and others offer a glimpse of justice or injustice in action, I would argue that the most important clues toward a Jewish vision of justice emerge from the laws given to the Jewish people as they prepare to enter the land of Israel and to establish an autonomous society there.

The Garden of Eden cannot offer us a model for justice in our own society, as the inhabitants of that place live in harmony only as long as they know no other alternative. The first human beings have no sense of positive responsibility toward one another, nor do they know that injustice is possible. Though we may long for such a naïve and peaceful existence, we cannot return to paradise once our illusions have been shattered.

Stories of individuals, such as Abraham and Joseph, who pursue justice, as well as the narrative of Jewish slavery in Egypt, provide invaluable insights into fighting for justice and the danger of not doing so. However, the most important evidence of a community's commitment to justice is not the actions of a few star individuals; nor is it the experience of oppression. Only upon gaining collective power does a community begin to demonstrate its approach to justice. Without a communal buy-in to a system of justice, well-meaning authorities may be able to move the society toward greater fairness, but malicious leaders may also lead the society toward evil.

With this emphasis on communal power, I turn now to the biblical passage that, for me, best articulates a Jewish vision of economic and social justice. In the book of Deuteronomy, Moses prepares the Jewish people for his imminent death by recounting the exodus narrative and by reminding the people of some essential divine laws. Significantly, this book—the last of the Torah—immediately precedes the Jewish people's entrance into the promised land of Israel. Moses' final instructions, then, may be read as an exhortation not to be corrupted by newfound power and wealth, but rather to use this new position to establish a just society. In the context of formulating this just society, Moses offers the following comments regarding the poorest residents of the land:

> There shall be no needy among you—for Adonai will surely bless you in the land which Adonai your God gives you for an inheritance to possess it if you diligently listen to the voice of Adonai your God, and observe and do the commandment that I command you this day. For Adonai your God will bless you, as God promised you; and you shall lend unto many nations, but you shall not borrow; and you shall rule over many nations, but they shall not rule over you. If there is among you a needy person, one of your brethren, within any of your gates, in your land which Adonai your God gives you, you shall not harden your heart, nor shut your hand from your needy brother; but you shall surely open your hand unto him, and shall surely lend him sufficient for his need in that which he wants. Be careful lest there be a hateful thing in your heart, and you say, "The seventh year, the sabbatical year, is coming" and you look cruelly on your brother, the poor person, and do not give him, for he will call out to God and this will be counted as a sin for you. Rather, you shall surely give him, and you shall not fear giving him, for on account of this, God will bless you in all that you do and in all that you desire. For the poor will never cease from the land. For this reason, God

commands you saying, "You shall surely open your hand to your brother, to the poor and the needy in your land." (Deut. 15:4–11)

A close look at this passage tells us much about biblical definitions of poverty, attitudes toward the poor, and suggestions for ending poverty. In the next few pages, we will look at this passage and at its interpretations in order to gain a foundation for our discussions of poverty and related issues.

Attitudes toward the Poor

The overarching Jewish attitude toward the poor is best summed up by a single word of the biblical text: *achikha* (your brother). With this word, the Torah insists on the dignity of the poor, and it commands us to resist any temptation to view the poor as somehow different from ourselves.

The concept of human dignity is well-ingrained in Judaism. The book of Genesis describes human beings as created *"b'tzelem elohim,"* in the image of God (1:26). At least one early Rabbi considers one of the verses expressing this idea to be the most important verse in the Torah (*Sifra K'doshim* 2:4). The insistence that human beings are creations in the divine image implies that any insult to an individual, by extension, is an affront to God. In reminding us that the poor person is our sibling, the Torah emphasizes that, like us, this person is a manifestation of the divine image and should be treated as such.

In addition to challenging us to see the poor person as a member of our family, the word *achikha* also disabuses us of any pretense that we are somehow inherently different from the poor. Those of us who do not live in dire poverty often protect ourselves from any sense of vulnerability by finding ways to differentiate ourselves from the poor: they must be poor because they don't work hard, because they drink or take drugs, because they come from dysfunctional families, and so forth. Seeing each poor person as our sibling cuts through any attempts to separate ourselves from him or her.

In a riff on the Deuteronomy 15 passage, Don Isaac Abravanel, a fifteenth-century Spanish commentator, identifies three primary reasons for giving *tzedakah*: to express mercy on the poor; to recognize the poor person as your relative; and to commit to sustaining your community.[1] With this list, Abravanel proposes a three-pronged approach to interacting with the poor. First, you may care for the poor out of pity. The word "mercy" suggests a stance toward the poor in which you give out of a sense of generosity, and not out of a belief that the poor person deserves the gift. Similarly, when Jews pray for divine mercy, the liturgy reflects the hope that God will have mercy even though we have done nothing to deserve God's beneficence. In the words of the High Holiday liturgy, "*Avinu Malkenu* (our father, our king), have mercy on us and answer us, even though we have done no good deeds."

Second, Abravanel asks us to recognize the poor as members of our own family, insofar as all people are descendants of a common ancestor. Like the concept of *achikha*, this demand forces us to see each poor person as an individual human being worthy of dignity and respect. Rather than view a poor person as an anonymous and undeserving beggar, we are asked to regard this person as a child of "Abraham, Isaac, and Jacob." As such, this person, though imperfect, is deserving of what the talmudic Rabbis call *z'chut avot* (the merit of the ancestors), the ancestral connection that guarantees God's mercy. With the reference to Abraham, Isaac, and Jacob, Abravanel seems to be speaking primarily of responsibility to the Jewish community; we can, however, expand his words to include all descendents of these three forefathers—this would certainly include *all* Christians and Muslims, but we might more generally say that we cannot be sure anymore who is descended from Abraham, Isaac, and Jacob, and thus should extend the definition of *achikha* to all of humanity.

Third, in Abravanel's formulation, we should consider the care of the poor as a means of building the community as a whole. In the most utilitarian formulation of this idea, we might say that contributing to the education of the poor helps to guarantee a better-educated and therefore more productive society; that helping the poor to buy property increases the number of homeowners in a given place and therefore raises the value of all housing stock; or that job training and small business loans for the poor increase the economic viability of an entire community.

A rabbinic story tells about a group of people traveling in a boat. One passenger takes out a drill and begins drilling a hole under his seat. The other passengers, quite understandably, complain that this action may cause the boat to sink. "Why should this bother you?" this man responds, "I am only drilling under my own seat." The others retort, "But the water will rise up and flood the ship for all of us!" (*Vayikra Rabbah* 4:6). The moral of this story is clear: one person's destructive action may literally drown the entire community. But we might add that the inverse is also true: a single positive change may transform an entire community. Thus, the alleviation of poverty, even in the smallest detail, may help the community as a whole to flourish.

Rather than consider the poor person a drain on our resources, we may regard a gift to this person as an investment in the future of the community. With monetary assistance, today's beggar may be tomorrow's community leader and himself or herself a giver of *tzedakah*.

The Paradox of Poverty

A striking feature of the Deuteronomy passage is the apparent contradiction between verse four, "There shall be no needy among you," and verse eleven, "For the poor will never cease from the land." We expect the omnipotent God of the Torah to keep promises; we are therefore surprised to hear the Torah promise to eradicate poverty and then, almost in the same breath, admit that this promise will never be fulfilled.

Noting the conditional nature of the promise to eradicate poverty "if you diligently listen to the voice of Adonai your God," most traditional commentators understand the passage as a prediction that the Jewish people will never fully obey the commandments. While holding out a utopian promise of the reward for full allegiance to the *mitzvot* (commandments), God, according to these commentators, simultaneously prepares for the inevitability of the people's disobedience.

If we accept that God's promise in this passage relies on a condition that humans can never meet, we encounter at least two problems. First, such an interpretation contradicts a basic principle of rabbinic exegesis—the idea that every word of the Torah has a purpose. Second, this suggestion raises an even more fundamental theological problem. If human beings are to hold ourselves responsible for observing the commandments of the Torah, we need to believe that God, at least, believes that we are capable of following these commandments. It would seem a betrayal of trust for the Torah to set out expectations that God already knows we will not fulfill.

Many commentators thus seek an alternative resolution of the apparent contradiction between the assurance that "there shall be no needy among you" and the warning that "the poor will never cease from your land." Rabbi Moshe ben Nachman (Ramban; Spain, 1194–1270) writes:

> "For the poor will never cease from the land" [means] it is impossible that the poor will permanently disappear. [Moses] mentions this because, having assured them that there would be no needy if they observed all of the commandments, he goes on to say, "I know that not every generation, forever, will observe all of the commandments to the point that there is no longer any need for commandments concerning the poor. For perhaps, at certain times, there will be needy, and therefore, I am commanding you for the case in which they are present. And the text says, "in your land," to refer to the entire area of habitation, for the promise that there will not be poor among you applies "in the land which God is giving you as an inheritance," as long as you fulfill all of the commandments there; then, it says that it is possible that, in some period or place in which you have settled, there may be a poor person among you. For the meaning of "in your land" refers to all of your settlements—in the land of Israel and outside of the land of Israel. And the meaning of "the poor person in your land"

is that this phrase refers both to your poor brethren and to all of the poor of your land. (Ramban's commentary to Deut. 15)

With this explanation, Ramban portrays the biblical text as optimistic but realistic. According to his reading of this passage, the Jewish people will generally observe the commandments, but will not always do so perfectly. Even if one generation succeeds in temporarily eradicating poverty, the possibility remains that poverty will resurface in another generation. Thus, the Torah anticipates a perfected world, but it plans for an imperfect one.

A common debate among those involved in antipoverty work concerns the relative value of direct service addressing immediate needs and of advocacy or organizing addressing the need for systemic change. Advocates of direct service argue that the hungry need to be fed *today* and that the homeless need somewhere to sleep *tonight*. Those who prefer organizing or advocacy point out that soup kitchens and shelters will never make hunger and homelessness disappear, whereas structural change might wipe out these problems.

The Deuteronomic response to this debate is a refusal to take sides, or better, an insistence on both. Rather than advocate exclusively either for long-term systemic change or for short-term response to need, this passage articulates a vision that balances the pursuit of full economic justice with attention to immediate concerns. In this reading, the text in question becomes a charge to work for the structural changes that will eventually bring about the end of poverty while also meeting the pressing needs of those around us.

Assigning Responsibility for Poverty and Poverty Relief

Common to most readings of the passage in Deuteronomy is an assumption that poverty results from the failure of the Jewish people to fulfill divine commandments. Where commentators differ, however, is on the question of whether poverty is a divine punishment or the natural result of disobedience.

A number of the writers discussed earlier suggest that the appearance of poverty represents an act of divine retribution. Because the people fail to obey the commandments, God sends poverty as a sign of displeasure. It is the act of disobeying God that brings about poverty, and not the nature of the disobedience. Thus, we prevent poverty by obeying *all* of the commandments (even the ones not directly connected with the alleviation of poverty), and we bring about poverty through committing *any* transgression.

Alternatively, poverty may be the natural result of the refusal to abide by the commandments directly related to the acquisition and use of wealth and power. One suggestion to this effect appears in the sixteenth-century commentary of Isaac Caro, who writes:

> The reason that the poor person is poor is because the rich person is rich; when your star ascends, his star descends. For this reason, the text says "the poor person *with you.*" What need is there to say "with you"? To indicate that you are the reason that he is poor. And if you do not give to him, what will God do? God will rotate the universe in such a way that the star that is on top will sink to the bottom, and the star that is on the bottom will rise to the top. (*Tol'dot Yitzchak, Parshat Re'eh*)

Caro here offers us a vision of a world in which fortunes are ever changing and in which the economic success of one person has an immediate impact on that of another. Today, few Jewish theologians share either Caro's cosmology, which ties individual fates directly to the movement of the stars, or his depiction of a God who intervenes directly in human affairs. Still, Caro's belief that the fate of the wealthy affects the fate of the poor corresponds with our contemporary experience, in which we find companies thriving by paying the lowest-level workers minimum-wage salaries while allowing CEOs to collect million-dollar paychecks. In some cases, wealth may "trickle down," such that all employees of a successful company thrive or all residents of a wealthy country live comfortably. More often than not, however, the rich make their fortunes by keeping the poor in poverty.

Wealth and Ownership

Significantly, alongside the promise of the eradication of poverty and the warning against ignoring the poor appears a mention of *sh'mitah* (the sabbatical year). During this year, debts are forgiven and no crops are planted. As a result, the gap between the rich and the poor necessarily closes, as landowners cease agricultural production while the poor free themselves from debt. Therefore verse nine above warns against refusal to lend to the poor as the *sh'mitah* year approaches, although the lender risks not getting his money back.

In addition to narrowing the gap between rich and poor, the *sh'mitah* year offers a glimpse of what a more equal distribution of wealth might look like. Living through the *sh'mitah* year without experiencing disastrous consequences may open people to a different sense of economic possibility. The wealthy may learn that they can get by with somewhat less, and that the increased fortunes of the poor may not directly affect the quality of life of the wealthy.

More broadly, the agricultural *mitzvot* associated with the land of Israel form the basis for the laws of *tzedakah* (gifts to the poor). Few Jews today own fields, part of whose harvest would be designated for the poor, per the biblical requirement. Laws governing the distribution of agricultural output have, however, left their mark on later *tzedakah* regulations. As we see here, and as we will see more explicitly in Chapter 4, *tzedakah* is considered a *mitzvah*—an obligation, rather than an act of charity.

It is no coincidence that the laws of *tzedakah* are deeply connected to the acquisition of land. Precisely at the moment at which the Jewish people, for the first time since before their enslavement in Egypt, are about to take hold of property, God chooses to remind the people of their obligation to eradicate poverty. The wilderness acts as the great economic equalizer. During their forty years of wandering, the Jewish people can own only what they can carry with them. While individuals may possess gold, silver, and rich linens, the wealth of each person is necessarily limited by the nomadic nature of the community. Once established in the land, however, some people will necessarily begin to acquire more land and wealth than others, and the wealthy may come to believe that they deserve their newfound fortune. Throughout the biblical discussion of the *sh'mitah* year, God constantly reminds the reader that "the land is mine" and that the land can literally throw up a community that ignores the received laws about how to live responsibly there.[2] Conscious of the human potential for greed, the Torah chooses the first moment of property ownership to remind the people that wealth ultimately belongs to God, and that human beings are simply sojourners in the land.

The timing of this commandment reinforces Caro's suggestion that the wealthy bear significant responsibility for the existence of poverty. If the people resist the effort to accumulate wealth at the expense of caring for others, then poverty will not arise among them. If, however, the opportunity to own land proves so tempting that the people single-mindedly pursue their own fortunes, then poverty will return.

In addition to the *sh'mitah* year, the Torah mandates a *yovel* (jubilee) every fiftieth year. The *yovel* year is a sort of "super *sh'mitah*" when, in addition to the other laws of the *sh'mitah* year, slaves are freed and land returns to its original owner. A person who becomes wealthy by accumulating much land, therefore, knows that he will possess this land for no more than forty-nine years. This periodic return of the land to its original owners reinforces God's assertion that "the land is mine" and can never fully belong to a human owner (Lev. 25:23).

The Torah conspicuously does not mandate a full redistribution of land every fifty years. If, as some have argued, the Torah were a fully socialist document, we might expect a biblical demand to divide the land equally among all residents. On the other hand, if, as others have suggested, the Torah advocated an unrestricted free-market economy, the periodic redistribution of land would be nonsensical. Rather, the Torah—as well as later Jewish law—favors a checked market system that permits the ethical acquisition of wealth, with measures aimed at ensuring that the market does not allow the poorest members of society to end up with close to nothing.

The Individual and the Collective

Until the book of Deuteronomy, the people operate in a post-slavery mentality. Their point of reference continues to be Egypt. They periodically remind Moses that they preferred the life of slavery, and they demonstrate little interest in the future. Now, however, the Jewish people stand just across the Jordan River, already able to see their destination, increasingly prepared to imagine building a new community there. By speaking to the people collectively, Moses challenges this band of former slaves to join together to create a communal response to poverty.

At the same time, the text addresses the people in the singular, rather than the plural form. We can understand this choice in two ways: first, we might say that the work of ending poverty necessitates a unified communal response, in which each person envisions himself or herself as a part of a whole, and not as a lone actor. One person working alone may contribute something to the eradication of poverty or to the welfare of a single individual, but ending poverty outright requires the agreement and participation of the entire community. Or, we might say that each person in a society needs to hear the command to end poverty as directed individually at him or her. That is, no person can sit back and say, "The government will take care of the poor," or "Someone else will care for the poor," but rather each person should feel personally responsible for the well-being of every member of the community.

Blessings and Curses

In our passage, God opens by promising to bless the people such that poverty will disappear, continues with warning that the failure to care for the poor constitutes a sin, and ends by promising to bless those who support the poor. God certainly promises blessings or threatens curses elsewhere in the Torah; the book of Deuteronomy, in particular, contains two long passages devoted to the blessings and curses through which the people will be rewarded or punished according to their adherence to divine law.

While our passage is not unique in its inclusion of divine blessings and curses, it is unusual in its tying of the fate of the people to a particular action. In a later section of the book of Deuteronomy, God specifies the blessings that will reward obedience to the law and the curses that will punish disobedience. Here, however, the blessings and curses follow from the people's success or failure in following the Torah as a whole, and not to the obedience of one commandment in particular (Deut. 28). In contrast, earlier in the Torah God promises often to bless the descendants of Abraham, Isaac, and Jacob but does not put specific conditions on this blessing. God does test the patriarchs and matriarchs, for instance by asking Abraham and Sarah to leave their ancestral home, but does not specify that the blessing promised to Abraham and Sarah's children is tied to obedience to a particular law or set of laws.

On the one hand, then, God appears to offer the people an easy means of achieving blessing, simply by caring for the poor and by working to eradicate poverty. On the other hand, those of us who have done any antipoverty work know the difficulty of succeeding in this task. Still, we may derive some comfort from believing that our actions are slowly leading toward a world filled with divine blessing.

Essential Principles

Deuteronomy 15 lays out both a vision of economic justice and the beginnings of a program for achieving this vision. The biblical vision of a perfected world begins with the eradication of poverty and the creation of a community that prevents any recurrence of poverty. Human beings are expected to work toward the creation of this eventual messianic state by caring for the poor within our communities, always with an eye toward ending poverty as a whole.

Failure to comply with God's instructions regarding the poor incites divine anger and moves the world a step away from the messianic vision.

In the course of offering a vision of a perfected world and mandating human participation in achieving this vision, this passage also lays out a series of principles that will underlie virtually all Jewish economic law. These principles, as we have discussed, are:

1. The world, and everything in it, belongs to God; human beings come upon wealth only by chance and do not necessarily "deserve" the wealth in their possession.
2. The fates of the wealthy and the poor are inextricably linked.
3. Corrective measures are necessary to prevent some people from becoming exceedingly rich at the expense of others. Jewish law does not propose a full redistribution of wealth, but rather, institutes controls against the gap between the rich and the poor becoming too wide.
4. Even the poorest member of society possesses inherent dignity; each member of the community is responsible for preserving the dignity of others.
5. The responsibility for poverty relief is an obligation, not a choice.
6. Strategies for poverty relief must balance short-term and long-term needs.
7. The eradication of poverty is an essential part of bringing about a perfected world, and each person has an obligation to work toward the creation of this world.

The promise that God will bless us according to our response to the poor also reminds us that there is more to Judaism than ritual observance. While some would define Jewish observance exclusively as adherence to ritual *mitzvot* such as prayer and *kashrut* (dietary laws), this passage emphasizes that ritual observance alone will not secure God's blessing. In response to those who consider "politics" outside of the sphere of Jewish observance, we can respond with the words of Solomon Schechter, one of the foremost Jewish scholars and theologians of the late nineteenth/early twentieth century, who commented, "If the disappearance of poverty and suffering is a condition of the kingdom of the Messiah, or, in other words, of the kingdom of God, all wise social legislation in this respect must help toward its speedy advent."[3]

2

Essential Terms
Tikkun Olam, Tzedek, and Prophetic Judaism

"In the beginning," God speaks the world into being. From the first moment of our history, language is central to the Jewish experience. In many of the countries in which Jews have lived, we have distinguished ourselves through our language—whether that language be Yiddish, Ladino, Judeo-Arabic, or an English peppered with Hebrew words and inflections. In using distinctly Jewish words and phrases, Jews simultaneously connect with other Jews and mark individual actions and commitments as Jewish.

Jews involved in social action or social justice often describe their work using the terms *tikkun olam* (fixing the world), *tzedek* (justice), and "prophetic Judaism." Synagogue social action committees are sometimes called "*tikkun olam* committees," and a well-known progressive magazine calls itself *Tikkun*. The biblical verse "*Tzedek, tzedek tirdof*" ("Justice, justice shall you pursue"; Deut. 16:20) has become almost ubiquitous in publicity materials across the political spectrum, and dozens of Jewish social action and social justice programs use *tzedek* in their names. The U.S. Reform Jewish movement has, for years, assumed "prophetic Judaism" as its mantra, and individual prophets have lent their names to more than a few social justice initiatives.

But what do these terms mean? In some circles, *tikkun olam*, *tzedek*, and "prophetic Judaism" have become overused to the point of losing

24

any real meaning. The tendency to conflate these three terms, or even to combine them into phrases such as "the prophetic concept of *tikkun olam*," has blurred almost any distinction among them.

In this chapter, I will consider the histories and meanings of these three terms in an effort to reclaim a distinct significance for each one. Clarifying the definitions of these terms will help us build a useful social justice vocabulary through which we can speak about our work in meaningful Jewish terms.

Tikkun Olam

The term *tikkun olam* has become a de facto pillar of progressive Judaism. Its incarnation, as a phrase interchangeable with "social justice" or "social action," began in the 1950s or later. But the term has existed for at least two thousand years, and it has changed meanings according to the needs of the hour.

The words *tikkun olam* themselves defy easy translation. The Hebrew verb *l'taken* (root: t-k-n) is generally translated as "to fix" in the sense of "to repair," but it can also mean "to establish."

As we will see, this word takes on more specific connotations in particular contexts. The word *olam*, usually rendered as "world," also signifies eternity, especially in biblical and other very early texts. Thus, *l'olam*, common in biblical, liturgical, and modern Hebrew, means "forever" (for an eternity). Even when referring to the physical world, the term *olam* also carries with it a sense of permanence. To these complications, we can add the question of which "world" any given use of the term *tikkun olam* might signify. In some cases, the term refers to the physical world, in others to the societal order, and in still others to the dream of a fully realized divine manifestation. Taken together, the two words form a phrase whose ambiguity and rich complexity make it tempting to overuse.

Establishing the Divine Kingdom

The term *tikkun olam* appears first in the *Aleinu* prayer, which may have been written as early as the second century CE. Originally part of the Rosh Hashanah liturgy, this prayer has concluded every Jewish prayer service since the thirteenth century. The move from the once-a-year appearance of this prayer to its current thrice-daily recitation speaks to the resonance of this composition for generations of Jews.

The first section of the *Aleinu* prayer speaks of the greatness of God and of the particular relationship between God and the Jewish people. The second section introduces the promise that divine sovereignty will eventually encompass the entire world. Within the second part of the prayer, we find the line *"l'taken olam b'malchut shaddai"* (to establish/fix the world under the kingdom of God). *"L'taken"* here is the infinitive form of the verb; *tikkun* is the noun form of the same root.

To understand the meaning of the term *l'taken olam* here, we need to take a step back and examine the context in which this line appears. As indicated, the second section of the *Aleinu* prayer focuses on the promise of God's ultimate sovereignty. Immediately before introducing the concept of *tikkun olam*, the text pleads that "idolatry will be swept away, and false gods will be utterly destroyed." Immediately following the promise of *tikkun olam*, the text speaks of a time "when all the people of the world will call out God's name." The triumph of divine sovereignty requires the elimination of any pockets of resistance to God's exclusive rule.

To contemporary North American ears, the rejection of other religions may sound intolerant and proselytizing. Most contemporary U.S. Jews who extol the value of *tikkun olam* certainly do not understand this term as a mandate to impose worship of the Jewish God on all other peoples.

Yet, for its time, the *Aleinu* text is comparatively universalistic. Given the numerous biblical commandments to wipe out idol-worshipping nations, we might assume that God's ultimate plan required the destruction of all those who do not accept divine sovereignty. Instead, the *Aleinu* prayer offers a gentler outlook. God, according to this text, does not demand the death of idol worshippers, but only their acknowledgment of God's own sovereignty.

Such a rereading does not reassure everyone. Indeed, the arrogance of the *Aleinu* prayer is one of the reasons that some communities revise or omit this prayer entirely, or at least reject the upbeat melody often sung with the prayer's final lines. Still, we can find meaning in the prayer if we put aside the specific issue of idol worship, or assume that idol worship as conceived by the Bible and early Rabbis does not refer to contemporary religious ritual, but only to a certain brand of paganism marked by problematic practices such as orgies and human sacrifice.[1] Then, we can derive from this prayer a sense that "fixing the world" means working toward the manifestation of divinity in every corner of the world. In our conception, this manifestation of divinity will not require the elimination of other means of religious worship, but rather the establishment of godly qualities throughout the world.

In a comment on the line in question, David ben R. Yosef Aboudraham, a thirteenth-century Spanish liturgical scholar, explains, "When the impurity is destroyed from the world, then the divine presence will return throughout the world, and the world will be repaired."[2] While Aboudraham presumably equated "impurity" with "idol worship," we can choose to read the notion of impurity a bit more broadly and say that the achievement of *tikkun olam* will require an end to all of the "impurities," such as poverty and discrimination, that hamper the manifestation of the divine presence.

The Preservation of the World

Some early rabbinic *midrashim* (elaborations on the biblical text) suggest a more literal understanding of *tikkun olam* as the physical repair or stabilization of the world. One such *midrash* appears in *B'reishit Rabbah*, a collection probably compiled around the fifth century CE. This particular *midrash* grapples with the question of why God does not proclaim "it was good" at the end of the second day of Creation, as God does at the end of all other days of Creation. The *midrash* assumes that this absence indicates that something created on the second day was, in fact, not good:

"And God made the expanse, and it separated the water that was below the expanse from the water that was above the expanse. And it was so. God called the expanse 'sky.' And there was evening and there was morning, a second day." (Genesis 1:7–8) Why is it that "it was good" is not written in connection with the second day?… Rabbi Chanina said, "Because on that day, a schism was created, as it is written, 'let it divide the waters.'" R. Tavyomi said, "If because of a division made l'taken olam and to stabilize it, 'it was good' is not written in connection with that day, how much more so should this apply to a schism that leads to the confusion of the world." (B'reishit Rabbah 4:7)

What interests us here is not so much the rabbinic explanation of why God does not declare the creation of the heavens to be good, but rather Rabbi Chanina's literalist use of the term l'taken olam to mean "to fix the world." According to this midrash, the world is "fixed" when it is physically viable, and not when it is spiritually or otherwise perfected, as other texts would have it. Similarly, another midrash explains that God created rain "to fix (l'taken) the world and to stabilize it" (B'reishit Rabbah 4:7). As in the first text, this midrash uses the phrase l'taken olam to refer only to the physical preservation of the world.

The Preservation of the Halakhic System and the Social Order

As we have seen, the term tikkun olam appears in some Jewish texts written in the first centuries of the common era. This term, however, gains real currency only within the Mishnah, where it appears in ten separate places and is rendered as tikkun ha'olam, "repair of the world." In most of these instances, the term is employed in relation to problems in traditional divorce law. Before we delve into the specifics of these cases, a few words of explanation about traditional divorce and family law are in order.

In Jewish law a husband may divorce his wife by giving her a get (divorce document), either in person or by means of a messenger. As soon as the woman accepts this get, she is divorced and free to marry another man. There is no way for a woman unilaterally to divorce her husband.[3] If a woman who is legally still married to her husband has a child with another man, this child is given the status of *mamzer* (illegitimate child) and is prohibited from marrying a Jew who is not also a *mamzer*.[4] Given the repercussions for a child born of an adulterous affair, the rabbis spend a great deal of time trying to ensure that there is no confusion about who is and is not married, and about who is or is not a *mamzer*.

With this context in mind, we can now look at some of the cases in which the term *tikkun ha'olam* appears in relation to questionable divorces. Many of these cases involve an indecisive husband who sends his wife a *get* and then changes his mind. The procedure for canceling a *get* is summed up in Mishnah, *Gittin* 4:1—

> If a man sends a *get* to his wife via a messenger, and then catches up with the messenger, or sends another messenger after the first to say to the first messenger, "the *get* that I gave to you is cancelled," then the *get* is cancelled. If the husband beats the messenger to the woman's home, or sends a second messenger who beats the first there, and says to her "the *get* that I sent you is cancelled," then it is cancelled. From the moment that the *get* reaches the woman's hands, it can no longer be cancelled.

This law as it appears here seems fairly straightforward: a man may cancel a *get* as long as his wife has not yet received the document. The moment that the *get* reaches the woman, the divorce goes into effect and can no longer be cancelled. The woman never has a moment of doubt about her marital status: until she receives the *get*, she has no reason to believe that she is divorced, and therefore cannot remarry; and from the moment that she holds the *get* in her hands, she is officially single and can remarry without concern that the divorce might somehow be undone.

Other *Mishnayot*, however, attest to legal loopholes that once gave rise to situations in which a woman might not know the status of her *get*. In these instances, the rabbis close this loophole "for the sake of *tikkun ha'olam*."

> At first, a man [who had already sent his wife a *get* by means
> of a messenger] would set up a *beit din* (court) in a different
> place [from where the wife lived] and cancel the *get*. Rabban
> Gamliel the Elder *hitkin* (established) that this should not be
> done, for the sake of *tikkun ha'olam*. At first, a man could use
> a different name for himself, his wife, his city, or her city.
> [That is, a man could use a nickname on the *get*.] Rabban
> Gamliel the Elder established that one should write one's
> name and any other name that he has and her name and any
> other name that she has for the sake of *tikkun ha'olam*. (Mish-
> nah, *Gitten* 4:2)

This text describes two circumstances that might lead to questions
about a woman's marital status. In the first example, a man sends his
wife a *get*, changes his mind about the divorce, and sets up a legal
court to annul the *get*. Soon afterward, the woman receives the *get*
and, not knowing that this *get* has already been cancelled, marries
again. The children of this second marriage are considered *mamzerim*,
and therefore unable to marry anyone who is not also a *mamzer*. Alternatively, a legally savvy woman might receive a *get*, recognize the
possibility that this *get* might already have been cancelled, and
refrain from marrying even though she is legally permitted to do so.
Given the rabbinic emphasis on the obligation to marry and procreate, this latter possibility also causes serious discomfort. Rabban
Gamliel therefore decrees that a man may no longer cancel a *get* by
means of a *beit din*, lest confusion over the status of divorces lead to
widespread unintentional adultery or unnecessary fear of remarriage.

The second situation is a bit more complicated. In this case, a
man writes a *get* using his nickname, or that of his wife or city. For
instance: a man named Charles, who lives in New York City divorces
his wife, Sarah, who lives in Chicago. On the *get*, Charles writes,
"Chuck of the Big Apple divorces Sally of the Second City." This
change of names may lead to confusion on the part of anyone who
looks at the *get*: Sarah might not recognize her or her husband's
name on the *get*, and she might therefore think that the document
has been delivered to her in error. Or, when Sarah shows the *get* to

someone else as proof of her divorce, this other person might either not believe that this *get* in fact belongs to Sarah, or may think that the use of nicknames renders the *get* invalid. Thus, Rabban Gamliel again steps in to guarantee that there will be no confusion about the marital status of the woman by ruling that a *get* must include all the names and aliases of the man and woman.

In these two cases, the term *mipnei tikkun ha'olam* (for the sake of the repair of the world) justifies forbidding a practice that, while technically legal, threatens to disrupt the system as a whole. In general, the Rabbis of the Talmud seek to explore every possible technicality in the law. If the stakes in this case were not so high, the Rabbis might have gone on to consider other legal loopholes that would allow a man to cancel a *get* in various creative ways. However, given the potential chaos caused by this particular loophole, the Rabbis take the unusual step of simplifying the law, rather than considering every possible complexity. What is at stake here is precisely maintaining the stability of the Jewish community, the "repair of the world."

Other Mishnaic appearances of the phrase *mipnei tikkun ha'olam* similarly attempt to solve large societal problems caused by legal technicalities. In one case, this phrase is used to allow a widow more easily to collect the amount of money stipulated in her *ketubah* (marriage contract) (Mishnah, *Gitten* 4:3). According to traditional Jewish law, when a man dies, his children inherit his estate. The children, however, owe their mother the amount of money agreed upon at the time of marriage. Ordinarily, someone who comes to collect a debt must first swear an oath that she or he has not previously collected this debt. Given the seriousness of oaths within Jewish law, the Rabbis recognize that a widow might be afraid to offer such an oath, and therefore may forfeit the money owed to her. Invoking the concept of *tikkun ha'olam*, the Rabbis free her from this serious oath. In this case, the Rabbis actually use the concept of *tikkun ha'olam* to eliminate a legally necessary procedure. The concern that widows will not receive the money owed to them thus becomes more important than the general rule for collecting debts.

Yet another case deals with a slave who is co-owned by two people. In biblical and talmudic times, people who owed money might pay this debt by indenturing themselves as servants to the creditor. In the situation in question, a man owes a debt to two people and indentures himself to both of them, working half-time for each. One of these masters frees the slave, either out of kindness or because the debt has been repaid. The other master does not follow suit. The Mishnah records a difference of opinion between the schools of Hillel and Shammai, two early rabbis, about the status of this servant:

> One who is half slave and half free should work for his master one day and for himself the next, according to the House of Hillel. The House of Shammai said to them, "You have solved the situation for his master, but not for him. He cannot marry a slave woman because he is already half free; and he cannot marry a free woman because he is still half slave. He will therefore not marry anyone. And wasn't the world created only for the sake of reproduction, as it says, 'It was not created for nothingness, but was created to be settled' (Isaiah 45:18). Therefore, for the sake of tikkun ha'olam, we force his master to free him, and [the slave] to write an IOU [to the master] for half his worth." The House of Hillel changed their minds and ruled in accordance with the House of Shammai. (Mishnah, Gitten 4:5)

Here, the strict letter of the law leads to an untenable situation. While it is legally permissible and even practically workable for a person to be half slave and half free, this status will create a situation in which a person becomes unable to marry. As in the case of the cancelled get, the rabbinic interest in encouraging legitimate marriages becomes reason to forbid a technically legal practice.

The Rabbis also use the term mipnei tikkun ha'olam to forbid practices that may lead to negative consequences. Thus, a person is forbidden to pay an excessive ransom to redeem captives, or pay non-Jews too high a price for Jewish religious objects, lest this willingness to overpay lead to a rise in prices for ransoms or for religious objects, or to an increase in kidnappings (Mishnah, Gitten 4:6). In these cases, the invocation of *tikkun ha'olam* does not override any particular law, but instead creates a new law aimed at protecting the Jewish community in the long run.

Perhaps the most radical use of the concept *mipnei tikkun ha'olam* appears within the context of the *sh'mitah,* or sabbatical year (Mishnah, *Sh'vi'it* 10:3). The Bible mandates that every seventh year, the land remain unplanted and all debts be forgiven. Foreseeing the possibility that people may refrain from lending in the year preceding the *sh'mitah* year, lest these debts not be repaid, the Torah specifies, "Be careful lest there be a hateful thing in your heart, and you say, 'The seventh year, the sabbatical year, is coming,' and you look cruelly on your brother, the poor person, and do not give him, for he will call out to God and this will be counted as a sin for you" (Deut. 15:9).

In rabbinic times, this biblical concern is apparently realized. Hillel, a major first-century rabbi, notices that the people of his time are refusing to lend to one another in the year preceding the *sh'mitah* year. For the sake of *tikkun ha'olam,* Hillel invents a procedure called *prosbul,* by which the creditor transfers ownership of the debt to the court. Since the court is not bound to forgive debts, the court may collect the debt after the *sh'mitah* year and then pay back the creditor. In this way, Hillel maintains the technical prohibition against collecting debts after *sh'mitah,* while simultaneously finding a way for the creditor to be repaid.

With the invention of *prosbul,* Hillel directly overturns a biblical law. Given that the Torah specifically forbids potential creditors from refusing to make loans in the year preceding the *sh'mitah* year, we might expect Hillel to respond to the widespread disregard for this prohibition by castigating his community for their sins. Instead, Hillel, perhaps recognizing that the entire system of lending and borrowing is at risk, devises a legal loophole that allows for the technical observance of the *sh'mitah* year while also protecting lenders from losing money as a result of this biblical institution.

In all of these Mishnaic cases, we might translate *mipnei tikkun ha'olam* as "for the sake of the preservation of the system as a whole." Within the Mishnah, this phrase is invoked in response to situations in which a particular legal detail threatens to cause the breakdown of an entire system. Divorces of uncertain status may lead to adulterous marriages or to unnecessary celibacy. Allowing individuals to be half free and half enslaved will prevent some people from fulfilling the biblical mandate to marry and procreate. Paying too much for religious objects or for the redemption of captives will result in an overall increase in prices and perhaps in a higher incidence of kidnapping. Ignoring the inherent challenges of debt forgiveness may lead to a wholesale disregard for the institution of *sh'mitah*. By invoking the concept of *tikkun ha'olam*, the Rabbis repair the flaw that endangers the stability of the system as a whole, and in doing so, they improve the system.

It is worth noting that these early invocations of the term *tikkun ha'olam* primarily involve an attempt to protect a vulnerable party. Prohibitions against certain methods of annulling a *get* prevent women from being trapped by an unclear marital status. Eliminating the possibility that a person might be half slave and half free guarantees indentured servants the right to marry. The institution of *prosbul* encourages the loans on which the poor often depend. This association of *tikkun olam* with efforts to care for vulnerable members of society will be further developed much later in Jewish history.

Restoring Divine Perfection

The best-known use of the term *tikkun olam* comes from Lurianic kabbalah, a sixteenth-century mystical school that revolved around Rabbi Isaac Luria in Tz'fat, a town in what is now northern Israel. Luria described Creation as a process by which God withdrew a part of the divine self in order to make room for the world. In the Lurianic Creation story, God then emanated Godself back into the world through ten *s'firot*—aspects of the divine presence. God contained these *s'firot* within vessels, but some of the vessels proved too weak to hold the more powerful of the *s'firot*. The vessels shattered, resulting in the mixture of divine light with the *k'lipot* (shells, or shards) of the vessels themselves. This process resulted in the introduction of evil into the world.

Lurianic kabbalah imagines that Adam, the first human being, could have redeemed the world and restored the divine light to its proper place. Through his sin, however, Adam lost the chance to achieve this repair, and the responsibility for restoring divine perfection fell to later generations. The attempt to free the divine emanation from the *k'lipot* is known as *tikkun* (repair), and is achieved primarily through the performance of *mitzvot*, as well as through contemplation and study. Before performing *mitzvot*, sixteenth-century kabbalists often recited *kavvanot* (intentions) in which they stated their intention that this *mitzvah* would help to reunify parts of the divine being. The kabbalists also instituted certain new rituals, including the practice of praying or studying at midnight, and a seder (ritual and liturgical meal) for the holiday of Tu B'Shevat, all intended to advance the process of *tikkun*.

The kabbalists' mystical notion of *tikkun* introduces into Jewish thought for the first time the idea that human actions can have an effect on the cosmos. Earlier biblical and rabbinic writings suggest that God demands certain behaviors, that human beings are rewarded or punished according to their behaviors, and even that God celebrates or mourns the appropriate or inappropriate actions of human beings. The innovation of kabbalah was the idea that God's being changes in response to human behavior. In deciding whether or not to perform a *mitzvah*, Jews thus must consider not only the potential consequences for themselves and their communities, but also the effect that a given action may have on the cosmos.

Given the current popular understanding of *tikkun olam* as describing ethical action in general, it is important to emphasize the connection, within Lurianic kabbalah, between *tikkun* and *halakhah*. It is no accident that Rabbi Joseph Caro, one of the key figures in the Lurianic circle, is the author not only of significant mystical texts, but also of the *Shulchan Arukh*, which became the most influential code of Jewish law. If the *tikkun* of the cosmos can result, in part, from precise adherence to *halakhah*, then an accurate guide to legal practice becomes even more necessary than ever.

Applying the kabbalistic notion of *tikkun* to contemporary ethical behavior is tricky. Contemporary social justice activists who make *tikkun olam* the focus of Jewish expression should be aware that, at least in the Lurianic perspective, *tikkun olam* cannot be divorced from ritual and other kinds of traditional observance. Furthermore, the mystics disagreed about what the world would look like once *tikkun* has been achieved. Given the focus on reuniting the divine self, it is not clear what place, if any, human beings will have in a perfected universe.

Even while advocating the practice of ethical commandments, such as *tzedakah* (gifts to the poor), the kabbalists maintained a focus on the effect of individual behavior on God. Lawrence Fine, a professor of Jewish Studies at Mount Holyoke College, explains:

> Although there is reference [in Lurianic text] to the actual giving of charity, and we have seen that Luria himself was meticulous about this obligation, the focus of contemplative attention is devoted entirely to its theurgical consequences. As individuals who were encouraged to be ethically sensitive—in conformity with rabbinic values—the Lurianic kabbalists doubtlessly believed in the intrinsic significance of *tsedaqah*. But the unmistakable inference one draws is that such mundane concerns were only the external dimension of deeper mystical goals. And yet, of course, the latter could not be satisfied except by means of the actual physical act—accompanied by the appropriate meditative intentions.[5]

The innovation of the Lurianic model of *tikkun* is the suggestion that human behavior can have an effect—positive or negative—on the world as a whole. *Mitzvot*, both ethical and ritual, have an impact far beyond the immediate result of the action. This emphasis on bringing divine perfection into the world, rather than on improving the condition of humanity, complicates the application of the mystical concept of *tikkun* to contemporary social justice work, especially as many contemporary Jewish social justice activists define their work as explicitly "secular."

Social Justice

The term *tikkun olam* more or less disappeared from popular usage between the sixteenth century and the 1950s, when the concept reemerged within liberal Jewish communities as the new shorthand for "social justice." The term gained currency in the 1970s and 1980s, as the progressive Jewish world began to emerge as an entity separate from the so-called mainstream organizational world. The New Jewish Agenda, a 1980s progressive Jewish organization, used *tikkun* as a rallying cry, as do contemporary local Jewish social justice organizations such as the Progressive Jewish Alliance in California and Jews United for Justice in Washington, D.C. By the 1990s, the term had entered the solid mainstream. For example, United Synagogue Youth, the youth group of the Conservative movement, calls its social action programming "Social Action Tikkun Olam."

More recently, the term *tikkun olam* has entered the popular American discourse. Both Hillary Clinton and Barack Obama referred to this concept during the 2008 election campaign.[6] Rabbi Michael Lerner, editor of *Tikkun*, has de-emphasized the magazine's specifically Jewish nature and has gradually reinvented it as an interfaith journal addressing a "network of spiritual progressives."

In its current incarnation, *tikkun olam* can refer to anything from a direct service project such as working in a soup kitchen or shelter, to political action, to philanthropy. While used widely by organizations on the left, the term also appears regularly in the rhetoric of more mainstream groups such as synagogues, camps, schools, and federations. In these contexts, *tikkun olam* more often refers to direct service projects, and less often to political initiatives, as synagogues and schools generally feel more comfortable dealing with immediate needs, for reasons of both politics and capacity.

At this point in Jewish history, the phrase *tikkun olam* is so often used by both Jews and non-Jews that it threatens to become nearly meaningless. Though once identified with the political left, *tikkun olam* has begun to appear frequently enough in mainstream and right-wing publications to blur its identification with any specific vision of what the world might be. In its popular usage, the origin of the term has become sufficiently confused that it is possible to find references to "the prophetic value of *tikkun olam*" and "the commandment of *tikkun olam*." As a post-biblical term, *tikkun olam* does not appear in any of the prophetic books, nor is it counted as a commandment.

As the meaning of *tikkun olam* has expanded to apply to virtually any action or belief that the speaker thinks is beneficial to the world, many Jewish social justice activists and thinkers have moved away from using the term at all. Complaining about the equation of Judaism with liberal politics, Rabbi Arnold Jacob Wolf comments, "All this begins, I believe, with distorting *tikkun olam*. A teaching about compromise, sharpening, trimming and humanizing rabbinic law, a mystical doctrine about putting God's world back together again, this strange and half-understood notion becomes a huge umbrella under which our petty moral concerns and political panaceas can come in out of the rain."[7]

Rather than reject this term altogether, I suggest a reimagining of *tikkun olam* that combines the four understandings of the term we have seen in traditional text: (1) the *Aleinu's* concept of *tikkun* as the destruction of any impurities that impede the full manifestation of the divine presence; (2) the literalist midrashic understanding of *tikkun olam* as the establishment of a sustainable social order; (3) the rabbinic willingness to invoke *tikkun ha'olam* as a justification for changing laws likely to create chaos; and (4) the Lurianic belief that individual actions can affect the fate of the world as a whole.

Even while rejecting or limiting the *Aleinu* prayer's condemnation of other nations, we can accept the belief that human behaviors determine the extent to which the world realizes its divine potential. To this emphasis on the achievement of a spiritually perfected world, we can add the midrashic emphasis on the physical maintenance of Creation. In recent decades, we have seen that human behavior can have a negative impact on global temperatures, hurricane systems, and other natural phenomena. Our definition of *tikkun olam*, then, can also include attention to the physical state of the world.

The dual emphases on the achievement of a spiritually and physically sustainable world offer a vision for what *tikkun olam* hopes to achieve but few concrete suggestions for the achievement of this vision. The rabbinic understanding of *tikkun ha'olam* as the creation of a workable social and religious system offers some suggestions about the nature of this process. In the rabbinic conception, *tikkun olam* constitutes the repair of systems that make the social order workable. *Tikkun olam,* for the Rabbis, refers to the closing of legal loopholes that lead to large societal problems. In this spirit, we might define *tikkun olam* as a mandate to correct the systems that make our own society dysfunctional. For instance, we may define as *tikkun olam* legal corrections to the systems that keep people in poverty, that distribute funding for education and other programs in unequal ways, or that allow for discrimination against whole classes of people.

Finally, the Lurianic belief that individual actions can have a permanent effect on the cosmos offers hope that our efforts toward *tikkun* will succeed. Unlike Luria, we may understand the repair of the social order not only as a means toward the restoration of the divine being, but also as a good unto itself. In accordance with Luria, though, we may maintain hope that our repair of systems will have a long-term effect on the world as a whole, and we may seek a reconciliation between the visions of social change activists and Jewish visions of God.

Each of these four strands taken alone has the potential to lead us into dangerous pitfalls when we try to apply it to contemporary thought. The *Aleinu* prayer risks directing Jews toward blaming the problems of the world on people outside of the Jewish community, or toward waiting passively for God to bring the messianic era. Likewise, the Lurianic emphasis on the restoration of divine wholeness easily leads to an otherworldly focus, and a minimization of our sense of obligation toward the here and now. The fact that the concept of *tikkun olam* is often cited as a product of mystical thought, combined with the current popularity of kabbalah as a means of spiritual seeking, increases the chance that the Lurianic definition of *tikkun olam* will lead to a focus on the relationship between the self and God, rather than on relationships between people in the world.

In contrast, the midrashic focus on the physical maintenance of the world might lead to an emphasis only on issues that affect the physical world—such as global warming, deforestation, or the extinction of animal species—and a concurrent disregard for human problems, such as poverty and health concerns. The rabbinic attention to fixing loopholes that disrupt the legal and social system may limit the definition of *tikkun olam* only to issues that are understood to interfere with the large-scale functioning of society.

For the purpose of crafting an approach to Jewish action in the public sphere, I lean toward resurrecting the rabbinic definition but modifying this approach by means of comparison to the other three strands. Ultimately, only the rabbinic definition permits—and perhaps even mandates—changing law in order to create a more functional and even equitable society. By itself, the rabbinic approach to *tikkun olam* risks reducing the work of *tikkun* to seeking small changes in specific laws. The more global approaches of the midrashic, Lurianic, and *Aleinu* models challenge us to see our obligation for *tikkun olam* as in the larger context of moving toward a more sustainable and divine world.

Tzedek

Like *tikkun olam*, the word *tzedek* has been stretched nearly to breaking by Jewish social justice advocates. The oft-quoted biblical command *Tzedek, tzedek tirdof* ("Justice, justice, you shall pursue"; Deut. 16:20) has been used to justify opposition to the war in Iraq, reproductive choice, universal health care, support for Israel's actions in the Palestinian territories, opposition to Israel's actions in the Palestinian territories, and hundreds of other issues. Often, a speaker will simply quote this verse and then go on to argue for a position or action that she or he believes is just. It is no wonder that the meaning of *tzedek* has become unclear and contradictory. Since *tzedek* derives from the same root as *tzedakah* (support for the poor), our understanding of *tzedek* may influence our attitudes toward the poor and our strategies for poverty relief. An examination of the development of this term over time can help us construct a modern understanding of the word.

Within ancient Semitic languages, words related to the Hebrew *tzedek* assume a number of meanings, including:

- legitimate, as in "a man's legitimate wife" (Ugaritic)
- loyal, as in reference to a subject's relationship to the king (Aramaic)
- true (Arabic)
- courageous, dependable, competent (second Arabic meaning)
- that which is right or responsible; one's duty (Syriac)[8]

In some ways, these definitions differ greatly from one another and from the popular understanding of *tzedek* as indicating simply justice or righteousness. Yet many of these ancient cognates emphasize *tzedek* as a relational term. That is, a person practices *tzedek* (alternatively understood as courage, legitimacy, loyalty, or responsibility) not abstractly, but within the context of a relationship with another person. To speak of God's *tzedek*, then, is not to describe an abstract divine quality, but rather to insist that God pursues a relationship of responsibility and loyalty with humanity. The Bible sometimes also describes the poor, the widow, and the orphan as a *tzaddik*, a word that seems to indicate that the person in question has not broken his or her contract with God. God, in return, remains loyal to this person by attending to his or her needs.[9]

Parallel biblical verses offer additional texture to this understanding of *tzedek* as referring to a relationship of loyalty, responsibility, and courage. Some of the words that often parallel *tzedek* in biblical text include *emet* (truth), *mesharim* (equity), and *chesed* (lovingkindness). From these parallels, we learn that *tzedek* refers not to a revenge-based justice, but to judgments made with love and in the interests of truth and equity.

More specifically, the many biblical pleas for God's justice or judgment indicate an assumption that such attention on God's part will necessarily improve the condition of the poor or suffering. Moshe Weinfeld, a professor emeritus of Bible at Hebrew University, comments:

> When the prophets speak of *tzedek umishpat*, they certainly are not referring to a settlement between the parties, or acts of charity associated with the judicial process, and they certainly do not mean merely *just* judicial decisions.... On the contrary, the concept refers primarily to the improvement of the conditions of the poor, which is undoubtedly accomplished through regulations issued by the king and his officials, and not by offering legal assistance to the poor man in his litigation with his oppressor.[10]

Weinfeld argues that *tzedek* and its related terms are associated with the actions of a just king who, upon ascending to power, establishes a new social order that produces salvation for the poor. He points, for example, to David and Solomon, who, upon assuming the throne, establish *"mishpat* (justice) and *tzedakah* (righteousness)" (2 Sam. 8:15 and 1 Kings 10:9). Similarly, the prophet Jeremiah describes the king Josiah, who did *"mishpat* and *tzedakah"* and "judged the judgment of the poor and needy," as the ideal monarch (Jer. 22:15–16).

Most tellingly, the Bible repeatedly uses the terms *tzedek* and *mishpat* to refer to three key moments in which God asserts sovereignty over humanity: the creation of the world, the liberation from Egyptian slavery, and the ultimate redemption of the messianic era. A major theme of these three events of *tzedek* is the salvation of humanity. In creating the world, God establishes the human being as exalted over other creations; in bringing about the exodus from Egypt, God saves the Israelites from their Egyptian oppressors; and in effecting the ultimate redemption, God promises to bring about a perfected world that allows for no poverty, suffering, or oppression.

The task of the just sovereign, whether human or divine, is to establish a system of government that protects the vulnerable. This assumption has strong parallels, as Weinfeld points out, in Mesopotamian texts, which describe the role of the king as proclaiming *misarum*. This concept of *misarum*, linguistically related to the Hebrew *mesharim* (equity), refers to "the establishment of social equity, i.e., improving the status of the poor and the weak in society through a series of regulations which prevent oppression" (Jer. 33).

The concept of *tzedek*, according to this understanding, extends beyond the basic legal requirements of the state, and beyond the execution of strict justice. Nor is *tzedek* a divine attribute, beyond human capacity. Again, *tzedek* appears as a relational term that describes a contract between God and humanity, or between humans of differing social or political status, to establish a system aimed at liberating the vulnerable from their oppressors.

One common form of the word *tzedek*, both in biblical and later text, is the term *tzedakah*, which in the Bible refers to a specific act of *tzedek*. Early Greek Bible translations render *tzedakah* as *agape*, the Greek word for an altruistically loving relationship, which was later translated into Latin as *caritas*, the root of our English word "charity."[11] While the Bible itself does not use the word *tzedakah* to refer to mandated monetary gifts to the poor, the early Rabbis—beginning in the first centuries of the Common Era—assume that *tzedakah* does refer to such financial assistance. Given that the Rabbis do not find it necessary to justify this definition of *tzedakah*, we may assume that the association of the term with charitable giving was already well established by the beginning of the Common Era.

It is popular to contrast the word *tzedakah* with the Christian concept of charity. Whereas the word "charity," from the Latin *caritas*, came to denote gifts made out of love and generosity, *tzedakah* refers to gifts made out of a sense of justice and in response to an objective obligation. Given our understanding of *tzedek* as a relational term that indicates the responsibility of the powerful for the powerless, and the pursuit of a society that establishes protections against oppression, we can now define *tzedakah* as a financial means of achieving these goals. In addition to being a means of meeting the immediate physical needs of the poor, *tzedakah* ideally aims to transform the system into one that is more equitable for the most vulnerable members of society.

Prophetic Judaism

The biblical prophets have long been favorites of Jewish social justice initiatives, and with good reason: the prophets remind the Jewish people of their responsibility to the poor and the vulnerable. Amos's call to "let justice roll down like water; righteousness like a mighty stream" (Amos 5:24) has become a rallying cry of both Jewish and Christian justice movements. Isaiah's admonition of those who prioritize ritual observance over the needs of the poor demonstrates evidence of Judaism's emphasis on ethical concerns (Isa. 58).

The Reform movement, in particular, has defined itself as the movement of "prophetic Judaism." For the early leaders of the Reform movement, this phrase described their commitment to "ethical monotheism" over ritual observance. In its inception, according to Rabbi Walter Jacob, prophetic Judaism was shorthand for "universalism, messianism, and a pioneering enthusiasm, as well as the desirability of changing the Jewish legal system in an evolutionary fashion."[12] In this context, "messianism" refers not to belief in the arrival of a human Messiah, but to the commitment to bringing about a messianic age. Later, the term acquired the narrower connotation of an activist commitment to social justice. While the Reform movement, in recent years, has reemphasized traditional practice, the movement has remained a leader in the social justice arena, and it continues to cite the prophets as inspiration for these commitments.

If we seek a usable contemporary "prophetic" perspective on Jewish social and economic justice, we must first understand who the biblical prophets were, what message they proclaimed, and to what audience they spoke.

In Hebrew, the Jewish Bible is known as the *Tanakh*. This word is an acronym that stands for Torah, *N'vi'im* (Prophets), and *K'tuvim* (Writings). As its name suggests, the section known as *N'vi'im* contains the prophetic books. The first part of *N'vi'im* covers the story of Joshua's conquest of Canaan around 1200 BCE and the establishment of Jewish sovereignty in the land of Israel. While prophetic figures appear in this section of the text, the focus is on the development of a political state in the land of Israel. The prophets who inspired the founders of Reform Judaism are those in the second part of *N'vi'im.* These fifteen prophetic books bear the names of their presumed authors: Isaiah, Jeremiah, Amos, and others, all of whom lived in the land of Israel between the eighth century and the fifth century BCE.

To judge by the words of these prophets, the Jewish people of the time had largely fallen into foreign customs of idol worship and were blatantly ignoring God's commandments. The prophets alternately warn the people of the destruction that will certainly result from continued disobedience and promise a redeemed and perfected world as the eventual reward for good behavior.

While the term "prophet" generally refers to these fifteen figures, Judaism actually defines as a prophet anyone who converses directly with God. While there is disagreement about the precise list of the biblical prophets, earlier figures such as Abraham, Moses, and Miriam are generally recognized as prophets by virtue of their direct contact with God.

What links all of these prophetic figures, beyond their ability to communicate directly with God, is their function as messengers between God and humanity. They primarily relay divine commands to humanity and chastise those who do not heed these commands, but they can also translate human needs to a God who sometimes appears deaf to the people's concerns. For example, when God threatens to destroy the Jewish people following their creation and worship of a golden calf at Mount Sinai, Moses successfully intervenes to save the people from annihilation (Exod. 32:11–14). When God reveals an intention to bring plagues of locusts and fire on the people, Amos persuades God to have mercy lest the people not survive this punishment (Amos 3).

Abraham Joshua Heschel, a prominent twentieth-century Jewish philosopher, convincingly argues that the prophets are distinguished by their ability to see the world through God's eyes. In Heschel's view, God suffers when human beings suffer. The prophet is able to feel this divine pathos, as Heschel names this quality of God, and to communicate the divine concern to other human beings:

> Sympathy is a prophetic sense. Compatible with God, the prophet is sensitive to the divine aspect of events. To be sure, such sensitivity is not regarded by him as an innate faculty. Sympathy is a response, not a manifestation of pure spontaneity. The prophet has to be called in order to respond, he has to receive in order to reciprocate.
>
> This moving awareness of God's cares and sorrows concerning the world, the prophet's communion with the divine in experience and suffering, is of such evident and striking power and authority, evincing such complete surrender and devotion, that it may offer a basic understanding of religious existence. Perhaps it is in sympathy that the ultimate meaning, worth, and dignity of religion may be found. The depth of the soul becomes the point where an understanding for God and a harmony with transcendent possibility spring to birth.[13]

This prophetic ability to feel and to communicate divine concerns is perhaps best exemplified by the biblical prophets, but it is not limited to them. If prophecy describes a human ability to be attuned to divine anguish, then this sensitivity is theoretically available to everyone.

The Rabbis of the Talmud, suspicious of those who would claim to hear the voice of God, declare that prophecy has been handed over to "children and fools." That is to say, the sanity of anyone who proclaims himself or herself a prophet should be assumed to be in question. Given widespread modern media coverage of people whose "God-directed" actions have been destructive or psychotic, we can well imagine that the Rabbis were wary of anyone who would claim direct access to the divine will. However, as Heschel suggests, the title of "prophet" may no longer be relevant, but the *quality* of prophecy remains available to anyone who seizes it. This prophetic quality consists of an ability to imagine the world as God might see it and to measure the existing world against the divine ideal of a world without oppression or inequality. A person who attains this prophetic ability sees beyond assumptions about what the world *is* and considers what the world *ought to be*. The modern-day prophet remains sympathetic simultaneously to the presumed suffering of God and to the everyday concerns of humanity.

While the term "prophetic Judaism" is often used to refer to a Jewish practice that prioritizes social justice concerns to the near exclusion of other modes of Jewish expression, the prophets themselves operated within a system that viewed ethical concerns and ritual behaviors as aspects of a single whole. Famously, in a text that now forms part of the Yom Kippur readings, Isaiah admonishes the people for their hypocrisy in observing the letter of the law while ignoring its spirit:

> Why, when we fasted, did You not see? When we starved our bodies, did You pay no heed? Because on your fast day you see to your business and oppress all your laborers! Because you fast in strife and contention, and you strike with a wicked fist! Your fasting today is not such as to make your voice heard on high. Is such the fast I desire, a day for men to starve their bodies? Is it bowing the head like a bulrush and lying in sackcloth and ashes? Do you call that a fast, a day when Adonai is favorable? No, this is the fast I desire: To unlock the fetters of wickedness, and untie the cords of the yoke to let the oppressed go free; to break off every yoke. It is to share your bread with the hungry, and to take the wretched poor into your home; when you see the naked, to clothe him, and not to ignore your own kin. (Isa. 58:3–7)

While this text is often invoked as evidence that the prophets valued ethics over ritual, it is important to note that Isaiah did not broadly condemn fasting, but rather criticized those who went through the motions of fasting without being personally affected by the process of fasting. The goal of ritual behavior, Isaiah argues, is to bring about an increased awareness of your surroundings, and not to substitute for ethical practices. The experience of fasting should attune the faster to the suffering of those who regularly lack food, and should inspire a type of reflection that makes you feel more—and not less—obligated to act in the world.

In their own way, the prophets answer the age-old question about the purpose of the *mitzvot*. For these figures, the commandments are not simply demands for ritual behavior that will, for one reason or another, please God. Rather, the ritual commandments are useless unless they sharpen our awareness of the condition of the world, increase access to the divine pathos, and engage us in working toward the biblical vision of a redeemed world.

The three concepts of *tikkun*, *tzedek*, and prophecy thus offer us a guide for what might constitute a uniquely Jewish approach to contemporary social and economic issues. Additionally, the ideal of *tikkun* presents us with a vision of a perfected world that can be achieved through human behavior. The rabbinic understanding of *tikkun ha'olam*, in particular, assumes that systemic change depends on legal solutions to problems that threaten the sustainability of the world as a whole. The concept of *tzedek* demands the establishment of systems of government that liberate the poor and the otherwise vulnerable. And the prophetic call sensitizes ordinary people to the divine perception of the world; it asks us to pursue a ritual practice that leads us toward ethical engagement with the world.

In the next chapters, we will consider the ways in which these concepts play out in relation to the specific issues of poverty and *tzedakah*, employer-employee relations, housing, health care, the environment, and criminal justice.

3

Defining Poverty and the Poor

In the United States, the public debate about poverty has managed to blame just about everybody. Conservatives blame poor people for taking drugs, not working, or perpetuating a "culture of poverty." Liberals blame the government or the market or society as a whole for keeping wages low, distributing educational funding inequitably, or failing to solve the American health care crisis.

Underlying these debates about the causes of poverty is the question of whether the poor and the wealthy are more different from or more alike one another. This tension marks the Jewish discourse on poverty as well. As we saw in Chapter 1, Jewish texts describe the poor as ordinary people in difficult circumstances, while acknowledging the impulse of the more fortunate to distance themselves from those who currently have less.

What Is Poverty?

Two Hebrew words describe the poor: 'ani and evyon. While more or less interchangeable, these two words are sometimes distinguished by degrees of need. Some commentators argue, for example, that the evyon is more desperate than the 'ani and that the biblical text chooses the term evyon when wanting to emphasize the need to care for even the poor who are least likely to evoke sympathy.[1]

The term *evyon*, generally translated as "needy," probably stems from a root meaning "to be in need" and implies an expectation that this need will be met, either by the community or by God.[2] In some cases, this term appears in conjunction with *tzaddik* (righteous person). This relationship between *evyon* and *tzaddik* can be understood in two ways. The *evyon* is, by definition, assumed to be righteous and to suffer economically for his or her refusal to pursue money-making at any cost. The Bible consistently describes God as siding with the poor over the wealthy and powerful. Like the *tzaddik*, the *evyon* enjoys special divine protection in this world and a promise of reward in the world to come. However, the *evyon* and the *tzaddik* similarly suffer from the absence of justice in the world. When injustice is rampant, and when many people resort to accumulating wealth at the expense of meeting human needs, both the *evyon* and the *tzaddik* suffer, and the *tzaddik* may even be likely to become an *evyon*.[3]

In reference to the prophet Amos's condemnation of the false piety of his time, Bible scholar Arvid Kapelrud comments, "They who should represent justice and righteousness, who should be [tsaddiqim] par excellence, did so no more.... Others had taken their place: the poor, needy people, who were trampled down by the mighty, they were the real [tsaddiqim]."[4] When those in power fail to prevent the exploitation of others, and when it becomes impossible for those who act fairly to become wealthy, there is a greater likelihood that the righteous will become poor, and that the wealthy will lose any commitment to righteousness.

The word *'ani*, which comes from the root meaning "humble" or "lowered down," describes a state of degradation, and may apply either to an individual who is suffering or to an entire people, as when God promises to redeem the entire Jewish people, who suffer—at different points—from slavery, expulsion, or other types of oppression.[5] The psalms regularly describe the *'ani* as suffering not only from financial need but also from illness, oppression, loneliness, and depression. This *'ani* calls out for divine help, on the assumption that God intervenes to redeem those who are suffering.

The words *'ani* and *evyon* regularly appear together in the phrase *'ani v'evyon* (a poor and needy person). The conjunction of these two parallel terms primarily serves a literary purpose, but it also reinforces the idea that someone who is in financial need is likely feeling degraded, abandoned, and in need of assistance from humanity and from God.

Who Are the Poor?

In most cases the Bible and Talmud seem to assume that the poor are those who were previously better off, but who have had a spate of bad luck that has cast them into poverty. This description of the poor is consistent with the reality of an agricultural society, in which a bad crop or an insect infestation might destroy a person's livelihood for an entire year. In many cases, rabbinic texts speak of the need to maintain an *'ani ben tovim*—a poor person from a good family—at his accustomed standard of living.[6] The prevailing portrait of the poor in Jewish text is that of a person who, by virtue of bad luck or circumstance, has landed upon hard times.

A number of texts refer to a "poor person from a good family"—meaning a person who was born into relative wealth, but who has fallen into poverty. In one of the best-known related texts, Hillel the Elder, a major rabbi of the first century, provides a newly poor person with a horse and a slave to run ahead of the horse and rider. On one occasion, Hillel cannot find a slave to hire and so he runs in front of the rider for three miles (Talmud, *Ketubot* 67b). Earlier in this discussion, the Talmud notes that the extra attention given to a poor person "from a good family" acknowledges the embarrassment this person must feel in front of the other, wealthier, members of the family, as well as the differing living standards that individual people can endure (*Ketubot* 66a). A midrashic text suggests offering this person a loan, lest he or she be embarrassed to accept outright charity (Midrash, *T'naim* 15:8). These discussions represent an attempt to step into the position of the other, and to acknowledge his or her individual experience of poverty and of accepting assistance. In addition, these texts correspond with contemporary research that demonstrates that relative poverty may be more difficult for the sufferer than absolute poverty.[7]

The agricultural assumption that poverty is a temporary condition is less reliable in modern industrial and post-industrial life, in which families may live in poverty for generations. Classical Jewish text does hint at a recognition that some people never escape poverty, and that some classes of people—notably *gerim* (sojourners), orphans, and widows—are more likely than others to find themselves permanently impoverished. However, the biblical and rabbinic understanding of poverty as a transitory state of being, while perhaps springing from the economic and social reality of an agricultural society, offers us a theology that discourages fatalistic approaches to poverty. If we understand poverty as an intrinsically impermanent condition, we are much less likely to throw up our hands at the impossibility of ending poverty and therefore to do nothing. In emphasizing the ease with which a wealthy person can sink into poverty, traditional texts further encourage readers to see themselves in the face of even the poorest person.

I once read an interview with a homeless man who earned his livelihood by begging for money on the New York City subway. The man noted that he generally earned more money when riding the trains through working class neighborhoods. The people in these neighborhoods, he noted, might themselves be just one job loss away from begging on the subway, and therefore more readily recognized themselves in the faces of the homeless. Residents of wealthier neighborhoods, in contrast, who could not imagine any catastrophe that would force them onto the streets, seemed less inclined to empathize with the beggars. The constant plea, within Jewish texts, to view the poor as members of your own family rails against this tendency, among the wealthy, to consider the poor as fundamentally different.

Stories of Poverty

Judaism communicates its attitudes about poverty and the poor most powerfully through stories. From biblical through contemporary times, Jewish texts have, more often than not, chosen to speak about poverty through the medium of narrative. This tendency is especially notable in the Talmud and in other early rabbinic texts. Whereas rabbinic discourse generally relies heavily on textual analysis and logical maneuverings, discussions about poverty more often than not incorporate an unusual number of stories.

This emphasis on storytelling is most likely not accidental. Stories, as we all know, are more powerful calls to action than the best researched policy brief could ever be. A story allows us to cut through the theory and the legal issues and to see the human effects of poverty. Sharing, if momentarily, in the experience of an individual's pain encourages us to empathize with, rather than rationalize away, this person's suffering.

Biblical and rabbinic texts are, in many cases, explicit about the need to listen to individual stories. Multiple times in the Torah, God promises to hear the cry of the poor, and threatens to exact vengeance on those who do not do the same. For example:

> You shall not ill-treat any widow or orphan. If you do mistreat them, I will heed their outcry as soon as they cry out to Me, and My anger shall blaze forth and I will put you to the sword, and your own wives shall become widows and your children orphans. If you lend money to My people, to the poor among you, do not act toward them as a creditor; exact no interest from them. If you take your neighbor's garment in pledge, you must return it to him before the sun sets; it is his only clothing, the sole covering for his skin. In what else shall he sleep? Therefore, if he cries out to Me, I will pay heed, for I am compassionate. (Exod. 22:21–26)

This passage appears within a litany of civil law regulations given during, or immediately after, the revelation at Mount Sinai. Here, God singles out three categories of vulnerable people: the widow, the orphan, and the poor, all of whom are likely to find themselves dependant on the goodwill of the wealthy. Twice within this passage, God promises to respond to the cries of the suffering; the implication, of course, is that human beings should similarly respond immediately to these cries.

The level of detail included in this biblical passage is both surprising and instructive. The Torah more often leans toward terse statements of law, with little justification or elaboration. Indeed, the Talmud and other bodies of oral law arose, in part, in response to lack of legal specifics within the Bible itself. It is unusual, then, to find both specific consequences for disobeying a particular law and an explanation of why someone may not hold a piece of clothing as collateral for a loan. Furthermore, the exclamation, "In what else shall he sleep?" demands that the reader place himself or herself in the shoes of a poor person struggling to make do with one set of clothing. Rather than simply dictate a straightforward law about the use of collateral, God appears momentarily drawn into the pain of the borrower, moved to respond emotionally to this person's distress.

Why Poverty?

There is, within traditional text, some attempt to extol the virtues of poverty and to explain poverty as a necessary test of faith. According to one midrashic text:

> God reviewed all of the positive qualities in the world, and did not find any fitting for Israel other than poverty, for through poverty, they come to fear God. If they have no food to eat, or clothing to wear, or oil for anointing, they will plead for mercy and will find it, and because of poverty they will come to fear God. Those who do acts of kindness come only out of poverty, those who do acts of righteousness come only from poverty, and those who do g'milut hasadim (lovingkindness) come only from poverty. Fear of God comes only from poverty.[8]

Poverty, according to this text, forces an appreciation of God's mercy that a wealthier person who feels entitled to his or her wealth may never experience. While this text may be extreme in its assumption that acts of lovingkindness and righteousness *always* stem from poverty, there is some truth to the observation that those who have experienced poverty are more likely to empathize with others in need of help.

Other texts propose a symbiotic relationship between the wealthy and the poor. For example:

> "In the day of prosperity, enjoy the prosperity" (Ecclesiastes 7:14). Rabbi Tanchum bar Chiyya said, "In the day of your fellow man's prosperity, rejoice with him. And in the day of adversity, reflect. If adversity confronts your fellow, consider how to do him a kindness and save him.... But why does God create both poor people and rich people? In order for them to draw riches from each other, as it says, 'God has made one for the other' (ibid.)."[9]

This explanation fits into a theological framework that understands God to have created a world that is imperfect, but that includes within it the instruments of its own perfection. The unequal distribution of wealth, according to this text, represents a purposeful decision to allow the rich and the poor to benefit one another through the giving and receiving of *tzedakah*.

Another rabbinic attempt to explain the existence of poverty pits Turnus Rufus, a Roman who often serves as the straw man in rabbinic stories, against Rabbi Akiva:

> The evil Turnus Rufus asked Rabbi Akiva, "If your God loves poor people, why does your God not support them?" He replied, "So that we may be saved through them from the punishment of Gehinnom." "On the contrary," Turnus Rufus said, "it is this which condemns you to Gehinnom. I will offer a parable. Suppose an earthly king was angry with his servant and put him in prison and ordered that he should be given no food or drink, and a man went and gave him food and drink. If the king heard, would he not be angry with him? And you are

called 'servants,' as it is written, 'For unto me the children of Israel are servants' (Leviticus 25:42)."

Rabbi Akiva answered him, "I will offer another parable: Suppose an earthly king was angry with his son, and put him in prison and ordered that no food or drink should be given to him, and someone went and gave him food and drink. If the king heard of it, would he not send him a present? And we are called 'children' as it is written, 'you are children to Adonai your God' (Deut. 14:1)." (Talmud, *Bava Batra* 10a)

This story first suggests that the purpose of poverty is to offer the wealthy a chance to give *tzedakah* and, in this way, to save themselves from being condemned to a punishing afterworld. Turnus Rufus, who assumes that God operates through a tit-for-tat system of reward and punishment, counters that God would not want human beings to assist those whom God has chosen to punish. Akiva, who gets the last word, compares the poor to someone whom God might want to punish in the heat of the moment, but whom God would not actually want to starve to death.

Akiva here simultaneously accepts Turnus Rufus's suggestion that poverty constitutes a divine punishment and yet asserts that God does care for the well-being of the poor. In comparing God to an angry parent, Akiva begins with the assumption that the poor have somehow infuriated God. But regardless of what a child has done to merit punishment, a parent does not normally stop loving this child and therefore, as Akiva points out, would be grateful to someone who took pity on the child.

As we saw in Chapter 1, other texts dispute Akiva's assumption that poverty comes as a punishment and suggest instead that poverty and wealth are matters of chance, and that a person's fortune may be reversed at any moment. Still, Akiva's insistence on the human obligation to care for the poor offers an important response to those who might argue that the poor deserve their fate and should bear the brunt of the responsibility for freeing themselves from this state of being.

In general, Jewish texts have portrayed poverty as an unjustifiable burden. In one of the more poignant discussions of poverty, one *midrash* notes that Job, who famously suffers from the loss of his family, his livestock, and his health, never loses his money:

> God said to Job, "Which would you prefer—poverty or suffering?" Job responded, "Master of the universe—I will take all of the sufferings in the world as long as I don't become poor, for if I go to the marketplace and don't have any money to buy food, what will I eat?"... This shows us that poverty is worse than all of the other sufferings in the world. (*Sh'mot Rabbah* 31:12)

This text makes no attempt to justify poverty as a means of achieving a divine reward or inspiring fear of God. Rather, poverty is an irredeemably negative experience, too horrible even for Job, the consummate sufferer. The composers of this *midrash* presumably knew of what they spoke. Like other texts about poverty, this passage exhibits an awareness of the extent to which poor people suffer and emphasizes the human element of poverty. Through Job's plea, we catch a glimpse of what life might be like for someone who is too poor even to afford food, and—if the text succeeds—we expand our capacity to empathize with the poor.

Parallel to the debates about the positive and negative aspects of poverty runs a rabbinic discussion about the merits of wealth. An oft-cited line of *Pirkei Avot* (*Ethics of the Ancestors*) defines wealthy as "one who is satisfied with one's lot" (Mishnah, *Avot* 4:1). Quoted alone, this line might suggest a rabbinic repudiation of monetary riches. However, other texts demonstrate that the Rabbis, of intangibles, also maintain a more practical approach to material wealth. One talmudic exchange about wealth captures both the idealist's notion that wealth is measured in terms of priceless possessions and the realist's understanding of wealth as a measure of material property:

> The rabbis taught: Who is wealthy? "One who is comfortable with one's wealth," said Rabbi Meir. Rabbi Tarfon said, "Anyone who has one hundred vineyards and one hundred fields

and one hundred servants to work in them." Rabbi Akiva said, "Anyone who has a wife who is good in her deeds." Rabbi Yose said, "Anyone who has a bathroom close to one's table." (*Shabbat* 25b)

On the one hand, Rabbi Meir and Rabbi Akiva here take the position that wealth should not necessarily be measured in material assets. Rabbi Meir astutely notes that even the wealthy do not always feel wealthy—a position that is certainly borne out by the modern day pursuit of greater wealth, even by those who will not be able to spend all of their money within their lifetimes. On the other hand, Rabbi Tarfon and Rabbi Yose assume more pragmatic, if vastly different, views of wealth, with Rabbi Tarfon imagining wealth as defined by extensive holdings of land, and Rabbi Yose settling for basic material comforts. While Rabbis Tarfon and Yose may differ on the extent of property that constitutes wealth, both understand wealth to refer to a certain measurable level of material comfort.

Beyond their theoretical discussions of wealth, the Rabbis also alternately describe themselves as wealthy or poor. Certain Rabbis pursue manual labor or rely on the support of the nonrabbinic population. In one episode, Rabban Gamliel, who until recently had been the rabbinic head of the community, visits Rabbi Yehoshua to apologize for publicly offending the latter. Upon entering Rabbi Yehoshua's home, Rabban Gamliel—who is elsewhere described as exceedingly wealthy—sees that the walls of the home are black. From this, he infers that Rabbi Yehoshua makes his living as a candlemaker. When he mentions this observation, Rabbi Yehoshua responds, "Woe to the generation whose leader you are, for you do not know the misery of the rabbis—how they must support themselves, and how they sustain themselves!" Though Rabban Gamliel may be oblivious to this reality, the Rabbis who are not independently wealthy find themselves resorting to draining manual labor or, at times, to requesting financial support from other members of the community.[10]

In some cases, however, the Rabbis describe themselves as being fabulously wealthy. Rav Huna is said to be so well-off that he is accustomed to being carried through the town in a golden chair, as a king would be (Talmud, *Ta'anit* 20b). Even more interesting are a series of texts that testify to Moses's wealth, and that define wealth as a precondition for communal leadership. A number of rabbinic traditions specify that Moses needed to acquire wealth in order fully to assume his status as a prophet and leader. One rabbinic text comments that "God grants prophecy only to one who is strong, wealthy, wise, and humble" and then goes on to justify Moses's leadership in these terms (Talmud, *N'darim* 38a). According to this text, Moses becomes wealthy through being allowed to keep the shards of the broken tablets, which, according to some traditions, are made of sapphire (*Vayikra Rabbah* 32:2). Other rabbinic texts explain that Moses acquired his wealth through keeping the spoils of Egypt and of the defeated kingdoms of Sichon and Og (*Vayikra Rabbah* 28:4). Given the tendency of the Rabbis to "rabbinize" Moses—that is, to ascribe to Moses the characteristics through which they define themselves—we can understand these discussions of Moses's wealth also as a comment on the rabbinic ideal. Whether they, in reality, were wealthy or poor, the Rabbis certainly aspired to wealth, even as they recognized the potential dangers of money. There is, within mainstream Jewish tradition, no idealization of poverty and no obligation for religious leaders to take a vow of poverty.

What Goes Around Comes Around

One recurring theme in rabbinic discussions of wealth emphasizes the interdependence between the rich and the poor, and the ease with which wealth can turn into poverty.

A standard rabbinic interpretation of the story of Ruth, for instance, suggests—against the literal translation of the biblical story—that the death and suffering with which the book begins constitute a punishment for neglecting the poor. As you may remember, the story begins with a famine that compels Elimelekh, his wife Naomi, and his two sons to leave Canaan for Moab. In Moab, Elimelekh and his two sons die of unexplained causes. According to *midrash*, Elimelekh and his family flee Canaan not because they themselves are starving as a result of the famine, but because they *have* food but do not wish to share it with those who do not (*Ruth Rabbah* 1:4). This *midrash* flips the biblical story on its head both to explain the bizarre coincidence of three of the main characters dying within the first few lines of the book and to emphasize the point made elsewhere in the *midrash* that the entire point of the book of Ruth is to teach *g'milut hasadim* (kindness to others) (*Ruth Rabbah* 2:14). The Rabbis here do not necessarily indicate a belief in a one-to-one system of reward and punishment, in which the generous enjoy long life and the miserly die early. Rather, the death of Elimelekh and his sons becomes an opportunity to teach the importance of responsibility to a person's own community.

Another *midrash* derives a similar idea from the biblical story of Joseph. After being sold by his brothers to a band of traveling merchants, Joseph finds himself in Egypt where he quickly rises to the position of second in command to Pharaoh. In this capacity, Joseph devises a food storage and rationing system that later saves Egypt from being ravaged by famine. When the famine strikes Canaan, Joseph's brothers come to Egypt in search of food. After a tearful reunion with Joseph, they return home and bring their father and the rest of their family back to settle in Egypt. The *midrash* in question begins with a verse that refers to Joseph's support of his father, his brothers, and their families, and then attributes Joseph's long-term success to his generosity to his family:

> "Joseph nourished his father and his brothers and all his father's household with bread according to [the needs of] their families" (Genesis 47:12). This is the meaning of the verse, "One who is merciful does good to one's own soul; but one who is cruel troubles one's own flesh." (Proverbs 11:17). When joy comes to a person and that person brings one's family along, that person does good for his or her own soul. And as for "one who is cruel troubles one's own flesh," Rabbi Alexander said: "When joy comes to a person and that person does not bring one's family along, that person comes into poverty." Rabbi Nachman said: "There is a cycle that operates

over everything, and who is the one who achieved joy and brought his family along? This is Joseph, for at the moment when Joseph made himself known to his brothers, he immediately sent for his father and his father's house in order that they should come to him and rejoice with him, and eat what was his.... For this reason, Joseph merited greatness all the days of his life." (*B'reishit Rabati, Vayigash*)

The strain of thought exemplified by these two *midrashim* understands poverty to be a temporary and cyclical condition. Those blessed with wealth are effectively being tried: those who share this wealth with others will merit long-term reward, while those who hoard the wealth for themselves may find themselves impoverished or worse. These texts correspond with a tradition that insists that "no one ever becomes poor as a result of giving *tzedakah*, and nothing bad or harmful results from giving *tzedakah*,"[11] thereby seeking to counter the instinct to hold on to your earnings lest misfortune require dipping into your savings. Also in this genre are numerous stories—both ancient and modern—in which poor people give away their last penny, only to be rewarded with a sizable treasure.

The Deserving and Undeserving Poor

In the United States, policy and public relations battles have long revolved around the competing portrayals of the poor as "deserving" or "undeserving." Television viewers in the 1980s and 1990s regularly encountered images of "welfare queens" who refused work in favor of having babies and collecting government checks. This stereotype and others succeeded in creating sufficient public support to pass a welfare reform act that dropped millions of families from the assistance rolls. During this time, discussions of the "culture of poverty" similarly shifted the blame for poverty to the poor themselves. As sociologist Herbert Gans and others have demonstrated, phrases such as "delinquents," "underclass," "paupers," and "vagrants" have long served to suggest that the poor are somehow fundamentally different from wealthier members of society.[12] From colonial times, these distinctions between the "deserving" and the "undeserving" poor have colored American economic policy. The Puritan "doctrine of the elect" suggests that God financially rewards righteousness; this theological strain still colors much American thinking about poverty and the poor. Historian Michael Katz writes:

> In his major report on the poor laws of the Commonwealth of Massachusetts in 1821, Josiah Quincy pointed out that the principle on which the laws rested divided the poor into "two classes": first, "the impotent poor; in which denomination are included all who are wholly incapable of work, through old age, infancy, sickness or corporeal debility." Second were "the able poor ... all who are capable of work, of some nature, or other; but differing in the degree of their capacity, and in the kind of work, of which they are capable." No one disagreed about helping the impotent, but the able poor were another matter: "From the difficulty of discriminating between this class and the former, and of apportioning the degree of public provision to the degree of actual impotency, arise all the objections to the principle of the existing pauper system."[13]

From early on, discussions of the "culture of poverty" and of the "undeserving poor" have been wrapped up in issues of race and ethnicity. Oscar Lewis (1914–1970), an American anthropologist, the first influential writer to suggest the existence of a "culture of poverty," based his conclusions on a study of Mexicans and Puerto Ricans, whom he describes as having a "way of life" that helps them to "cope with feelings of hopelessness and despair which develop from the realization of the impossibility of achieving success in terms of the values and goals of the larger society."[14] While extolling the adaptive nature of this "culture," Lewis also blames the culture for perpetuating poverty from one generation to another. He further suggests that the poor share certain psychological features, including "a strong feeling of marginality, or helplessness, or dependence ... a high incidence of maternal deprivation ... confusion of sexual identification, a lack of impulse control, a strong present-time orientation with relatively little ability to defer gratification and to plan for the future ... a widespread belief in male superiority and a high tolerance for psychological pathology of all sorts."[15]

While the "War on Poverty" of the 1960s emphasized rural poverty, the discourse around welfare reform in the 1980s shifted to urban poverty. Even though the majority of welfare recipients and the poor are white, media portrayals perpetuated a belief that poverty is a "black problem," brought on by an inferior work ethic and an unwillingness to assimilate to white cultural norms.[16] The success in casting poverty as a function of the moral failings of the African American community helped to turn public opinion against continuing welfare at its previous level.

More recently, the term "working poor" has emerged to describe those who are struggling to get by on minimum-wage pay-checks. This term represents a conscious attempt to recast the debate about poverty in systemic terms by highlighting the near impossibility of supporting a family on wages earned in the service industry. This recasting of poverty as a societal problem appears to have gone far in terms of building support for instituting higher federal, state, and local wages. As of 2007, thirty-two states had adopted a minimum wage higher than the federal minimum, and more than 140 cities and municipalities had passed a "living wage ordinance" that attempts to tie wage levels to household expenses.

This debate runs counter to the Jewish emphasis on obligation to help the poor regardless of the source of their poverty. In fact, a series of rabbinic texts chastise those who attempt to distinguish between "deserving" and "undeserving" poor. For example:

> Rabbi Chanina had a poor man to whom he regularly sent four *zuz* every Friday afternoon. One day, he sent that sum through his wife, who came back and told him that [the man] didn't need it. "What did you see?" [Rabbi Chanina asked]. "I heard him being asked 'With what will you dine? With the silver settings or the gold ones?'" He said, "This is what Rabbi Eliezer meant when he said, 'Come, let us be grateful to the cheaters, for if not for them, we would be sinning every day,

as it is said "And [the poor person] cries unto God against you, and it will be a sin on you" (Deut. 15:9).'" (Talmud, *Ketubot* 67b)

Here, Rabbi Chanina's wife argues that the recipient of her husband's *tzedakah* is not only undeserving but also a cheat. Without disagreeing with his wife's assessment of the situation, Chanina responds that the very presence of cheaters among the poor frees the wealthy from being held liable for not giving to everyone. That is, given the infinite obligation to help the poor, a person escapes being punished for insufficient generosity only by virtue of the fact that not everyone who asks is actually poor.

Rabbi Chanina responds to evidence of the presence of cheaters not by resolving to investigate more closely future recipients, but rather by concluding that it is better to occasionally give to cheaters than to curtail your giving. This attitude finds legal expression in the principle that you should verify the need of someone who applies for clothing assistance, but not of someone who applies for food assistance (Talmud, *Bava Batra* 9a). The fear of a person's starving to death overshadows any concern about theft.

A number of rabbinic stories criticize those who purport to be able to assess the needs of the poor. Two examples of this genre appear in a page of Talmud devoted to stories about poverty and *tzedakah:*

> A certain man once came before Rabbi Nechemiah [looking for *tzedakah*]. "Of what do your meals consist?" [Nechemiah] asked him. "Of fatted meat and aged wine," the other replied. "Will you consent to live with me on lentils?" [Nechemiah asked]. [The man] lived with him on lentils and died. "Alas," Nechemiah said, "for this man whom Nechemiah has killed!" On the contrary, he should have said, "Alas for Nechemiah who has killed this man!" However, he should not have gotten used to stuffing himself to such an extent.

> A man once came before Raba [looking for *tzedakah*]. "Of what do your meals consist?" he asked him. "Of fatted chicken and aged wine," the other replied. "Are you not concerned

about the burden of the community?" [Raba] asked him. He said to him, "Am I eating what is theirs? I am eating [the food] of the All Merciful, for we have learned, 'The eyes of all wait for you, and you give them their food in his season' (Psalms 145:15). Since it does not say 'in *their* season,' but 'in *his* season,' this teaches that the Blessed Holy One provides food for each individual in accordance with that person's habits." Just then, Raba's sister, who had not seen him for thirteen years, arrived and brought him a fatted chicken and aged wine. "What chance!" Raba exclaimed. He said to him, "I apologize to you. Come and eat." (*Ketubot* 67b)

In both of these stories, divine intervention signals approval of the poor person's gourmet preferences. In the first, the death of a poor man serves as a cruel rebuttal to Rabbi Nechemiah's confidence in his own ability to judge the needs of another. In the second, a miraculous coincidence indicates that it is the poor man, and not the great rabbi, who correctly intuits God's approach to wealth. This latter story further turns the tables on Raba, who tries to shame the poor person into frugality, but instead finds himself beaten at his own game, as the poor layperson teaches Torah to the rabbi. With little subtlety, these two Talmudic stories assert that the poor alone are qualified to judge their own needs, and that the wealthy should respond according to the self-defined needs of the poor.

Other rabbinic texts similarly chastise those who would declare certain people to be undeserving of support. For example:

If the rich man says to this same poor man, "Why do you not go and work and get food? Look at those hips! Look at those legs! Look at that fat body! Look at those lumps of flesh!" I, the Blessed Holy One say to him, "Is it not enough that you have not given him anything of yours, but you must set the evil eye upon what I have given him?" (*Vayikra Rabbah* 34:4)

The text here has God rebuking the wealthy for judging the poor. By way of responding to the assumption that excess flesh signifies a well-fed body, God claims responsibility for determining the physical makeup of each person. In calling attention to a poor person's girth, then understood as a sign of health, the wealthy only tempts "the evil eye," which, in Jewish superstition, brings disaster to those who are too beautiful or too healthy. In the contemporary United States, when the poor are more likely to be overweight than the wealthy, and when the cheapest food is the most calorie dense, we may no longer equate weight with riches. Still, it is not unusual to assume that a person's physical appearance or habits offer an accurate picture of his or her financial needs. Like the stories discussed above, this text challenges the reader to respond to the poor person's stated need, and not to his or her own projections about this person's need.

The twentieth-century scholar Rabbi Moshe Feinstein takes up the question of whether you are obligated to give *tzedakah* to a person who quits working in order to study Torah full-time. While the specific question of Torah study raises particular issues that are outside of our area of inquiry, Feinstein's more general comments reiterate the rabbinic distaste for dividing the poor into "deserving" and "undeserving." He writes:

> Even if he caused himself [to lose all of his property] not for the sake of studying Torah, though he is a sinner, we are obligated to give him *tzedakah*.... One who refrains from working his fields, even out of laziness, and sells them and consumes the profits and becomes poor may collect *leket, shikh'chah* and *pe'ah* [certain types of agricultural *tzedakah*]; we are also obligated to give to this person from the communal *tzedakah* fund. (*Igg'rot Moshe, Yoreh De'ah* 4:37)

Defining a Poverty Line

Even while establishing an ideal of always allowing the poor to define their own needs, and of erring on the side of giving, even to potential cheaters, the Rabbis recognize the need to establish some sort of poverty line in order to ensure the proper distribution of communal *tzedakah*.

On a practical level, the ways in which a society responds to the question, "Who is poor?" affects the type and level of assistance available to the needy. Perhaps even more importantly, our answers say much about our society's attitudes toward the poor. Implicit in our answers to the question, "How much is enough?" is a statement about the level of dignity and quality of life that we consider the poor to deserve.

Rabbinic texts establish at least three "poverty lines," each of which determines a person's eligibility for various types of financial and/or food assistance. These poverty levels are based on the type and the immediacy of someone's need. Those without enough food even for a single day may receive emergency food assistance, whereas those with more resources are eligible only for longer-term help.

Each of these rabbinic "poverty lines" corresponds to one of the three types of mandatory *tzedakah* programs: *tamchui*, *kuppah*, and agricultural *tzedakah* (of which there are four subtypes). The *tamchui* provides emergency food to those without enough food to survive a day, and the *kuppah* provides emergency money to those without enough to feed themselves for a week. The four agricultural types of *tzedakah*, which will be discussed in depth in the section Agricultural Assistance, offer longer-term assistance to those unable to support themselves for a year.

In contrast to U.S. poverty thresholds, rabbinic texts do not define poverty per se, but offer guidelines for the purpose of distributing certain kinds of assistance. Rabbinic discussions of who should be permitted to accept *tzedakah* are most concerned with the issue of *gozel 'aniyyim* (stealing from the poor)—the worry that if an undeserving person takes *tzedakah*, there will not be enough resources left for those more in need. Thus, the apparent goal is not the classification of the poor, but the fair distribution of limited resources. Even so, early rabbinic sources and later commentaries have defined poverty in various ways. The values and obligations implicit in each of these definitions can inform our own attempts to define and respond to contemporary poverty.

Meeting Immediate Needs

Rabbinic texts describe two types of emergency food assistance—the *tamchui* and the *kuppah*. The *tamchui* appears to have been a type of mobile food pantry. Every day, three collectors, appointed by the community, would go door-to-door to collect leftover food, which would then be distributed to those in need. Only those without enough food for a particular day could collect from the *tamchui* on that day. As the *tamchui* was distributed every day, those with limited food security knew that they would be able to collect food whenever they needed it, and therefore did not need to stockpile food on any given day. Furthermore, the *tamchui*, which depended on the donations of local residents, was necessarily a limited fund. If those who did not need emergency food assistance accepted donations from the *tamchui*, there might not be enough food left for those truly in need.

Similar in structure to the *tamchui* was the *kuppah*, a monetary fund collected and distributed by two members of the community. While the *tamchui* was distributed daily, the *kuppah* was distributed only once a week, on Fridays. Only a person without sufficient food for the week could collect money from the *kuppah* (Talmud, *Bava Batra* 8b; Mishnah, *Pe'ah* 8:7).

Both the *tamchui* and the *kuppah* responded to immediate need, and eligibility for both of these *tzedakah* programs depended on a person's ability to survive until the next distribution. In both cases, the sole determinant of need was access to food. Other expenses, such as housing, health care, and education, were not taken into consideration. As a number of later commentators suggest, the limited size of both the *tamchui* and the *kuppah* presumably necessitated the restriction of these funds to the poorest of the poor—those at immediate risk of starvation.[17]

Agricultural Assistance

While the eligibility criteria for the *tamchui* and the *kuppah* seem relatively straightforward, the conditions for participation in the agricultural *tzedakah* programs are somewhat more obscure. Most post-talmudic codes and *teshuvot* (legal rulings) assume that the institutions of *tamchui* and *kuppah* no longer exist, and that the laws pertaining to the four forms of agricultural distributions offer the precedents for contemporary *tzedakah*.[18]

The Torah specifies that three types of produce must be left for the poor: *pe'ah* (corners of the field), *shikh'chah* (forgotten sheaves that are left behind), and *leket* (produce that falls during harvesting). In addition, a certain percentage of each person's crop is designated as *ma'aser 'ani*—a tithe for the poor. The Torah does not, however, address the question of who is considered poor enough to collect from these agricultural gifts. The one biblical example of this system of agricultural *tzedakah* put into practice appears in the book of Ruth. In this story, Ruth and her mother-in-law, Naomi, find themselves destitute following the deaths of their husbands. With no other potential source of income, and no capital, the women depend on the gleanings of Boaz, a distant relative.

There is, of course, a wide range of economic circumstances between total destitution and the ability for someone to support himself or herself fully. Assuming limited communal resources, the question of where, within this spectrum, to draw a "poverty line" becomes crucial.

The Mishnah, the earliest written incarnation of the oral law, defines the poverty line as 200 *zuzim* (an ancient unit of currency). Although we no longer know what that sum is really worth, clues within the Mishnah itself, as well as the interpretations of later commentators, offer some possibilities for defining this threshold in a way that may inform our understanding of contemporary measurements of poverty:

> One who has 200 *zuzim* should not take *leket, shikh'chah, pe'ah*, and *ma'aser 'ani*. If one has one *dinar* (equal to two *zuzim*) less than 200 *zuzim*, even if 1,000 people give to him, he may take from all of them. [One whose 200 *zuzim*] are owed to a creditor or to his wife's *ketubah* may take. We do not obligate him to sell his house or his vessels [in order to acquire the 200 *zuzim* that would disqualify him from taking from the *leket*, etc.]. One who has fifty *zuzim* with which he does business should not take [from the *leket*, etc.]. (Mishnah, *Pe'ah* 8:8)

This *mishnah* offers a number of hints that point us toward the definition of a poverty line for the purposes of agricultural forms of *tzedakah*. First, the restrictions on eligibility for these types of *tzedakah* do not necessarily depend on whether someone will starve to death before the next distribution. While it is possible that 200 *zuzim* is the Mishnah's estimation of the cost of food from one harvest to another, such an explanation does not appear within the text itself. In contrast, the Mishnah specifies that a person may take from the *tamchui* and the *kuppah* only if he or she cannot afford meals for the day or for the week, respectively. With its omission of a parallel statement about agricultural *tzedakah*, the Mishnah leaves open the possibility that the sum of 200 *zuzim* includes costs other than food.

Second, the Mishnah recognizes that not all money is equally accessible or equally valuable. Thus, the Mishnah distinguishes between money that is wholly a person's own and money owed to another party, and between money stored away and money with the potential to make more money. It seems obvious to point out that someone whose money is owed to a creditor does not, in practice, have the same amount of money as someone with no debt. However, in calculating eligibility for services, many contemporary antipoverty programs count as assets cars, homes, and other items on which applicants owe money. In contrast, the Mishnah is primarily interested in a person's ability to purchase necessities, and not in the amount of money he or she has in the bank.[19] Similarly, the Mishnah distinguishes between money with no growth potential and money with which a person does business. Again, the relevant issue is financial security, not the value of the person's initial savings.

Even more striking is the Mishnah's distinction between liquid assets and material possessions. Instead of compelling a person to sell his or her property in order to avoid taking *tzedakah*, the Mishnah insists on a certain standard of living even before beginning to calculate a poverty line. Poverty, according to the Mishnah, is defined as having no more than a home, cooking vessels, and either 200 *zuzim* or 50 *zuzim* with which the person does business. To this list, the *Yerushalmi* (Palestinian Talmud) adds two garments, one for weekdays and one for Shabbat.[20] The *Tosefta*, another early rabbinic source, differs somewhat from the Mishnah in mandating that a person who owns gold dishes sell these and replace them with silver dishes. Similarly, silver dishes must be exchanged for bronze ones, and bronze dishes must be exchanged for glass ones (*Pe'ah* 4:11). With this ruling, the *Tosefta* attempts to balance a desire to prevent those with access to wealth from wrongly taking *tzedakah* with a wish to preserve the dignity of the newly poor by allowing them to maintain a standard of living similar to that to which they are accustomed. The *Bavli* (Babylonian Talmud) tries to reconcile the Mishnah and the *Tosefta* by suggesting that the two rulings apply either to two different kinds of dishes or to two different situations.[21] While disagreeing on the details, all three of these texts assume that the poor must be permitted to maintain a standard of living that preserves their dignity.

While limiting eligibility for *tzedakah*, the Mishnah acknowledges that even a person with 200 *zuzim* may not be able to support himself or herself. Thus, a person whose net worth falls just below the 200 *zuzim* threshold may take *tzedakah* from multiple people, even if the cumulative value of this *tzedakah* will lift him or her above the poverty line. As if to illustrate this point, the *Yerushalmi* tells the story of one of Rabbi Yehuda haNasi's students, who is one *dinar* short of the 200 *zuzim* that would place him over the poverty line. Some of his fellow students maliciously give him this final *dinar*, thus making him ineligible for *tzedakah*. When Rabbi Yehuda tries to give the student *tzedakah*, the student refuses, saying that he already has 200 *zuzim*. Rabbi Yehuda escorts the student into a store, directs him to spend more than a *dinar* there, and then proceeds to give him the originally intended *tzedakah*.[22] A net worth equal to the Mishnaic poverty line, this story suggests, does not necessarily guarantee self-sufficiency.

Interpretations of the Mishnah

Halakhic (Jewish legal) sources written after the Talmud preserve the Mishnah's distinction between material necessities and the wealth that determines someone's poverty status. Jacob ben Asher (Spain, 1270–1343), the author of the law code *Arba'ah Turim* (the *Tur*), revisits the question raised by the Mishnah and *Tosefta* of whether a person is forced to sell gold and silver dishes before receiving *tzedakah*:

One who has a house and many utensils but does not have 200 *zuzim* may take *tzedakah* and does not need to sell his utensils, even if they are of silver and gold. This applies to utensils for eating and drinking and such, but if he has a silver menorah or table or such things, he must sell it and not take from the *tzedakah* fund. The statement that we do not force a person to sell his silver and gold utensils applies only in the case that the person does not need to take from the *kuppah*, but is taking only from individuals or from relatives—they may give *tzedakah* to him, and he does not need to sell his utensils. However, if he comes to take from the *kuppah*, we do not give to him, but rather, we force him to sell his [gold and silver] utensils. (*Yoreh De'ah* 253:1)

While insisting that a poor person be able to keep his home and utensils, even if the latter are very expensive, the Tur worries that a person with material wealth may deplete the communal *tzedakah* funds, thereby depriving more deserving people of assistance. For the purposes of accepting donations from individuals, however, the definition of poverty is more lenient, as the size of individual donations has less of a direct impact on the amount of assistance available for other poor community members.

In our time, we can say that government assistance programs are comparable to the *kuppah* in that they are communally administered funds whose size is necessarily limited.[23] Applying the *Tur* to contemporary assistance programs, we might argue that the calculation of a person's eligibility should not take into account basic possessions, but should consider material wealth.[24]

In an attempt to understand the exclusion of a person's property from calculations of wealth, Rabbi Menachem ben Pinchas of Merseberg (known as the Nimukei Menachem; Germany, fourteenth century) speaks of the precarious nature of someone's home and land (*Dibbur haMatchil "Din d'ein"*). Land may or may not produce fruit, he says, and a house may burn down. While it is possible to protect other forms of wealth from loss, you cannot always guarantee the long-term stability of land or a house. With this interpretation, the Nimukei Menachem introduces into our discussion the idea that income security determines poverty status. That is to say, the classification of a person as poor or not poor depends on whether that person can expect to remain self-sufficient for at least a year—and not on his or her current economic situation. Thus, given the contemporary system of property insurance, we might suggest, based on the Nemukei Menachem, that in determining poverty status today, property for which someone has insurance *should* be included in the calculations, but property for which that person has no insurance should not. This emphasis on financial security—rather than on the possession of a specific amount of money—will become even more pronounced in post-talmudic discussions of the value of the 200 *zuzim* mentioned by the Mishnah.

The Value of 200 *Zuzim*

Having established that, according to the major halakhic sources, a person's home and utensils are not factored into the determination of poverty status, we next must consider the value of the 200 *zuzim* that define the poverty line for the purposes of agricultural *tzedakah*. Because little is known about monetary values in Roman Palestine, I will not even venture a guess about the real worth of this amount of money.[25] More important for our purposes is an examination of the ways in which this amount has been understood in halakhic sources and in commentaries on the Mishnah.

From the assumption within the Mishnah that the poor person in question already owns a house and utensils, we can assume that the 200 *zuzim* that would disqualify this person from taking *tzedakah* is not expected to pay for these items. The figure of 200 *zuzim* must then be based on other expenses.

In his commentary on the *Yerushalmi*, Moshe ben Simeon Margoliot (known as the P'nai Moshe; Lithuania, ca. 1710–1781) explains that 200 *zuzim* is the value of food and clothing for an entire year.[26] Rabbi Yitzchak ben Moshe (known as the Or Zarua; Vienna, ca. 1180–ca. 1250) suggests that this amount also includes food for the person's wife, dishes, shoes, and other necessities.[27] However, he argues that the amount of assistance will necessarily vary from person to person and from situation to situation:

> I say that everything depends on what a person needs to support his household, for we find that if a person is a wine drinker, we need to double the limit to 400 *zuzim* according to that to which he is accustomed.[28]

For the Or Zarua, poverty is defined as the inability to provide for the basic physical needs of a person and his family. These needs may include food and clothing, but they may also be extended to luxuries such as wine. The fundamental goal of *tzedakah*, in his articulation, is the preservation of a person's dignity and comfort, even beyond the provision of basic necessities. Like most of the sources we have seen, the Or Zarua understands poverty as a temporary condition, caused perhaps by a bad agricultural yield or a personal disaster. He therefore worries about maintaining a person's accustomed standard of living, even during this aberrant year, and does not address the case of chronic poverty. It is unclear whether the Or Zarua would allow a poverty threshold higher than 200 *zuzim* for a person who has always been poor but who has expensive tastes. Regardless, the primary contribution of the Or Zarua is the acknowledgment that different people have different levels of need. In the contemporary world there would be little support for a definition of basic needs that included a wine allowance. However, we can imagine creating a poverty line that takes into account individual medical, educational, child care, or transportation expenses.

The Tur offers an even more liberal interpretation of a person's eligibility for *tzedakah*, whose laws he equates with the laws of *leket*, *pe'ah*, *shikh'cha*, and *ma'aser 'ani*. He writes:

> All of these values (200 *zuzim* or 50 *zuzim* with which one does business) apply only in their time (in the rabbinic period), when the institutions of the *kuppah* and the *tamchui* existed and when *ma'aser 'ani* was distributed yearly, and when the poor would take the *leket*, *shikh'cha*, and *pe'ah*. Therefore, one who had 200 *zuzim* would not take [*tzedakah*], since this person would

be able to survive for a year on this amount, and the following year, he would have whatever he had. However, today, when we do not have these institutions, one may take until he has enough capital that he is able to live off of the profit. You should know that there is a distinction between one who does business with his money and one who does not, as it says, "One who has 50 *zuzim* with which he does business should not take," as it is possible for him to live off of the profit. Similarly, all laws of *tzedakah* follow this principle. It is possible that, in their time, salaries were low and one could live on the profit made from 50 *zuzim*. However, today, this is not possible, and everything goes according to the place and the time.[29]

Most striking in the Tur's discussion is his permission to take *tzedakah* until the point at which a person can live off of his or her business profit while, presumably, retaining some capital. A contemporary application of this principle might extend the definition of poverty to anyone without any money in savings.[30] While the amount of money that should remain in this savings fund remains undefined, the Tur's essential innovation is the characterization of poverty as determined by economic insecurity. A person may take from the communal *tzedakah* fund as long as she or he is not absolutely certain of being able to survive on her or his year's profits.

Furthermore, the Tur emphasizes that the 200 *zuzim* specified by the Mishnah represents not a fixed amount, but rather an approximation of the cost of living during the rabbinic period. The poverty line, according to the Tur, should reflect the cost of living in a particular place in a particular time.

Joseph Caro echoes this insistence that the definition of poverty change according to time and place. In a *teshuvah* (legal response) about the permissibility, when funds are limited, of giving *tzedakah* to Torah scholars who have more than fifty Venetian coins, he defines 200 *zuzim* as twenty Venetian coins, but argues that the cost of living in his time exceeds this 200 *zuzim* limit:

This 200 *zuzim* is only twenty Venetians (type of coin), and if the intention [of the questioner] was to refer to what is written

in the Tur—that one may take *tzedakah* until he has enough
that he can live off of the profit—does he think that fifty Venetians is enough money that one can live off of the profit from
this? This, too, has no limit, as not all places or all people are
the same. There are some places where one who does business with a small amount of money can live off of the profit,
and there are places where even four times this much would
not be enough. Similarly, there are people who are talented at
business and succeed in it, and there are people who are not.
Also, there are people who have few needs and are happy
with very little, and people who need more.[31]

The poverty line should vary, Caro suggests, according to individual
situation and ability, as well as according to time and place. In contemporary terms, we might understand his position as support for
local or regional, rather than national, poverty lines, and/or for differences among the poverty lines of urban, rural, and suburban
areas. Based on Caro's distinction between those "who are talented
at business ... and people who are not," we might also suggest different levels of assistance for those with college degrees or career
skills and those unlikely to secure lucrative jobs. However, the difficulty of determining a person's potential earnings, as well as other
mitigating factors such as job availability and physical and mental
health, serves as a caution against implementing such an approach.

Going a step further than either of these earlier sources, Rabbi
Yair Chaim ben Moses Samson Bachrach (known as the Chavvot
Yair; Germany, 1638–1702) argues that in his time there may be no
limit on who can take *tzedakah*:

As it says in the Mishnah at the end of *Pe'ah*, "one who has
200 *zuzim* or 50 *zuzim* with which he does business may not
take"—this is the limit set by the rabbis, as this is the amount
of money necessary for supporting oneself and one's family.
From this, we can say that the Mishnah refers to their time
[the rabbinic period], when they did not have all of the injustice of the king's burden, and when everything was cheap, as
is clear from several places and as is explained in another
responsum that I wrote in my book, *Chut haSheni*. But in our

time, there is no limit at which one says, "I have enough for myself, my wife, and my children."[32]

The Chavvot Yair may speak to a reality in which everyone in the community actually is deserving of *tzedakah*. In our society, it would be hard to argue that there is nobody who has enough for their families. However, this text does remind us that the definition of poverty changes according to time and place, and that even a higher poverty line may never be able to take into account every individual need.

Contemporary Applications

All of the texts that we have examined, from the Mishnah through the early modern *teshuvot*, calculate a person's wealth, for the purposes of defining a poverty line, by excluding basic material necessities such as a house and eating utensils. This rule presumes that even the poorest of the poor are entitled to have a home and basic utensils. A contemporary translation of this principle would suggest that when determining the poverty line, we should first calculate the price of housing and food and consider other costs afterward. Such a strategy might produce definitions of a poverty threshold that parallel the National Low Income Housing Coalition's proposed "housing wage"—the amount of money someone must earn in order to afford adequate housing in various places.[33]

Next, virtually all of the sources examined here understand 200 *zuzim* to include at least the cost of food, clothing, and other necessities for the year. Based on later legal texts, we may also insist that the poverty threshold take into account regional and individual differences and reflect rising costs. According to these sources, we should, perhaps, have no federal poverty threshold, but should instead have separate poverty thresholds for individual regions, states, or cities, and should link this poverty threshold to the rate of inflation. Caro's differentiation among the differing needs of individuals may also call for a poverty threshold that takes into account medical costs, child care, and educational expenses. Finally, based on the *Tur*, we might suggest that the poverty threshold be high enough that a family living exactly at this line will always have some amount of savings in the bank.

A few themes emerge from the texts examined prior. Most importantly, throughout Jewish tradition there is an insistence that the poor are fundamentally like the wealthy, as well as a refusal to distinguish between the "deserving" and "undeserving" poor. As creations in the divine image, and as descendents of the same ancestors, the poor are entitled to the same level of dignity, and the same quality of life, as the wealthy.

Embedded within these texts is a recognition of the desperation, loneliness, and suffering of the poor. Beyond merely commanding material support for those in need, Jewish sources also demand empathy from those better off. God's own declared empathy with the poor drives home the obligation not only to give *tzedakah*, but also to do our best to understand the suffering of the other. Multiple times in the Bible, God notes an intention to listen to the voice of the poor over the voice of the wealthy.[34] When the Israelites are slaves in Egypt, God hears their cries and takes mercy on them (Exod. 2:3–5).

In addition to the individual responsibility to care for the poor, there is also a collective obligation to meet the needs of all members of the community. Even more specifically, some texts posit a direct connection between the fortunes of the wealthy and the poor, such that one person's wealth may directly contribute to another's poverty, and vice versa. Within each community, and perhaps within the world as a whole, the distribution of wealth may directly affect the well-being of all members of the collective, and not only that of the most desperate.

In the next chapter we will see some of the ways in which these general ideas about poverty are translated into specific instructions for the distribution of *tzedakah*.

4

Sufficient for One's Needs
The Collection and Allocation of *Tzedakah*

W hether we have a few dollars to give away or control a multi-million-dollar foundation, we all hope to give our *tzedakah* money in a way that is both effective and consistent with our values and priorities. With instant global communications, we also have easy access to information about the latest crises and the ongoing suffering in every part of the world. It can be difficult to focus our attention or to find useful ways for our money to make positive change in the world.

In this chapter we will consider the definition and nature of *tzedakah*, the amount that a person is expected to give, various means of giving, and priorities and strategies for giving. We will also ask how the realities of globalization might affect our notions of community and obligation.

What Is Tzedakah?

The word *tzedakah* is derived from the term *tzedek*, discussed in depth in Chapter 2 of this book. Whereas *tzedek* indicates a general principle that encompasses justice, compassion, and mercy, *tzedakah* refers to a specific, active expression of this principle. Within the Bible, *tzedakah* may refer to any act of mercy performed either by God or by humanity. This term, though, quickly took on the more specific meaning of financial assistance to the poor. Even as early as the third century CE, the first translation of the Bible into Greek rendered the term *tzedakah* using the Greek word for gifts to the poor. By the time of the Talmud, the equation of *tzedakah* with poverty support was well established.

The theme of justice remains central to the understanding of *tzedakah*. Within Judaism, support for the poor is understood as an obligation and as a means of restoring justice to the world, and not as an altruistic or voluntary gesture. This approach is consistent with the general outlook toward poverty and the poor described in the previous chapter. If the poor are entitled to the same dignity and quality of life as the wealthy, and if the fortunes of the wealthy and of the poor are understood to be interconnected, then it stands to reason that the better off would be expected to care for the needs of the less well-off.

In contrast with philanthropy, *tzedakah* specifically refers to financial support for the poor. Other kinds of giving—to communal institutions such as synagogues, museums, schools, and cultural organizations—are important responsibilities, but are not necessarily considered *tzedakah*.

In our day and age, it is not always simple to differentiate between institutions that support the poor and those that do not. Given that many institutions whose primary purpose is not poverty relief also serve the spiritual needs of the poor, as well as the wealthy, it can be difficult to draw lines between what might constitute *tzedakah* and what would constitute philanthropy or the fulfillment of communal obligations. Does a gift to a hospital that provides charity care count as *tzedakah*? What about a donation to a university or private school that offers financial aid? What if one earmarks such a donation for financial aid? What about a museum that offers free admission one night a week, or that offers programs for schoolchildren from low-income neighborhoods?

These questions defy any easy answer. In distributing *tzedakah*, however, we might take into account the degree to which a given institution prioritizes poverty relief. Some of us may choose to devote our *tzedakah* money only to organizations that meet the direct needs of the poor, or that advocate or organize communities around issues that disproportionately affect the poor. Others of us might also classify institutions that are, in any way, involved in meeting the physical or spiritual needs of the poor. We should, in either case, begin from an understanding that *tzedakah* money is designated for the poor, and that other types of philanthropy fall into the category of support for communal institutions.

The Value of Tzedakah

Judaism speaks in the language of *mitzvah*, commandment. In the most traditional understanding of this concept, a Jew keeps kosher, observes Shabbat, prays, maintains fair business practices, and even gives *tzedakah* in direct response to the divine commandments given at Mount Sinai. Rabbinic and medieval Jewish thought seeks to divine the reasons for the commandments, as well as to distinguish between commandments that have a rational explanation (known as *mishpatim*) and those whose purpose is beyond human understanding (known as *chukim*). Even so, the traditional understanding is that Jews are to observe *mitzvot* because it is God's will, and not for personal gratification, or even for specific, knowable, external results. The idea that *mitzvot* can be a means of self-fulfillment, of creating community, and of creating a better world, and should be performed for those reasons, becomes much more important in modern Jewish thought.

That said, it is notable that even the early Rabbis go out of their way to declare *tzedakah* to have value beyond the fulfillment of a divine obligation. Presumably in response to the natural human resistance to parting with hard-earned money, traditional texts spend significant time extolling the virtues and rewards of *tzedakah*.

We learn that "no one ever becomes poor from *tzedakah*" and that harm cannot befall one who is on one's way to do *tzedakah*.[1] This latter principle has led to the custom, among some Jews, of giving *tzedakah* money to a person embarking on a journey for delivery to a needy person at the destination, in the belief that the transformation of the trip into a *tzedakah* mission will protect the traveler from the dangers of the road.

Some texts even threaten that harm or financial loss will befall a person who refuses to give *tzedakah*. One *midrash* has God saying, "If you do *tzedakah* with your property, your property will be maintained for you; if a poor person comes and says, 'Give me *tzedakah*,' and you do not give, your property will go into that person's hands" (*Shir haShirim Zuta* 1:15). Based on the verse in Ecclesiastes, "Send your bread forth upon the waters, for after many days you will find it" (11:1), the *midrash* explores ways in which *tzedakah* may produce a benefit for the giver.

In one such story, the early rabbinic figure Bar Kappara generously clothes and feeds the Roman survivor of a shipwreck. Years later, when the Roman Empire captures the land of Israel, Bar Kappara goes to Rome to beg mercy for the Jewish people and finds that the man whose life he saved has become the governor of Rome. This man recognizes Bar Kappara and agrees to relieve the Jews' suffering (*Kohelet Rabbah* 11:1).

As this story implies, *tzedakah* is considered to have redemptive possibilities, even beyond offering benefit or protection to an individual giver. Thus, God explains that if the generation drowned by the great flood or the people of Sodom had done *tzedakah*, they would not have been destroyed (*Shir haShirim Zuta* 1:15). Furthermore, the *midrash* promises that "through the merit of *tzedakah*, redemption will come, the Temple will be rebuilt ... and the exiles will be returned" (1:15). Beyond simply fulfilling a particular divine commandment, or even meeting the needs of a particular individual, *tzedakah* is understood to play a central role in the larger project of redeeming the world and bringing about the messianic age.

Tzedakah *as a Spiritual Practice*

We give money for many reasons. We give out of passion for causes, out of love or concern for others, out of gratitude for our own good fortune, and out of a desire to create a better world for ourselves and our children. Many of us also give because giving makes us feel good: *tzedakah* helps us to feel more connected to other individuals or organizations, to advance causes in which we believe, and to achieve a sense of purpose. Economist James Andreoni has deemed this motivation the "warm glow" theory of giving.[2]

There is nothing wrong with giving as a means of personal fulfillment. In commenting that "more than the wealthy person does for the poor, the poor person does for the wealthy" (*Vayikra Rabbah* 34:8), the Rabbis acknowledge that the spiritual benefits that the giver enjoys often exceed the material benefits for the recipient. Similarly, the commands for even the poorest person to give *tzedakah* and the instructions to give to the same person even one hundred times suggest that the practice of *tzedakah* aims, in part, to condition the giver to giving.[3] Giving even a small amount of *tzedakah* forces us to recognize the extent of poverty in the world, awakens our compassion toward others, and helps us to see our wealth as God's loan to us, rather than as a tribute to our own worth.

As a resident of Manhattan, I struggle with whether and how often to give money to people on the street, especially when I've seen many of the same faces on my street corner for ten years or more. In general, I choose to give, even knowing that my spare change will have little impact on any individual life, and that the recipients may use the money for drugs or alcohol. In this way, *tzedakah* is distinct from *tikkun olam*: I can give freely, even knowing that the system is not fully repaired. In cases where I am not able to give cash at all, I strive to give at least an acknowledgment of the other as a person, rather than seek comfort in shutting out his or her pain and suffering.

In *Orchot Chayyim*, a fifteenth-century work of *mussar* (ethics), the anonymous author explains that the discipline of giving regularly should become a spiritual practice that will awaken the compassion of the giver:

Our sages of blessed memory have stated further that the trait of generosity resides in habit, for one is not called generous until one becomes accustomed to giving, in every time and season, according to one's ability. For one who gives to a deserving person 1,000 gold pieces at once is not as generous as one who gives 1,000 gold pieces one by one, each gold piece to an appropriate recipient. For one who gives 1,000 gold pieces at once is seized with a fit of generosity that afterwards departs.... About this, the sages said, "all is according to the abundance of deeds" (Mishnah, *Avot*: 3: 15). They did not say "according to the greatness of deed."[4]

The mystical tradition imagines that our own compassion for the poor awakens divine compassion. The eighteenth-century Hasidic teacher Rabbi Levi Yitzchak of Berditchev comments:

Just as a Jew gives *tzedakah* to the poor and robes himself in the attribute of lovingkindness, and shows lovingkindness toward a poor person, similarly this causes God to robe Himself in the attribute of lovingkindness and to make divine lovingkindness flow ... to all of the worlds and the worlds below, as the rabbis said: "Anyone who shows mercy to humankind brings mercy on oneself from the heavens." (Talmud, *Shabbat* 151b)[5]

The goal of *tzedakah* is, first and foremost, to lift individual people out of poverty and to create a more equitable world. At the same time, giving *tzedakah* should also increase our own awareness of the world around us, and should arouse in us compassion for those in need. Like other spiritual practices, conditioning ourselves to give *tzedakah* can bring us into closer relationship with God or divinity, and has the potential to increase the sense of divine compassion in the world as a whole.

Who Needs to Give?

Depending on which survey you believe, between 60 and 90 percent of Americans give to charity, with the average household giving between 2.2 percent and 3.5 percent of its after-tax income.[6] Surprisingly, families in the highest and the lowest income brackets give the greatest percentage of their income to charity. Not surprisingly, the largest beneficiaries of Americans' charitable impulses are religious institutions, particularly churches that require or advise tithing.[7]

While Americans in general tend to be generous in their charitable giving, much of the media portrayal of philanthropy focuses on large gifts by the super rich or by major foundations. Bill Gates, Warren Buffet, and others have made national news with their commitments to spend billions of dollars on their charitable priorities. In the Jewish world, virtually every synagogue, Hillel building, JCC, day school, and camp is filled with plaques thanking donors who have funded capital projects. Many communal institutions bear the names of major donors. With all of this emphasis on large gifts by the wealthy, it would be easy for middle- and low-income individuals to see their own giving as inconsequential.

Judaism emphasizes that *tzedakah* is obligatory upon every member of the community, even those who themselves accept *tzedakah*.[8] A person who has lived in a community for thirty days becomes obligated to contribute to the *tamchui*, a system for distributing food to the hungry; and someone who has lived in a community for three months must donate to the *kuppah*, a fund that gives financial assistance to the poor. Someone who buys a home, thus declaring an intention to stay in a given community, becomes obligated to contribute to these funds immediately (Talmud, *Bava Batra* 8a).

By requiring that every member of the community contribute according to his or her ability, these texts establish a standard of shared responsibility for the well-being of the community. In the process described by the Talmud, community members do not independently, or according to their own inclinations, decide how much to give to *tzedakah*; rather, *tzedakah* collectors appointed by the community make the rounds of people's homes, do an assessment of wealth, and determine how much each individual owes to the *tzedakah* fund. Specifically, there is an expectation that each person should give at least 10 percent of his or her yearly income to *tzedakah*. According to traditional sources, you should not give more than 20 percent of your income to *tzedakah*, lest you find yourself dependent on the communal fund.[9]

Maimonides (Rambam) once exclaimed, "We have never seen or heard of a Jewish community without a *tzedakah* fund."[10] The question of whether Rambam *actually* had never seen such a community, or whether he was making a prescriptive point, is open for debate. Regardless, the fact that he considers a *tzedakah* fund to be the defining institution of a Jewish community gives us a sense of the centrality of *tzedakah* in Jewish law and history.

As we saw in the previous chapter, Judaism tends neither to venerate the wealthy nor blame the poor for their misfortune. Rather, the dominant strain of thought suggests that poverty and wealth are matters of chance, that fortunes can easily be reversed, and that the well-off therefore have a responsibility to share their wealth with the poor. In one statement of this concept, Rabbi Yechiel Epstein (Russia, 1829–1908), the author of the legal code known as the *Arukh haShulchan*, comments, "One should not say, 'How can I take away from my own money to give to the poor?' For this person should know that the money is not his own, but rather is a *pikadon* (a deposit left for safekeeping) in his hand in order that he may do the will of the one who left it. And [God's] will is that the person should give *tzedakah*."[11]

This admonition demands a fundamental shift in the way in which most people view charitable giving. Rather than praise those of us who give to the poor, Epstein emphasizes that our money is not ours to begin with, and that through *tzedakah*, we simply redistribute the money that God has given to us for safekeeping.

To facilitate *tzedakah*, my husband and I have set up a separate bank account into which we automatically move 10 percent of any income we receive. This strategy marks *tzedakah* money as fundamentally different from the money in our checking or savings accounts. No matter how well or poorly we're doing financially, we never touch the *tzedakah* money—it simply doesn't feel like ours to use. And rather than wait until December to distribute *tzedakah* all at once, we write checks throughout the year, whenever a substantial sum accumulates in that account.

Determining Tzedakah *Priorities*

We are surrounded by nearly infinite opportunities to change the world with our financial giving, to individuals and organizations, locally and worldwide. But our resources are not infinite, and dividing our gifts among too many recipients risks helping no one. How then can we choose?

At first glance, Jewish texts appear to offer a practical summary of our responsibilities. One Talmudic text develops a clear hierarchy of priority for loans:

> Rabbi Yosef taught, [the meaning of the verse] "If you lend money to my people, to the poor among you, do not act as a creditor toward them (Exod. 22:24)." In the case of a Jew and a non-Jew, the Jew takes precedence; a poor person and a wealthy person, the poor person takes precedence; a poor person of your own city and a poor person of another city, the poor of your city take precedence. (*Bava Metzia* 71a)

Although the focus here is on loans, later legal writers used this text as precedent for a hierarchy of *tzedakah*, and we will do so as well. This hierarchy is simple, but problematic. We *could* give all of our *tzedakah* to poor Jews in our own cities, but such behavior would fail to recognize any obligations beyond those physically and ethnically closest to us. Giving only to Jews might make sense in a world in which Jews are, as a whole, worse off than those around them, and in which non-Jews are, at worst, hostile and, at best, indifferent (as has been the case in many times and places). Giving in your own town makes sense in a world in which the next town is a several-hour, or even multi-day horse ride away; but in a globalized world in which we can access the news from Liberia as quickly as we can hear the news from New York, and in which many of us move from city to city multiple times over the course of our lives, the definition of "your city" becomes somewhat less clear.

When we look at other traditional texts, the seemingly simple equation becomes even more complicated. A number of sources challenge the conclusion that the Jewish responsibility of *tzedakah* extends only to other Jews. The Talmud elsewhere comments that you should "sustain the non-Jewish poor along with the Jewish poor and visit the non-Jewish sick along with the Jewish sick, and bury the non-Jewish dead along with the Jewish dead *mipnei darkhei shalom* (for the sake of the ways of peace)" (*Gitten* 61a). The precise meaning of *mipnei darkhei shalom* has generated significant debate. Some read this phrase simply as a nod to the political reality that a refusal to contribute to the care of the general population may provoke the wrath of non-Jews; others read the term more sympathetically, as an appeal to pursue peace among all peoples. This latter interpretation may be what Rambam had in mind when he wrote, in reference to the concept of *mipnei darkhei shalom*, "For this reason, it is said, 'God is good to all, and merciful to all of God's creations' (Psalms 145:9), and it is said, '[the Torah's] ways are ways of pleasantness, and all its paths are peace' (Proverbs 3:17)."[12] Caring for non-Jews may thus be understood as a means of imitating the divine quality of mercy to all, and/or as a fulfillment of the Torah's ideals of pleasantness and peace.

An additional warning against prioritizing those closest to yourself comes from Joseph Caro, who writes:

> The Mordekhai (a commentator on the Talmud) wrote: "Rav Kahana said, 'Anyone who gives all of his gifts to a single *kohen* (member of the priestly clan) brings anger to the world.' (Talmud, *Eruvin* 63a)." From this, we learn that one should not give all of one's *tzedakah* to a single relative, abandoning all other relatives, nor should one give all of one's *tzedakah* to a single person and not to anyone else.
>
> He also wrote that one who doles out *tzedakah* must be careful not to give more to one's relatives than to anyone else. Similarly, elsewhere in the Talmud (*Shabbat* 118b), Rabbi Yose said, "May I be among the collectors of *tzedakah* and

not among those charged with distributing it." Rashi explained, one who distributes *tzedakah* is likely to give more to one's relatives and thereby to steal from the rest of the poor. (*Beit Yosef, Yoreh De'ah* 257:9–10)

Three notable principles emerge from Caro's comment. First, despite the principle stated elsewhere that you should care first for the poor of your own household,[13] you should not prioritize a single, presumably closer, relative over all others. Second, you should distribute your *tzedakah* among multiple recipients rather than try to fulfill all the needs of a single individual. Finally, distributors of communal *tzedakah* funds should guard against allowing their own family commitments to interfere with the equitable distribution of *tzedakah*.

The first two of these three principles serve as a corrective against the potential tendency to view yourself as the savior of a single poor person. Faced with a needy relative or other individual, you may be tempted to divert all of your *tzedakah* money toward caring for this person. Such focus, however, threatens to lessen your sense of responsibility toward those outside of your immediate circle. According to Caro, then, it is preferable to provide smaller amounts of support to more people than to lift one person entirely out of poverty. Adding to this conversation, the *Arukh haShulchan* suggests that a person should give *more* to those closest to him or her, but should always reserve some *tzedakah* money for those farther away (*Yoreh De'ah* 251:4).

Looking back at the question of whether to prioritize the needs of Jews or non-Jews, we may find in Caro encouragement to give *tzedakah* beyond our immediate community. Even when the needs of the local Jewish community make major and legitimate demands on our *tzedakah* money, we might challenge ourselves to look beyond the needs of the "relatives" closest to us. In accordance with Rambam, we understand giving beyond our immediate community as a means of increasing peace and of emulating the divine quality of mercy, and not simply as a concession to political reality.

A more serious challenge to the preference for the poor of your own community comes from Rabbi Moshe Sofer (known as the

Chatam Sofer; Germany, 1762–1839), who complicates the talmudic hierarchy by defining need and geography as competing categories of priority:

> "If there is a poor person within your gates." *Sifre* [a collection
> of legal *midrashim* on the book of Deuteronomy] expounds
> this verse saying, "When one is starving, the one who is starv-
> ing takes precedence," and then expounds, "The poor of your
> city take precedence over the poor of another city." That is to
> say—this applies if both poor people need food or clothing.
> However, if the poor of your city have what they need to live,
> but just don't have any extra money [and the poor of the other
> city don't have food or clothing], then the poor of the other
> city take precedence over the poor of your city, for the needi-
> est takes precedence.[14]

Along similar lines, Rabbi Moshe Feinstein, a twentieth-century
authority, suspends the traditional preference for giving first to a
Kohen or *Levi* (descendents of the priestly tribes) in favor of giving to
the neediest:

> In regard to the issue of giving a *Kohen* precedence over a
> *Levi* and a *Levi* over a *Yisrael*, this applies only when all of
> them have the same need for food or clothing. For this rea-
> son, the text does not just say "there are many poor before
> you and you do not have enough for all of them" but rather,
> it says "you don't have enough to feed or to clothe all of
> them." The reason for this phrasing is that if one of them
> needs food and another needs clothing, the one who needs
> food takes precedence over the one who needs clothing,
> even if the one who needs food is a *Yisrael* and the one who
> needs clothing is a *Kohen*.... All discussions of precedence
> apply only when all of the poor people have the same
> needs. (*Igg'rot Moshe, Yoreh De'ah* 1:144)

While the traditional distinction between the status of a *Kohen* or *Levi*
and that of a *Yisrael* has ceased to have real meaning outside of a few
areas of ritual or marriage practice, Feinstein and Sofer's larger point
stands: the extent of need trumps both geography and social status.

Based on Feinstein and Sofer, as well as on Caro's warning against prioritizing family, we might then construct a different hierarchy of *tzedakah,* in which we give first to the neediest and only then worry about questions of geography, identity, or closeness. But this new hierarchy would be as oversimplified as the one that prioritizes the local Jewish community above all else. Attention to relative need above all else might lead us to give *tzedakah* only to the poorest residents of the developing world, and to ignore members of our own communities entirely. Such an approach might result in a decrease of economic opportunity in our own communities, and may send us into a seesaw approach to poverty, in which we focus on one community until another falls into desperate straights, and then switch our attention fully to this other community.

Instead of distributing *tzedekah* strictly according to need, geography, or Jewishness, we might view these categories as competing priorities. Rather than elevate one of these categories over the others, we might look for a means of balancing these sometimes competing categories. In allocating *tzedakah* over the year, for instance, I designate certain percentages to New York (my city), the rest of the United States (my city according to an expanded sense of geography), Israel (considered like a Jew's own city by a number of commentators), and the rest of the world. For each geographic area, I then assign target percentages to Jewish and non-Jewish organizations. Within each category, I focus on areas of greatest need: the poorest individuals or the causes most likely to be struggling for support. The percentages assigned to each category change each year, and are not scientific. Rather, in thinking through my relative commitments to people in various geographic areas, to Jews and non-Jews, and to different types of needs, I strive for a balance among competing responsibilities.

What Counts as Tzedakah?

A literalist reading of the sources cited above might conclude that *tzedakah* money should be used first and foremost to provide food to the hungry. Based on this interpretation, we might postpone giving to nonhunger-related programs until every person in the world had been sufficiently fed. Economic realities being what they are, this approach to *tzedakah* would lead all of us to give only to soup kitchens, food pantries, and other emergency food programs. More people might be less hungry, but we would make little progress toward ending poverty.

The potential conflict between caring for the immediate needs of the most desperate and working toward an end to poverty has not escaped Jewish thinkers. Famously, Rambam designated as the highest level of *tzedakah* "strengthening the hand of a fellow Jew by giving a gift or a loan or entering into partnership with him."[15] The long history of Jewish mutual-aid and free-loan societies in the United States—which have helped numerous Jews and non-Jews to start businesses, get through crises, and pay college tuition—pays tribute to Rambam's example. We should note that even as Rambam specifies "strengthen[ing] the hand of a fellow Jew," he offers as a proof text for this position a verse that indicates an obligation to the *ger,* or non-Jewish sojourner (Lev. 25:35).

Some legal thinkers explicitly allow *tzedakah* money to be used for nonmaterial needs. Commenting on Rabbi Meir of Rothenberg's (Germany, 1215–1293) statement of permission to use *tzedakah* money to purchase books, Rabbi Eliezer Waldenberg (Palestine/Israel, 1915–2006) explains:

> One can say that he permits this because the books will be lent for study to those who need them, and anyone who needs these books is considered poor, insofar as this person lacks them. This is like distributing spiritual food, and is no less desirable than distributing physical food to those who need it. However, as for using this money for a *mitzvah* (such as buying candles for the synagogue)—in this case, the money does not go to either physical or spiritual food for those who need it ... and one should not use the money in this way. I have seen an opinion that ... one may certainly use this money to buy books for the children of the poor, for providing spiritual food to the poor is also considered to be *tzedakah.*[16]

In a modern context, we might define "spiritual food" as education, access to the arts, public libraries, and other nonmaterial resources that improve individual lives and reduce poverty. We should notice, though, that Waldenberg's definition of *tzedakah* includes only items purchased primarily for the use of the poorer members of the community, and not for general communal use. As mentioned earlier, separate obligations mandate contributing to building communal institutions, but these gifts do not fall under the rubric of *tzedakah* unless the poor will benefit significantly or primarily from the result.

Jewish organizations that address poverty generally pursue a combination of direct relief and advocacy for systemic change. Mazon, a Jewish organization that focuses on hunger relief, supports not only emergency food programs but also advocacy for better food policies. The Federation system, which acts as a central distribution system for the needs of local, national, and international Jewish communities, as well as for non-Jews in need, provides funds both for direct relief and for legislative advocacy. Organizations such as Jewish Funds for Justice, New Israel Fund, and American Jewish World Service, which respectively address economic and social inequality in the United States, Israel, and the rest of the world, prioritize initiatives to organize low-income people around issues of concern, to provide microloans to those trying to buy first homes or to start small businesses, and to advocate for legislative change. These approaches allow people to improve their lives immediately, through starting a business, securing a home, or developing the political capital that comes with citizen action. At the same time, recipients help to transform their communities for the long term by accumulating wealth, providing long-term employment, and changing the political systems that engender inequity.

Three times a day, traditionally observant Jews pray for the arrival of the messianic age. But multiple traditions insist that prayer alone does not suffice. In one Talmudic story, Rabbi Yehoshua ben Levi asks Elijah the prophet—a constant advocate for the poor—when the Messiah will arrive. Elijah instructs Rabbi Yehoshua to pose this question directly to the Messiah, who stands among the lepers outside of the gates of Rome. Rabbi Yehoshua finds the Messiah and asks, "When will you come?" "Today," the Messiah answers. When the Messiah fails to appear as planned, Rabbi Yehoshua complains to Elijah. Rabbi Yehoshua has misunderstood, Elijah explains. By "today," the Messiah meant, "Today if only you will listen to God's voice (Psalms 95:7)" (Talmud, *Sanhedrin* 98a). The point is clear—the messianic age will arrive only when we bring it. The description of the Messiah as standing among—and presumably comforting—the lepers reminds us of the importance of caring for the individual sufferer. At the same time, the emphasis on bringing about the messianic era keeps our sights on large-scale, systemic change.

The Responsibility of the State

The traditional discussions of *tzedakah* assume a situation in which a semi-autonomous Jewish community has the power to collect and allocate *tzedakah* funds, and in which individuals also regularly make choices about *tzedakah*. If considered at all, the larger government is seen as an impediment or an active threat. At best, the government leaves the Jewish community alone. At worst, the government demands excessive taxes or even sponsors persecution. There is, therefore, little or no attention in the traditional sources to the question of the government's responsibility toward the poor.

The establishment of the state of Israel in 1948 generated new interest in civil law among Jewish legal thinkers. While modern Israeli law is based on British common law and not *halakhah*, in an independent state run by Jews, once-theoretical discussions of civil law become increasingly relevant. In a state with a built-in—if imperfect—welfare structure, are the responsibilities of individual citizens fulfilled instead by the state? If individual citizens became, in the words of former president George H. W. Bush, "a thousand points of light," and actually managed to alleviate most immediate needs, would the government's responsibilities toward the most vulnerable citizens diminish?

Mitzvot include two different kinds of obligation. *Chovat gavra* refers to *mitzvot* that every individual is obligated to observe on a regular basis, such as praying, eating *matzah* on Passover and observing Shabbat. A *chovat cheftza* is an obligation that comes into play only if the occasion arises; for example, saying a blessing when eating fruit, but there is no obligation to eat an orange in order to say this blessing. Israeli rabbi Ya'akov Ariel suggests that the *mitzvah* of *tzedakah* is both types of *mitzvot* at once. It is a *chovat gavra* in the sense that each individual Jew is obligated to give *tzedakah* regardless of the presence or absence of people in need. Even if there is no one to whom to give the *tzedakah*, each person should contribute to the communal fund, which will be held in trust until a need arises. In contrast, the community's obligation is a *chovat cheftza*: if there are poor, their needs must be fulfilled. For Ariel, now that the government takes on responsibility for its citizens, the term "community" can be understood as "government." In his reading, a state is judged according to the kind of society it produces, and not according to how much money has been spent. Ariel writes:

> An individual is not obligated to carry alone the burden of ... (fulfilling the needs of the poor person)—this is, rather, the responsibility of the community.... Today, the economists believe that the state is not able to carry all of this heavy burden that it has taken upon itself. A part of the responsibility has now been passed on to the volunteer sector within the community—in my opinion, this is not the preferred situation.... Citizens should not think themselves exempt from the *mitzvah* of *tzedakah*, for as stated, this is also an individual *mitzvah*.... [But] only the community is able to do this in a widespread way.[17]

That is to say that the volunteer sector will always remain important, but should not take on full responsibility for the well-being of society. Per Ariel's suggestion, we might think of two streams of caring for societal needs. In designing social systems, we should strive to prevent extreme poverty, to allow each member of society the opportunity to support himself or herself in a dignified and productive way, and to care for those who still fall through the cracks. Some of our *tzedakah* money should go toward creating this society. But even in this ideal society, some people will still need emergency assistance, especially in the face of health challenges, job loss, or other crises. A combination of governmental assistance and individual *tzedakah* would then address these issues. And even if, against all expectations, we create a world in which there is no poverty at all, we should still maintain our practice of giving *tzedakah* both to reap the spiritual benefits of cultivating generosity and to ensure that a system of *tzedakah* will be available to respond to needs that might arise in the future.

5

Servants to Servants or Servants to God
Workers, Employers, and Unions

The Rabbis of the talmudic period were deeply ambivalent about the value of work. Rabbinic debate about labor most often concerns the relative value of *derekh eretz* (the way of the world, i.e., work) and *talmud Torah* (study). The Rabbis also discuss whether the divine punishment that Adam must acquire food "by the sweat of [his] brow" (Gen. 3:19) designates all work as a curse. On the one hand, they certainly view the need for market labor as a potential interference with the study of Torah. On the other hand, they recognize that individuals must earn a living, and that the life of the community depends on certain types of work and workers.

One early source suggests that work for pay is not only economically necessary, but even morally beneficial to the worker, and that the life of the fully supported scholar is not the ideal:

> "Great is *talmud Torah* (Torah study) that is combined with *derekh eretz*, as the two together will lead to the abandonment of sin. All *talmud Torah* that is not combined with *derekh eretz* will, in the end, be nullified and will lead to sin."
> (Mishnah, *Avot* 2:2)

Here, the term *derekh eretz*, literally "the way of the land," is understood to mean ordinary human affairs, specifically work. Similarly,
one rabbinic passage equates the obligation to work during the six
days of the week with the obligation to rest on Shabbat. Expanding
on the command in Mishnah, *Avot* 1:10 (also known as *Pirkei Avot*, or
Ethics of the Fathers) to "love work," *Avot d'Rabbi Natan*, an early commentary on Mishnah, *Avot* states:

> "Love work." How? This teaches that a person should love
> work, and not hate work. Just as the Torah was given through
> the covenant, so too, work was given through the covenant,
> as it says, "For six days you shall labor and do all of your
> work, and the seventh day is a Sabbath to your God." (*Nusach*
> 1, ch. 11)

Or, in the words of Rabbi Chaim David HaLevy, a twentieth-
century Israeli rabbi, "In the Jewish worldview, work is sacred—it is
building and creating and is a partnership with God in the work of
creation" (*Aseh L'cha Rav* 2:64).

In contrast to these praises of work, other rabbinic texts
declare *talmud Torah* to be the only worthwhile endeavor. For the
purposes of this discussion, however, I will not focus on texts that
debate the relative merits of work and of *talmud Torah*, but rather I
will examine texts that assume the necessity of working and that
address the preferred nature of this work.

In some places, the Rabbis depict certain types of work,
notably skinning animals and tanning hides, as inherently undigni-
fied, presumably because these trades are notoriously dirty and
smelly (Talmud, *Kiddushin* 82b). Similarly, a person should avoid
engaging in trades associated with criminality, such as donkey or
camel handling (*Kiddushin* 82a). However, in other places, the Rabbis caution against shunning any kind of work. In one talmudic
episode, Rav instructs Rav Kahana, "Skin carcasses in the marketplace and collect your wages, and do not say, 'I am *a kohen* (priest)
and a great man, and this is below my dignity.'"[1] Even more strik-
ingly, the Talmud reports:

> Rabbi Yehuda used to go into the *beit midrash* (house of study) carrying a pitcher on his shoulders. He would say, "Great is work, as it gives honor to the one who does it." Rabbi Shimon would carry a basket on his shoulders, and would say, "Great is work, as it gives honor to the one who does it." (*N'darim* 49b)

Here, the Rabbis not only glorify working, but also introduce everyday work into the *beit midrash*, a place that some might expect to remain a sanctuary from "everyday" intrusions.

The episode in the *beit midrash* confuses our notions of the sacred and the ordinary. We expect the Rabbis, who declare *talmud Torah* to be one of the greatest *mitzvot*, to present Torah study as the only means by which someone acquires honor. Furthermore, we expect a clear division between the domains of work and of study. Instead, the *beit midrash* becomes a meeting point for these two pursuits, and the locus for a declaration about the honor of work. By locating inside the *beit midrash* Rabbi Yehuda's and Rabbi Shimon's exaltations of work, the text challenges our previous notions about the relative value of study and work and about the existence of a separation between the spheres of "religious" and "ordinary." Not only can "ordinary" work enter the *beit midrash*, but the honor that we might consider the exclusive property of the religious world, represented by the *beit midrash*, is also accorded to everyday labor.

Another talmudic text not only unites the sacred and the ordinary, but goes even further, elevating work over religious belief. According to this text:

> Rabbi Chiyya ben Ammi said in the name of Ulla: Greater is the one who benefits from the work of his hands than one who fears heaven. In regard to the one who fears heaven, it is written, "Happy is the man who fears God" (Psalms 112). But in regard to the one who benefits from his own work, it is written, "When you eat from the work of your hands, you will be happy, and it will be well with you" (Psalms 128). "You will be happy" refers to this world; "It will be well with you" refers to the world to come. In regard to the one who fears

heaven, the text does not say "it will be well with you."
(B'rakhot 8a)

Again, this text challenges our assumptions about the relationship between the sacred and the ordinary. We might expect to reap the rewards of work in this world and of religious faith in the world to come. Instead, Rabbi Chiyya asserts the opposite. While both the worker and the person of faith enjoy rewards in this world, only the worker automatically merits a place in the world to come. We can read this text in a number of ways. It may serve as a corrective to statements that value spiritual practice over physical labor, or as a means of affirming a sacred dimension to the work that people are compelled to do. However we read it, the text reminds us of the impossibility of drawing hard boundaries between the sacred and the mundane. Not only can work enter the *beit midrash*—it can even lead the worker into the world to come. Religious practice may lead us into a messianic age, but it may just as easily trap us in the present world.

Dignity in the Workplace

Despite their ideological ambivalence about the value of work, the Rabbis insist on the dignity and honor of the worker. The Rabbis also sought to articulate ways to ensure that workplaces manifest and uphold that dignity.

The story of the exodus and its associated rabbinic commentary offer the most extensive insight into traditional Jewish understandings about work and working conditions. While the biblical account of the Israelites' slavery in Egypt focuses on the difficulty of the imposed physical labor, *midrash* and other rabbinic commentaries understand the difficulties of slavery to arise primarily from spiritual, rather than physical, oppression. For instance, in rabbinic expansions of the slavery narrative, the Egyptians prevent Israelite husbands and wives from seeing one another and view the Israelites as "thorns" rather than human beings (*Sh'mot Rabbah* 1:11–12).

The emphasis in these texts on the loss of dignity as the primary condition of slavery mirrors the experience of many modern
low-wage workers who, when asked to describe their working conditions, invariably reply, "they don't respect us," alongside more
concrete concerns such as low wages, long hours, or the lack of
health insurance. In the words of Marie Pierre, a Haitian nursing
home assistant interviewed by Human Rights Watch (HRW), "We
know our job, we love our job, we love our patients, but management doesn't respect us." Although Pierre and her co-workers twice
voted to accept a union, HRW reports, the company has refused to
accept the union and fired Pierre for speaking Creole with other
employees.[2] Together, the midrashic text and the real-life examples
help explain why so many strikes concern people's desire for a voice
at work, and not only the wage issues that we most often associate
with labor disputes.

According to one well-known *midrash*, the Egyptians placed:

> A heavy burden on a child and a light burden on an adult; a
> man's burden on a woman and a woman's burden on a man;
> the burden of an elderly person on a youth, and the burden of
> a youth on an elderly person.[3]

I began to understand this *midrash* only upon hearing workers at a
plastics factory in Paterson, New Jersey, describe a manager who
purposely assigned the company's oldest employee, a seventy-four-
year-old woman, to the heaviest machines. Even when this woman
was on the verge of fainting from exhaustion, the manager refused
to allow another worker to take her place.[4]

From an initial reading of this last *midrash*, and from our immediate reaction to the story of the Paterson workers, we understand that
placing a heavy burden on an elderly person compromises the health
and the dignity of the worker. The problem with placing "the burden
of an elderly person on a youth" may not, however, be immediately
clear. We might speculate that it is degrading to perform work that
does not challenge our abilities. But the story of the Paterson workers reveals another indignity to which the *midrash* hints. These

factory workers reported begging to trade places with the elderly woman, only to meet with the manager's insistence that they continue their own, less strenuous work. Instead of exercising their compassionate instincts, these women were forced to remain helpless as a co-worker and friend suffered. The initial indignity to one elderly worker thus results in an insult to the humanity of all of the workers.

I would further suggest that the offense to the dignity of a worker also compromises the dignity of the employer, whether the employer realizes this or not.[5] When local Catholic priests organized a prayer vigil outside of the Paterson plastics factory, the owners hired a surveillance team to photograph the vigils and to record the names of the workers speaking with the clergy.[6] In their determination to maintain the status quo in their factory, the owners became increasingly less receptive to the needs of others and willing even to interfere with the activities of local clergy. Through their actions these owners made themselves look ridiculous and damaged their own ability to earn the respect of third parties. Additionally, in degrading others, the employers implicitly suggested that human beings do not inherently deserve respect. In treating their employees poorly, these employers, by extension, questioned the inherent value of all humans, including themselves.[7]

The case of the Paterson factory workers therefore reveals the more general principle that insulting the dignity of another brings with it an affront to your own dignity. Someone who degrades another denies the essential dignity of all people and therefore necessarily reduces his or her own claim to dignity. With this in mind, we can perhaps read the biblical statement that God "hardened Pharaoh's heart" not only as an indication of divine intervention, but also as a description of the inevitable effect of enslaving or mistreating another. In mistreating his slaves, Pharaoh introduces into Egyptian society the possibility of human degradation, and thus necessarily calls into question the inherent dignity of all members of the society, including himself.

Another *midrash* further understands the ways in which employers can degrade their employees. In a bit of wordplay, it recasts the unfamiliar Hebrew word *perach*, used in the Torah to describe the Egyptian enslavement of the Israelites, as *peh rach*—a gentle mouth. According to this *midrash*:

> At the moment when Pharaoh said, "Come, let us deal wisely with them ... and they set taskmasters over them" (Exod.1:10–11), [Pharaoh] gathered all of the people of Israel and said to them, "Please, will you work with me today?" For this reason, the text says "The Egyptians oppressed the children of Israel *b'ferach* (with hard labor)" meaning *b'peh rach* (with a gentle mouth). Pharaoh took a basket and trowel. When the children of Israel saw Pharaoh taking the basket and trowel and working with bricks, they came hurriedly and worked with him with all of their strength, as they were strong and mighty people. When night came, Pharaoh placed taskmasters over them and said to them, "Count the bricks." Right away, they stood and counted them. Pharaoh said to them, "This is what you must produce every day." He appointed Egyptian taskmasters over Israelite supervisors, and appointed the supervisors over the rest of the people of Israel.[8]

The *midrash* is perceptive in its understanding of the subtle ways in which employers exert power over employees. In the contemporary world, when workers request changes in working conditions or attempt to organize, employers often discourage these efforts by questioning employees' commitment to the company "family" or by offering assurances that the company has workers' best interests in mind. Describing the Wal-Mart employee training video, Barbara Ehrenreich writes:

> Here, various associates testify to the "essential feeling of family for which Wal-Mart is so well known," leading up to the conclusion that we don't need a union. Once, long ago, unions had a place in American society, but they "no longer have much to offer workers," which is why people are leaving them "by the droves." ... Think of what you would lose with a union: first, your dues money, which could be $20 a month "and sometimes much more." Second, you would lose "your

voice" because the union would insist on doing your talking for you.[9]

The *midrash* offers yet another insight about intimidation. Slavery, the *midrash* implies, becomes even more degrading when the slave believes himself or herself to be responsible for bringing about this condition. If the Israelite slaves complain about their situation, the Egyptians can reply that the Israelites willingly accepted servitude. Later generations may accept the Egyptian account of events and direct anger at their parents and grandparents, rather than at their enslavers. Similarly, contemporary employers convince workers that unpleasant working conditions and firings result from the disloyalty of certain employees, and from the interference of unions, rather than from any wrongdoing on the part of the employer.

When Sara Flores, a janitor in New Jersey, testified before the National Labor Relations Board about her company's unfair labor practices, she returned to work to learn that she had been fired. The following day her eight co-workers went on strike to protest Flores's firing, and they too lost their jobs. When company employees throughout the region walked out in protest of these initial firings, the company responded by dismissing all of the striking workers.[10] If Sara Flores's employer succeeded in persuading employees to hold Flores responsible for the mass firings, the company would effectively have silenced further complaints and guaranteed a permanently degrading workplace.[11]

If we understand the biblical and rabbinic account of Egyptian slavery to represent the primary example of unacceptable working conditions, then we can assume a general prohibition against mimicking the practices of Pharaoh and his taskmasters. This assumption gains support from the repeated biblical assertion that the memory of slavery creates an obligation not to subject others to the conditions the Egyptians imposed on the Israelites.[12] If we understand these historical reminders as general admonitions against enslaving others, and not only as justification for specific commandments such as the obligation to protect strangers, widows, and orphans, then we can read the rabbinic descriptions of Egyptian slavery as obligating us to avoid similar workplace models.

Thus, in contrast to the Israelite workers described by the *midrashim* discussed above, the workers we hire should be permitted to continue regular family relations and should perform jobs suited to their abilities. Drawing on midrashic interpretations of the verse, "When your brother sells himself to you" (Deut. 15:12), Ben-Tzion Meir Chai Uziel (Palestine, 1880–1953), the Sephardic chief rabbi first of Palestine and then of the state of Israel, comments, "Employers are obligated to behave with love, honor, goodwill, and generosity toward their workers."[13]

One of the best-known and most powerful statements of the responsibility of employers toward their workers demands that employers go above and beyond the letter of the law in caring for their workers:

> Some porters working for Raba bar bar Chanan broke a jug of wine. He seized their clothes. They came before Rav, and Rav said to Raba bar bar Chanan, "Give them their clothing." Raba bar bar Chanan said to him, "Is this the law?" Rav said, "Yes, because of the principle, 'You should walk in the ways of the good' (Proverbs 2:20)." He gave them back their clothes. They said to him, "We are poor, and we troubled ourselves to work all day, and we are needy—do we receive nothing?" Immediately, Rav said to Raba bar bar Chanan, "Go, give them their wages." He said to Rav, "Is this the law?" Rav said, "Yes—'you should keep the ways of the righteous' (ibid.)." (Talmud, *Bava Metzia* 83a)

Rav's answer to Raba bar bar Chanan here is both unusual and instructive: a reader accustomed to the intricate style of talmudic discourse would expect Rav to respond by deriving a law from a biblical verse, or by quoting an earlier authority. Instead, Rav dodges legal discourse altogether by quoting a general principle—answering, effectively, that the letter of the law is irrelevant to the case at hand. As an employer, Raba bar bar Chanan is responsible for the welfare of his needy workers, and not simply for fulfilling his contractual obligations toward them. According to Rav, the principle, "You should walk in the ways of the good; you should keep the ways of the righteous," compels employers to recognize their privileged and powerful position vis-à-vis their workers, and to act in such a way as to protect the interests of the workers.

Traditional sources also indicate an awareness of the unclear boundaries between work and slavery. Workers are specifically permitted to quit a job in the middle of the day, because "the children of Israel are [God's] servants and not servants to servants."[14] Likewise, Moshe Isserles (known as the Rema; Poland, 1520–1572), the author of a gloss on the *Shulchan Arukh*, rules that a person may not accept employment in the household of another for more than three years, as such a position may take on the appearance of servitude (*Choshen Mishpat* 333:3).

Today, when the institution of slavery is illegal, it is unlikely that anyone would confuse long-term employment, even for domestic servants, with slavery. Even so, we should be aware that some low-wage employment situations do become, de facto, slavery. In my own organizing work in New Jersey, I was shocked to encounter a nursing home that employed Filipino nurses who were brought to the United States illegally and forced to work as indentured servants to pay off their traffickers' fees. The nurses lived in the nursing home and were on call twenty-four hours a day. Without documentation, the nurses could not take the risk of leaving the home. When the local health care union sent Tagalog-speaking organizers to speak with the nurses, nursing home administrators prevented these organizers from entering. In 2008, the issue of human trafficking from the Philippines jumped into the newspapers with reports of a California nursing home's attempt to smuggle six Filipino health care workers into the country by presenting these workers as tae kwon do students.[15]

While *midrashim* on Egypt offer insight into unhealthy workplaces, one biblical episode offers us a more positive workplace model. The second chapter of the book of Ruth begins with Boaz, a wealthy field owner, visiting his fields to speak to the workers. This interaction offers a few insights into appropriate employer-employee relations. First, it is clear that Boaz visits the field often. He is familiar with the workers, and he even notices the appearance of a new gleaner. Second, Boaz invokes God's name in greeting his workers. The Talmud understands the interaction between Boaz and his workers as the precedent for always invoking God's name in asking about the well-being of another (*B'rakhot* 54a). It is significant that the precedent for using God's name as a greeting appears in a workplace situation, and not in a religious context. Perhaps it becomes even more important to introduce God into a situation in which we might not expect to sense God's presence. In this way, the episode parallels the stories of Rabbi Yehuda and Rabbi Shimon bringing their work into the *beit midrash*. Third, Boaz's insistence on enforcing the biblical permission for the poor to glean shows his awareness that his wealth is not his own, but is a loan from God, meant to be shared with those who do not enjoy such wealth.

While the Rabbis remain ambivalent about the inherent value of work, they push us toward the conclusion that work, when necessary, should confer dignity upon the worker. Employers should, like Boaz, maintain close contact with their workers, recognizing them as individuals. Most importantly, the Rabbis insist that God's presence should manifest itself in the workplace, both through the literal pronouncement of God's name and through the interactions between employers and employees. A person's work environment should offer the same kind of dignity and honor we associate with religious spaces such as the *beit midrash*.

The "Working Poor"

Jewish law differentiates between two types of workers—the *po'el*, who is paid by the day, and the *kablan*, who is paid by the task. Generally, the *po'el* is a low-skilled worker who is hired for agricultural or other manual tasks. The *kablan* is more often a skilled craftsman who performs tasks such as dying cloth or repairing household items. This chapter will focus on the *po'el* as a closer parallel to the contemporary low-wage worker, who is paid an hourly wage rather than by the task, and who does not necessarily have specialized skills or training.

Most Jewish employment law revolves around the concept of *minhag hamakom*—the idea that the custom of the place determines workers' salaries, as well as other working conditions. This principle is laid out most clearly in the Mishnah:

> One who hires workers and instructs them to begin work early and to stay late—in a place in which it is not the custom to begin work early and to stay late, the employer may not force them to do so. In a place in which it is the custom to feed the workers, he must do so. In a place in which it is the custom to distribute sweets, he must do so. Everything goes according to the custom of the land.
>
> A story about Rabbi Yochanan ben Matya, who told his son, "Go, hire us workers." His son went and promised them food [without specifying what kind, or how much]. When he returned, his father said to him, "My son! Even if you gave them a feast like that of King Solomon, you would not have fulfilled your obligation toward them, for they are the children of Abraham, Isaac and Jacob. However, as they have not yet begun to work, go back and say to them that their employment is conditional on their not demanding more than bread and vegetables." Rabbi Shimon ben Gamliel said, "It is not necessary to make such a stipulation. Everything goes according to the custom of the place." (*Bava Metzia* 7:1)

Within this text, we find two voices: on the one hand, the dominant voice twice asserts that the "custom of the place" (*minhag hamakom*) is the deciding factor in all areas of labor law. The second voice—that of Rabbi Yochanan ben Matya—insists that the inherent dignity of the workers transcends any entrenched customs, and that the employer theoretically bears infinite responsibility toward the workers.

It is unusual for a *mishnah* to offer the level of detail included in this text. In general, the Mishnah consists of concisely stated case law. In some cases, two schools of opinion appear in the Mishnah, but there is rarely any explanation of the reasoning of either side.

This *mishnah* stands out both because of the relatively long list of practices that might be governed by the *minhag hamakom* and, even more significantly, because of the story included within the text.

Some major contemporary writers on Judaism and business ethics have understood the principle of *minhag hamakom* as evidence of halakhic support for a free-market system.[16] The custom of the area determines wages, hours, and other working conditions, but no one may set those terms—they are assumed to derive "naturally" from the market. The *mishnah* prohibits employers from forcing employees to work long hours, but it leaves open the possibility that an employer may stipulate long hours in the initial contract. The talmudic commentary on this *mishnah* suggests that Torah law technically permits long hours, but that local custom may be stricter (*Bava Metzia* 83b).

The *Yerushalmi* offers a new and significant perspective on the question of the payment and treatment of workers. Commenting on the same *mishnah* discussed above, the *Yerushalmi* supports the initial conclusion that rabbinic law prefers an unregulated free-market system. There, Rabbi Hoshea concludes that "the custom overrides the law," because even though the Torah allows employers to insist on long working hours, local custom takes precedence (*Bava Metzia* 7:1). The *Yerushalmi* then offers the story of the people of the city of Beit Maon who, unlike the people of the city of Tiberius, were accustomed to starting work early and ending late. According to the *Yerushalmi*:

> The people of Tiberius who went up to Beit Maon to hire themselves out would hire themselves according to the custom of Beit Maon. The people of Beit Maon who came down to Tiberius to hire themselves out would hire themselves according to the custom of Tiberius. However, when one went from Tiberius to hire workers in Beit Maon, he could say to them, "Do not think that I could not find workers to hire in Tiberius. Rather, I came here to hire workers because I heard that you will start work early and end late." (Talmud Yerushalmi, Bava Metzia 7:1)

From this story we might infer that market forces are the only factor governing working conditions and that employers may demand any conditions that workers will accept. This story supports the claim by many employers that workers unhappy with their wages should find higher-paying work. Disturbingly, this story also seems to justify the current practice of employing workers in developing countries at wages that would be illegal in America.

A few elements within the *mishnah* and its accompanying *gemara* in the Babylonian Talmud challenge this initial conclusion. We are first struck by the number of apparently superfluous details in the *mishnah*. Instead of simply offering the concise statement that "everything goes according to the custom of the land," the *mishnah* offers numerous examples of conditions determined by the accepted *minhag*.

The *gemara* notices the expansive nature of the *mishnah* and questions the necessity of specifying that an employer may not force workers to begin early and stay late. The Talmud responds:

> We need [this statement] for the case in which the employer raises the workers' wages. In the case in which he says to them, "I raised your wages in order that you would begin work early and stay late," they may reply, "You raised our wages in order that we would do better work." (*Bava Metzia* 83a)

With these words, the *gemara* establishes wages and hours, and presumably other working conditions, as categories that are not inherently dependent on one another. Raising a worker's salary does not necessarily obligate this worker to work longer hours or to accept new responsibilities. Employers and workers presumably may stipulate longer hours when they negotiate a contract, but an employer who fails to make such a stipulation before raising wages may not, post facto, demand a longer workday. In its use of the plural form of "workers," this text hints at a collective bargaining process through which workers negotiate a shared contract. The workers, as a group, also have the power to enforce this contract in a way that a single worker may not have the power to do.

The Talmud is also surprising in its suggestion that workers may adjust their production rate or quality to salary levels. The *gemara* implicitly permits an employee who earns low wages to work less hard than one who earns a higher salary. In this allowance, the text calls to mind the common labor tactic of a "work to rule" strike, in which workers refuse to exceed the precise job requirements and slow production by painstakingly observing every regulation. In this text, I hear the voice of historian Robin Kelley, who reminisces about himself and his friends as African American teenagers, without union representation, quietly challenging the management of the McDonald's where they worked by conducting work slowdowns, or by finding other ways to compensate for the indignity of their jobs.[17] When we pay people minimum wage, we can expect a low level of production. To increase work quality, we must also increase wages and improve other working conditions.

In the Mishnaic story of Rabbi Yochanan ben Matya, we also find a challenge to the idea that the local *minhag* governs all workplace conditions. Rabbi Yochanan assumes not only that the employer must stipulate the exact working conditions, but also that vague statements should be interpreted in favor of the worker.

With the comment that the workers are "the children of Abraham, Isaac and Jacob," Rabbi Yochanan ben Matya simultaneously asserts the dignity of these workers and denies any separation between himself and his son and those they employ. Many employers fail to recognize the humanity of their workers and, accordingly, show little interest in the workers' history or personal situation. In contrast, Rabbi Yochanan forces his son to confront the humanity of the workers, and to acknowledge the shared narrative of employer and employee. Although the *gemara* does not eventually accept Rabbi Yochanan ben Matya's demand for clear stipulations regarding food quality and quantity, the inclusion of this aggadic text problematizes our acceptance of *minhag hamakom* as the sole determinant of worker contracts.

The specification that the workers in Rabbi Yochanan's story are Jewish is problematic for our discussion, both because our modern sensibilities resist legal separations between ethnic and religious groups, and because most low-wage workers in America are not Jewish. We can read this text either as evidence that the Rabbis imagine a separate body of law for Jewish and non-Jewish workers, or as a reflection of the rabbinic inability to conceive of non-Jews working for Jews. The absence of a separate body of rabbinic law for non-Jewish workers supports the latter conclusion. However, we must admit that biblical law does recognize separate categories for Jewish and Canaanite slaves, and that the Rabbis may consider this fact precedent for creating separate labor laws for Jews. While we may be inclined to argue that the Rabbis simply cannot imagine a situation in which Jews employ members of other ethnic groups, we need to admit that the interpretation of this aspect of the text remains open.

The talmudic texts we have examined so far therefore leave us with questions and paradoxes. On the one hand, some textual evidence points to a bias in favor of workers. On the other hand, the conclusion of the text instructs us to follow the *minhag* of the place in all areas of labor law. Additionally, we have no clear statement about appropriate wage levels beyond the necessity that these levels conform to the regional *minhag*. Furthermore, it is not clear whether halakhic labor laws apply to non-Jews as well as to Jews. To sort out these issues, we must expand our inquiry into the assumptions of labor law.

The Conditions of Work

Two biblical verses provide the basis for much of Jewish labor law:

> Do not oppress your neighbor and do not rob him. Do not keep the wages of the worker with you until morning. (Lev. 19:13)
>
> Do not oppress the hired laborer who is poor and needy, whether he is one of your people or one of the sojourners in your land within your gates. Give him his wages in the daytime, and do not let the sun set on them, for he is poor, and

> his life depends on them, lest he cry out to God about you, for
> this will be counted as a sin for you. (Deut. 24:14–15)

These biblical verses are significant in their acknowledgment of the essential imbalance of power and wealth between employer and employee. The texts understand both the employer's power to rob the employee and the employee's dependence on the wages. From these verses, we understand workers to be a protected category, perhaps similar to widows, orphans, and sojourners, whom the Torah also prohibits oppressing.[18] The verses from Deuteronomy further include sojourners among the protected workers, thereby prohibiting us from distinguishing between Jewish and non-Jewish workers.[19]

From the biblical text, we can derive a few general principles. First, workers are understood to be poor—or at least without wealth, relying on daily income—and thus vulnerable and deserving of our protection. Second, both Jews and non-Jews are considered to be included in the category of protected workers. Third, the texts assert the need for specific legislation to prevent the oppression of workers.

Still, these biblical verses offer little assistance in determining appropriate wages or other labor conditions. Tardy payment of wages may have been an important labor issue in biblical times, and it still afflicts day laborers and other contingent workers. However, most contemporary labor debates focus on wage levels and working conditions. We must explore further to determine a Jewish response to these modern-day concerns.

Two rabbinic texts do explicitly legislate against the gross underpayment of workers. One *mishnah* forbids an employer from telling an employee paid to handle straw, "Take the result of your labor as your wages" (Mishnah, *Bava Metzia* 10:5). The *Tosefta* considers a case in which an employer hires someone to bring fruit to a sick person. If the employee goes to the home of the sick person and finds that this person has died or gotten better, the employer must pay the worker's wages in full and cannot say, "Take what you are carrying as payment" (*Tosefta, Bava Metzia* 7:4).

While it might be tempting to compare straw and fruit with today's low wages, we must acknowledge the difference. The current federal minimum wage of $7.25 per hour as of July 2009 may not buy much, but we cannot equate it with straw and fruit, which are not even forms of currency (Talmud, *Bava Metzia* 112a). Furthermore, in these early rabbinic texts, as in the biblical commands, we assume that the employer originally agreed to reasonable wages and now wishes to break the contract.

As in the biblical verses we have discussed, these early legal texts are most significant in their understanding of the employer's inherent power over the employee. Because the employee may not have the power to refuse the straw and fruit and to demand monetary compensation, the texts legislate against the attempt on the part of the employer to take advantage of the employee.

This text, like the biblical texts cited earlier, does address the still-relevant situation in which a worker is not paid for the work that he or she has completed. It still happens that employers take advantage of low-wage workers by refusing to pay these workers, by disappearing, or by paying less than the agreed-upon salary. In 2006, the Mississippi Immigrants Rights Alliance won three-quarters of a million dollars in back wages from contractors who hired immigrants to rebuild Biloxi following Hurricane Katrina and who then left the state without paying these workers. A bit closer to home, a Jewish professional I know recently sent a copy of the *Tosefta* text to an institution that had hired her to teach a class, cancelled the class the day before it was to start, and then refused to compensate her for her preparation time. Moved by the text, the leaders of the institution changed their minds and mailed her a check.

Considering the assumptions of rabbinic texts offers us additional insight into the employer's responsibilities toward the employee. Returning to the biblical text, we may perhaps assume that the focus on delayed payment reflects the central concerns of laborers in the biblical period. As Ramban says in his comment on Deuteronomy 24:15, "The text speaks in the present." In singling out one labor law, the text does not imply that delayed payment is the only issue worthy of our consideration. Rather, in addressing the issue most relevant to workers of its own time, the Bible invites us to consider ways to ameliorate the situation of workers in our own time. Paying workers promptly constitutes only one means of fulfilling the more general commandment, "Do not oppress the hired laborer." Today, adherence to this general commandment may take many other forms.

Rabbinic commentary on the biblical verse helps us to understand the emphasis on prompt payment of wages, rather than on the amount of the wages themselves. In interpreting the phrase "his life depends on [the wages]," the Talmud explains, "Why does he climb a ladder or hang from a tree or risk death? Is it not for his wages? Another interpretation—'His life depends on them' indicates that anyone who denies a hired laborer his wages, it is as though he takes his life from him."[20] This reading is surprising in its suggestion that the employer assumes responsibility for the health and well-being of his workers. Even more radical is the statement of Jonah Gerondi (Spain, d. 1263), the author of the *Sefer HaYirah*:

> Be careful not to afflict a living creature, whether animal or fowl, and even more so not to afflict a human being, who is created in God's image. If you want to hire workers and you find that they are poor, they should become like poor members of your household. You should not disgrace them.[21] (*Sefer haYirah, Dibbur hamatchil "Hishamer militza'er"*)

Given this emphasis on the employer's responsibilities toward the worker, the absence of specific legislation about appropriate wages is puzzling. While we still have no clear statement about appropriate wages, this text hints at an assumption that wages, when paid on time, will be sufficient to lift a person out of poverty.

This point becomes even clearer in Ramban's commentary to Deuteronomy 24:15. He writes:

> For he is poor—like the majority of hired laborers—and he depends on the wages to buy food by which to live ... if he

does not collect the wages right away as he is leaving work, he will go home, and his wages will remain with you until the morning, and he will die of hunger that night.

Like Gerondi, Ramban holds the employer responsible for the health and sustenance of the worker. If the worker and/or his family die of hunger as a result of nonpayment of wages, Ramban implies, fault for the death lies with the employer.

In commenting that a person who does not receive wages on time will "die of hunger that night," Ramban takes for granted that a person who *does* receive payment on time *will* be able to provide sufficiently for himself and his family and will not die of hunger. This assumption also forms the premise for Rambam's designation of the highest level of *tzedakah* as "the one who strengthens the hand of his fellow Jew by giving him a gift or a loan or entering into partnership with him or finding him work in order to strengthen his hand so that he will not need to ask in the future" (*Mishneh Torah, Matanot l'Aniyim* 10:7). For Rambam, a person who has permanent employment or a share in a business will never find it necessary to ask for *tzedakah*.

A second Rambam text offers an even clearer statement of the responsibility to pay workers enough to support their families. In regard to certain communal workers, he writes:

> The correctors of books in Jerusalem would take their salaries from [funds collected primarily to cover the cost of sacrifices]. The judges who judged cases of theft in Jerusalem would take their salary from these funds. And how much would they take? Ninety *maneh* per year; and if this was not enough for them, [those responsible for distributing the money] would increase the amount. Even if [these communal workers] did not want to take more, they would increase the amount according to the needs of the workers, their wives and their families. (*Mishneh Torah, Sh'kalim* 4:7)

By way of explaining this text, Rabbi Chaim David HaLevy (Palestine/Israel 1924–1998), a former Sephardic chief rabbi of Tel Aviv and a major legal authority of the twentieth century, comments that the salaries of these workers would be increased, "In order for [these workers] to devote their full energies to their important tasks and in order that they will be able to focus on fulfilling their duties, without concerns about the needs of their families weighing on them."[22] HaLevy also infers from Rambam that a communal worker's salary should go up as the size of the worker's family increases. A person unable to support his or her family cannot possibly be an effective worker, either because of anxiety or because it will be necessary to take a second job in order to make ends meet.

The assumption that employed people will be able to support themselves and their families may respond to the reality that Ramban and Rambam describe, but does not reflect the current situation. In a time when 36 percent of families who apply for emergency food support include at least one employed adult, we can no longer assume that providing jobs will eradicate poverty.[23]

The contemporary situation, then, differs from the reality upon which biblical and rabbinic wage laws are based. The Rabbis are familiar with workers who live "paycheck to paycheck," but they do not imagine that a day's wages might prove insufficient to buy food or other necessities for that day. We therefore find ourselves in a difficult position. As discussed earlier, traditional *halakhah* remains relevant for many areas of employment law. However, in regard to wages, the rabbinic premise does not correspond with our current reality. This discrepancy suggests that the application of traditional *halakhah* to present-day labor issues first requires raising wages to a level at which rabbinic assumptions hold true.

Can and Should We Interfere with Market-Determined Wages?

Having established that our current *minhagim*—including the minimum wage of $5.15 per hour and the failure to grant health benefits to all employees—do not enable employers or employees to fulfill their halakhic obligations toward one another, we must ask whether there is precedent for changing the *minhag hamakom* in response to new economic realities.

A few texts do indicate a need to adapt employment laws to changing conditions. The laws concerning a worker's right to quit a job in the middle of the day, as enumerated in the Talmud and later codes of law, change according to the availability of other workers. The principle that "The children of Israel are [God's] servants and not servants to servants" theoretically grants the worker permission to quit midday without penalty. However, in a case in which the work in question will be lost if not completed immediately and in which no other workers are available, a worker may not be able to quit early, or may face penalties for doing so.[24]

Here, the texts stipulate one law for an ideal situation, then offer alternate laws for different economic conditions. These laws further establish a general principle that the law should favor the person in the more precarious position. Most commonly, the law protects the worker, who stands in danger of becoming like a servant to the employer. In the words of Shillem Warhaftig, a contemporary Israeli scholar and the preeminent authority on Jewish labor law, "The purpose [of Jewish labor laws] is to protect the weaker side in these relationships—the worker who is exposed to injustice and exploitation by the stronger party—the employer. We can say that the labor laws attempt to correct the socio-economic discrimination that exists in society against workers by instituting a legal discrimination against employers."[25] Similarly, HaLevy comments, "The sages of Israel and their courts always knew to side with the worker."[26] Presumably, if workers were in a position of power, the law would favor the employer; however, as Warhaftig notes, the worker is more likely to be dependent on the employer and therefore in danger of exploitation.

Other texts more explicitly allow communities, and even groups of workers, to change the *minhag hamakom*. The *Tosefta* permits the "people of the city" to stipulate workers' wages, as well as prices and measurements (*Bava Metzia* 11:23). Here, we have an explicit break with the controlled free-market system that some other texts describe. In granting individual communities the authority to determine wages, the Rabbis indicate an understanding of the failures of a free-market system. While certain economic conditions might enable such a system to succeed, other conditions will make this system unworkable. To maintain stability, the local authority must have the power to adjust wage rates as necessary.

Some traditional texts extend to members of a trade this ability to set wages and regulate work. The clearest statement of this allowance appears in the *Tosefta*:

> The wool workers and the dyers are permitted to say, "We will all be partners in any business that comes to the city."
>
> The bakers are permitted to establish work shifts amongst themselves. Donkey drivers are permitted to say, "We will provide another donkey for anyone whose donkey dies." If it dies through negligence, they do not need to provide a new one; if not through negligence, they do need to provide him with another donkey. And if he says, "Give me the money, and I will purchase one myself, they should not listen to him, but should buy a donkey and give it to him."
>
> Merchants are permitted to say, "We will provide another ship for anyone whose ship is destroyed." If it is destroyed through negligence, they do not need to provide another one; if it is not destroyed through negligence, they do need to provide another. And if he departs for a place to which people do not go, they do not need to provide him with another ship. (*Bava Metzia* 11:24–26)

Interpreting this *Tosefta*, Rabbi Shlomo ben Aderet (known as Rashba; Barcelona, 1235–1310) comments, "All members of an organization are, unto themselves, like 'the people of the city' in regard to these things. Similarly, every community is permitted to make enactments for itself and to establish fines and punishments beyond those mandated by the Torah" (*She'elot u'Teshuvot* 4:185). This opinion also appears in several other authoritative books of Jewish law, including the *Mishneh Torah* (*Hilkhot Mekhirah* 14:10) and the *Shulchan Arukh* (*Choshen Mishpat* 231:28). The Rema narrows the application of this provision, saying that members of a single trade can make stipulations "all together," and that "two or three of them cannot make a binding stipulation" (*Choshen Mishpat* 231:28). That is, while "two or three" members of a trade may not enforce a new condition, a significant majority may have such power.[27]

Halakhic debate about the ability of individual communities to set wages generally revolves around the question of the necessity for an *adam chashuv*, a communal leader who is a wise or important person, to approve changes. In the Talmud, a rabbi named Rava suggests that members of a trade may make economic stipulations among themselves only when there is no *adam chashuv* in the town (*Bava Batra* 91). Commenting on this passage, Rabbi Asher ben Yechiel (known as the Rosh; Germany/Spain, 1259–1328), says:

> From here, we learn that all artisans are able to make stipulations amongst themselves, and they are considered as "the people of the city," in regard to work issues. When we speak about an *adam chashuv*, we refer specifically to someone like Rava, who was the head and leader of the city. When there is such a person, even all of the people of the city together do not have the authority to make stipulations without the consent of this important person.[28]

Later medieval scholars similarly require that an *adam chashuv* approve any changes to employment law. The identity of this *adam chashuv* remains unclear. From the Rosh's comment, this person appears to be a rabbi and scholar who also has political power. Other legal scholars define this figure as a scholar who is responsible for making enactments for the community, or as the person who is the appointed head of the community.[29]

Regardless of the precise identity and role of the *adam chashuv*, we can probably safely say that such a person does not exist in contemporary America, where the Jewish community does not have a separate political structure. We can therefore also say that our situation is one in which there is no *adam chashuv* and in which townspeople—ordinary citizens—have the authority to determine wages and working conditions. Even if we were to argue that the equivalent of the *adam chashuv* does exist in contemporary America, we would notice that the medieval *halakhists* do not require that the impetus for the change in wages or other laws originate with the leader, but only that this leader consent to the change. These writers therefore implicitly encourage townspeople and members of a trade to determine appropriate regulations and then seek communal and official approval.

In accordance with the assumptions of Ramban and Rambam, we can say that the wages set by a community should be sufficient for a person to support himself or herself, and on a single job with a forty-hour workweek. In American political discourse, this wage is commonly referred to as a "living wage." Currently, approximately 140 cities, towns, and municipalities have passed living wage ordinances that seek to ensure that workers are able to support themselves on a single job.[30] The living wage has variously been determined according to estimates of the real cost of living in an area, 80 percent of the median income of the area, or approximately three times the cost of a two-bedroom apartment at fair market rent. Often, local living-wage laws are based more on political expediency than on a real measure of the cost of living in a place.[31]

Moonlighting and Its Consequences

Traditional sources compel employees to work diligently, to be precise in their work, and to avoid wasting the employer's time. Workers may even recite abbreviated prayers and excuse themselves from certain religious obligations in order not to detract from their work (Talmud, *B'rakhot* 17a, 46a). According to Rambam:

> Just as the employer must be careful not to steal the salary of the poor [worker], so too must the poor person be careful not to steal the work of the owner by wasting a little time here and there until the entire day is filled with trickery. Rather, he should be careful about time. For this reason, the rabbis specified that workers do not need to recite the fourth blessing of *Birkat HaMazon*. Similarly, the worker is obligated to work with all of his strength, for behold, Jacob the righteous said [to Laban], "I have served your father with all my might."[32]

Workers are also prohibited from working both during the day and at night, as taking on a second job interferes with a person's ability to perform the first job well.[33] Furthermore, workers must care for their own health. According to the *Tosefta*, "[a worker] may not starve or afflict himself in order to feed his children, as this is considered stealing work from the employer."[34]

In theory, these regulations offer the employer reasonable guarantees that workers will be efficient and productive. However, as in the above discussion of appropriate wages, the assumptions that generate these laws do not reflect our current reality. For many Americans, holding multiple jobs is an economic necessity, particularly for low-wage workers. The Bureau of Labor Statistics estimates that 5.2 percent of Americans hold multiple jobs.[35] Some have suggested that the actual rate may be closer to 15 or 20 percent.[36] As with any labor statistic, the number of undocumented workers and "under the table" jobs makes it difficult to determine accurately the frequency of multiple employment, particularly among low-wage workers. Anecdotal evidence suggests that a high percentage of the lowest-paid workers supplement their primary jobs with weekend and evening work. One union organizer reports coming to grips with the frequency of this phenomenon only when she asked a janitor what he planned to do with the higher wages promised by a new contract. His reply? "Quit my third job."[37]

A strict reading of the *Mishneh Torah* and other sources might suggest that these workers cheat their employers when accepting second and third jobs. However, given the near impossibility of supporting a family on a few hundred dollars a week, we cannot reasonably expect low-wage workers to confine themselves to a single, forty-hour-a-week job. Again, we find ourselves caught between the halakhic ideal and the contemporary reality.

Other factors also make it difficult for workers to fulfill the expectations of Rambam and other halakhic sources. In the case of the New Jersey janitors, who clean the equivalent of six residential homes in each twenty-hour shift, the requirement to perform a full-time job in part-time hours virtually ensures that these workers will not be able to complete their work satisfactorily. In the field of health care, workers are most concerned about providing adequate patient care in understaffed hospitals and nursing homes. While other workers may strike over wages and benefits, nurses and doctors most often strike over issues of patient care. At a June 2001 public forum, one Bergen County, New Jersey, nurse sobbed as she told the audience, "It used to be that when I had to give a patient a shot, I would explain why he needed a shot, and then give him a hug afterward. Now, I only have time to administer the shot, and move on." Other nurses spoke of working sixteen-hour shifts five or more days a week, sometimes while their children waited in the nurses' station.[38]

The lack of adequate health benefits for many workers makes it particularly difficult to fulfill the *Tosefta*'s requirement that workers maintain their health. Without health benefits, workers forgo regular doctors visits, and instead use the emergency room as their first line of medical care. The lack of adequate health care not only leads to missed work days, but also constitutes a drain on the public, as communal funds pay for the workers' emergency medical care.[39]

Given the discrepancy between halakhic obligations on workers and the contemporary reality, we are confronted with two possibilities. We can either reconsider the halakhic prohibition against taking multiple jobs and the requirement that employees work at full capacity, or we can accept the current reality as a challenge to traditional *halakhah* and, in turn, use *halakhah* to critique the present-day situation.

In his analysis of Jewish labor issues, David Schnall, dean of Yeshiva University's Azrieli Graduate School of Jewish Education and Administration, takes the former approach. He suggests that in American society, multiple employment may have assumed the status of *minhag hamakom*, and therefore may be acceptable.[40] He also cites evidence that those who work second jobs "appear no more likely to underperform or to behave in an undesirable fashion [than those who work only one job]." Furthermore, Schnall classifies as "substantial" the argument that permitting multiple employment "is a means of retaining and satisfying talented workers when an employer cannot continue to raise salary or benefits."[41]

Schnall's analysis may appropriately respond to certain instances of multiple employment, including the examples he cites of teachers who tutor after school or during the summer, and professionals who consult in their free time.[42] Within certain professions, such additional part-time work may be a reasonable and accepted practice. Teachers who take on one or two weekend or after-school tutoring jobs will not necessarily be less effective in their full-time jobs.[43] However, it does not seem reasonable to assume that a low-wage worker holding more than one *full-time* job will be as effective as a person working a single job. Furthermore, as noted earlier, other factors, including unreasonable production expectations and the lack of access to health care, make it even more difficult for many workers to perform their assigned tasks adequately. We can therefore suggest that the halakhic requirements that the employee maintain his or her health, eat properly, and work only one job implicitly obligate the employer to enable the worker to fulfill these conditions.

As we have seen, the traditional obligations placed on the employer and on the employee presuppose a situation that differs significantly from the contemporary work environment. In the halakhic ideal, a person who works full-time and receives wages promptly will be able to buy food and other necessities and maintain his or her health. In return, this person is expected to work efficiently and reliably. In the United States, the forty-hour workweek, put into effect by the Fair Labor Standards Act of 1938, is one of the early products of the labor movement. Today, working hours have increased for people across the economic spectrum; Americans currently work more hours than people in any other industrialized country.[44] In our time, a low-wage worker may work sixty or eighty hours a week and remain unable to purchase basic necessities. The prohibitive costs of medical care for those without health benefits make it virtually impossible for many of these workers to care for themselves sufficiently. Requirements that some workers, particularly those in the health professions, work long shifts in understaffed facilities further prevent employees from meeting the standard.

Our current situation, then, violates the most basic assumptions of *halakhah*. Applying Jewish labor laws to contemporary America requires first creating a system that mirrors the ideal upon which traditional sources are based. Most importantly, we need to ensure that even the lowest-paid workers earn enough to provide their families with food, shelter, health care, and other basic necessities. Only then can employers sufficiently fulfill their obligations toward the workers simply by paying salaries on time; and only then can we expect employees to work a single job, and to perform this job to the best of their abilities.

When it is financially possible to support themselves through a single full-time job, Jewish workers should be responsible for upholding the *halakhot* that apply to workers—namely, the prohibitions against working multiple jobs and against stealing time from the employer. To the best of their abilities, Jewish union leaders should ensure that employers who sign union contracts receive the best possible work. In the halakhic ideal, the employer and employee become equal partners, each of whom has responsibilities toward the other, and each of whom benefits from the other.

The Permissibility of Unions

Based on early rabbinic discussions of stipulations among members of a single trade, Jewish scholars overwhelmingly permit workers to establish labor unions. Rabbi Eliezer Waldenberg (1915–2006), a judge on the Israeli Supreme Rabbinical Court and a leading legal authority, rules that the people of a town—or their elected officials—may enact labor laws, which then become the *minhag hamakom*, incumbent on employers and employees.[45] If a particular employer fails to comply with these regulations, workers may strike in order to force the employer to adhere to the established *minhag*. As justification for the permissibility of striking, Waldenberg takes the radical step of invoking Rambam's statement that "a person who

is able to do so may take the law into his own hands."[46] Contemporary rabbinic authorities such as Ovadiah Yosef, Moshe Feinstein,
Eliezer Waldenberg, and Chaim David HaLevy understand the
workers' guilds described in the Talmud as precedent for today's
labor unions, and even go beyond this basic permission to allow
unions to strike in order to enforce working standards. Yosef permits
the leaders of labor unions to call strikes "in order to raise wages or
to ease work conditions, or other such things" (*Yechavvah Da'at* 4:58)
on the basis of the establishment of the principle, within the
Yerushalmi, that the *minhag* overturns the *halakhah* (*Bava Metzia* 7:1).

A few rabbinic authorities require workers to bring their case to
a *beit din* (a religious court made up of three rabbis) before calling a
strike. Rav Avraham Yitzchak haKohen Kook (known as Rav Kook;
Latvia/Palestine, 1865–1935), Rabbi Chaim David HaLevy, and
Rabbi Rafael Katznelbogen (Palestine/Israel, 1894–1972), for
instance, permit strikes only when the employer refuses to appear
before a *beit din*.[47] Once a strike has been called, Katznelbogen
declares scabbing to be illegal and permits striking workers to prevent others from entering the premises to work. Even while considering strikes to be "against the spirit of the law," HaLevy permits strikes
"in a time of need" but prefers for the two sides to enter into binding
arbitration (*Aseh L'cha Rav* II:64). Rabbi Ben-Tzion Meir Chai Uziel
similarly suggests that labor disputes be brought before a court made
up of experts in *halakhah* as well as experts in economics. If, however,
a strike is declared, Uziel forbids employers to fire striking workers
without the agreement of a *beit din* (*Mishp'tei Uziel* III:42).

In contrast, Waldenberg does not require workers to bring the
employer to a *beit din*, as he considers the workers to be acting in
accordance with *halakhah*. The question of the necessity of a *beit din*
may be relevant in Israel, where all of the above-mentioned rabbis
live or lived, but is less important in America, where it is rare that
both owners and workers are Jewish. When—as in most cases in
contemporary America—there is no possibility of taking the case
before a *beit din*, it is likely that all of the authorities mentioned
would permit employees to strike.

While Waldenberg requires unions to make labor stipulations in partnership with an elected or appointed official, Moshe Feinstein requires such consultation only when the stipulations run counter to the law.[48] As we have seen, Feinstein dismisses the category of *adam chashuv* as irrelevant in America.

Feinstein further permits union members to prevent nonunion members from working during a strike. As a basis for this ruling, he invokes the principle of *ka pasakta l'chayuti*—that one person may not take away the livelihood of another. He also compares the union to a *m'arupiya*, a person with whom you have an exclusive, and binding, business agreement. A company that has agreed to hire union workers may not, during a strike, contract with other, nonunion workers. While generally supportive of strikes, Feinstein is more cautious about teachers' strikes, which he permits only if the teachers "do not have enough for their needs, so that as a result, it becomes difficult for them to teach the students well, and if it is clear that if they do not teach for a day or two that the employers will pay them on time or raise their salaries."

Hiring Union Workers

While most of the authorities mentioned explicitly permit labor unions and allow at least some forms of strikes, none of these rabbis address the question of whether Jewish owners must hire union workers. They focus only on the process of declaring strikes, arbitrating disagreements, and preventing scabbing. This focus may reflect the cultural milieus in which each of the authorities cited was writing. For Feinstein, the only American mentioned, the focus on Jews as union members may reflect the realities of 1950s America, when Jews were more likely to be workers than business owners. The Israeli scholars, for their part, address a situation in which both employers and employees are assumed to be Jewish (though, of course, there are many non-Jewish workers working low-wage jobs in Israel) and in which the existence of a strong national union means that most employers do not have a choice about hiring union workers.

An oral statement by Rav Kook begins to lead us toward this next step of obligating employers to hire unionized workers. Kook says:

> Within the workers' organization, which is formed for the purpose of guarding and protecting the work conditions, there is an aspect of righteousness and uprightness and *tikkun olam*.... Unorganized labor brings damage and loss of money to workers. For the unorganized worker works under worse conditions—both in regard to wages and in regard to working hours, etc. And this is likely to make working conditions worse in general.[49]

To understand this statement, we must first determine the meaning of the phrase *tikkun olam*. It is unlikely that Kook intends these words as we often use them today, as a general imperative for social action work. The kabbalistic notion of *tikkun olam* would also be out of place here. Rather, based on the final words of the paragraph, "this is likely to make working conditions worse in general," we can compare Kook's use of the phrase *tikkun olam* to the Mishnaic phrase *mipnei tikkun ha'olam*, discussed in Chapter 2. In the Mishnah, this phrase introduces a change in law aimed at correcting a loophole that threatens to undermine the system as a whole.

Through this Mishnaic lens, we can understand Kook as indicating that unions, though perhaps not specifically mandated by *halakhah*, help preserve the halakhic system as a whole. As I have argued, traditional *halakhah* governing the relationship between employers and employees cannot hold in a market in which workers do not earn enough money to provide their families with basic necessities, and in which workers may not be able to fulfill their obligations toward their employers. As Rav Kook suggests, unions may provide the only means of rectifying this situation. While legislation, including living wage laws and the institution of national health care, may eventually create a market in which employers and employees can fulfill their obligations to one another, it is unlikely that such legislation will be in place soon. Nor is it likely that enforcement of such legislation could be ensured without strong workers' organizations that would hold employers and regulatory agencies accountable. In the meantime, unions appear to be the most efficient means of guaranteeing that workers can live on their salaries, care for their health, and avoid taking second and third jobs.

Rabbi Ben-Tzion Meir Chai Uziel echoes this understanding of unions as a necessary means of protecting workers. He writes:

> The law allows [for the existence of unions] in order that the individual worker not be left on his own, to the point that he hires himself out for a low wage in order to satisfy his hunger and that of his family with a bit of bread and water and with a dark and dingy home; in order that the worker may protect himself, the law gives him the legal right to organize, and to establish stipulations that benefit the members of his profession regarding the fair distribution of work among the workers, and to achieve fair treatment and a wage appropriate for the work and sufficient to sustain his household at the standard of living as the other residents of his city…. all of these things can only be fulfilled through a workers' union. Therefore, the Torah gave the Jewish people the full and legal right to organize these, even though it is possible that [such unions] will result in a financial loss for the employers (*Mishp'tei Uziel, Choshen Mishpat* 52:6).

The imperative articulated so forcefully by Uziel reaches yet another level when we look, for instance, at highly competitive industries such as office cleaning. Cleaning companies engage in constant bidding wars for business, and thus are reluctant to pay workers higher wages. Therefore, the unions working in this industry generally agree not to hold companies to a union contract until the majority of companies in the region also agree to sign. The decision of each individual company thus has an impact on all other companies in the area, and on all of the associated workers. For the sake of *tikkun ha'olam*, as I have defined the term, we may insist that Jewish employers allow workers to unionize in order to help all workers in the industry attain higher wages and benefits. To maintain the halakhically desired equality in the employer-employee relationship, we may also insist that Jewish employees and union leaders endeavor to provide employers with the highest possible quality of work.

No human institution functions perfectly, and unions have been guilty of corruption and other scandals. In the past decade or so, the AFL-CIO has put significant energy into reforming certain problematic member unions, notably by installing new leadership. The 2005 split within the AFL-CIO and the emergence of the Change to Win Coalition highlighted differences within the labor movement about the extent to which unions should focus on organizing low-wage minority workers. Even given all of these concerns, unions remain, as Uziel points out, the only way for workers not "to be left on [their] own" without any collective bargaining power.

The Historical Experience

Many Jews have a particular affinity for unions because of the Jewish involvement in the early labor movement in America. Jews have been deeply involved in the American labor movement since its inception. The Triangle Shirtwaist Factory Fire of 1911, in which 146 workers—primarily Jewish and Italian women—lost their lives, led to a successful effort by the largely Jewish International Ladies Garment Workers Union to secure legislation mandating workplace safety protections. Many of the giants of the U.S. labor movement, including Emma Goldman, Samuel Gompers, and Samuel Hillman, have been Jews. Even today, Jews are at the helm of some of the largest and most influential labor unions, including SEIU (Andrew Stern), UNITE HERE! (Bruce Raynor), and United Federation of Teachers (Randi Weingarten).

The significance we assign to this historical involvement depends on the broader question of the obligatory nature of history. The Bible offers some precedent for deriving legal obligations from history, particularly from Egyptian slavery. Multiple times, the Torah instructs the reader that the experience of slavery in Egypt imposes obligations to care for the stranger, the widow, and the orphan, and to observe Shabbat as a time of rest for all members of the household, including sojourners, servants, and animals. Some later rabbinic texts obligate the community, following the destruction of the Second Temple in Jerusalem, to observe certain Temple-based rituals *zecher l'mikdash* (in remembrance of the Temple). However, it is not clear whether this precedent establishes history in general as an obligating force.

If we do consider the command to remember our slavery in Egypt and other admonitions to remember as general statements of the obligatory nature of history, we might argue that our early experience of low-wage work, combined with the relief brought about through labor unions, compels us to support unions, even once we have taken on more managerial positions. The lessons of labor history challenge Jewish union leaders to ensure that today's unions, like the early unions, are focused on creating a workplace that protects the interests of both employee and employer.

Our tradition upholds an ideal in which the workplace offers dignity both to employers and to employees. But in our society, the workplace instead often becomes a degrading place that fails to acknowledge the humanity of either the workers or their bosses. Workers often have no way of voicing their concerns, and may not even be able to provide their families with food, housing, and medical care. Unfavorable conditions, in turn, prevent employees from doing their best work. An unregulated market further tempts even well-meaning employers to violate *halakhah* and basic principles of dignity in order to remain competitive with those who have no such scruples. Unions may not be the sole means of ameliorating this situation, but for now, they are the most effective way of creating workplaces in which traditional *halakhah* can operate as intended. Thus, demanding that Jewish employers hire union workers and permit their workers to unionize represents a first step in creating a system in which it will be possible to institute traditional *halakhah* in such a way that these laws will protect both employer and employee.

6

They Shall Tremble No More
Housing and Homelessness

Housing has become one of the hottest topics in social policy, as subsidized housing vouchers expire, urban neighborhoods struggle with gentrification, and millions of families face foreclosure or declining home values as a result of the subprime mortgage crisis. Much of the attention on housing focuses on the growing, and increasingly visible, incidence of homelessness, a single symptom of America's much deeper housing problems. According to a 2004 report by the National Low Income Housing Coalition, more than 95 million Americans—one-third of the population—suffer from housing problems, defined as overcrowding, poor housing quality, homelessness, or a "high cost burden." High cost burden is defined as spending more than 50 percent of the household income on housing costs. A report by the Millenial Housing Commission, appointed by the U.S. Congress, reports that more than 1.7 million Americans live in housing so inadequate that it threatens their health and safety.[1] While the full consequences of the recent subprime mortgage crisis have yet to be felt, we can expect that the number of Americans with insufficient, insecure, or unsafe housing will only rise over the next few years.

Given that homelessness is the most obvious manifestation of poverty in our own society, we might expect that the laws of *tzedakah* or other discussions of poverty in Jewish texts would also focus on the provision of housing as a primary responsibility toward the poor. Surprisingly, other than the oft-cited command from Isaiah to "take the poor into your homes" (Isa. 58:7) and scattered later mentions of housing as a type of *tzedakah*, few sources directly consider housing as an element of poverty relief.

Five basic questions lie at the root of virtually all contemporary housing issues:

1. What is the relationship between housing and other aspects of life?
2. Is housing a basic human right?
3. What constitutes sufficient housing?
4. What responsibilities do landlords and tenants have toward one another?
5. What responsibility does the government have to provide housing for its citizens?

Housing and the Rest of Life

Housing conditions can have a dramatic impact on many other aspects of a person's life, from health to educational success, from job status to family stability. Summarizing some of the research on the effects of inadequate housing, the Millenial Housing Commission report comments:

> The physical condition of housing makes a difference for families as well. Better-quality housing is related to lower levels of psychological distress, which in turn reduce health care costs and improve productivity. In contrast, housing that exposes families to hazards such as lead paint can limit lifelong educational and economic achievement. The presence of dust, molds, and roach allergens in the home increases the incidence of asthma and allergies, while electrical problems, poor lighting, and other system deficiencies increase the risk of illness, injuries, and even death.[2]

At times, the recognition of the impact of housing on other parts of life has led some housing reformers to a condescending belief in environmental determinism. Central to the tenement reform movement of the nineteenth and early twentieth century was a conviction that the filth of the tenements both resulted from and contributed to a general immorality among the residents. According to E.R.L. Gould, a prominent housing reformer of the time, "Strong-willed, intelligent people may create or modify environment," but "the weak-willed, the careless, and the unreflecting ... are dominated by environment."[3] Both the pre–World War I Garden Cities movement, which aimed to create ideal urban areas, and the subsidization of suburbia during the 1940s and 1950s assumed that open space and beautiful surroundings would contribute to the health of the American family. Gwendolyn Wright has suggested that by its very design, the suburban home, centered around the family room and distant from neighboring houses, acted as "an architectural expression of family togetherness"[4] and was meant to reinforce the ideal of the nuclear family with a stay-at-home mother. The current trend toward demolishing public housing high-rises and constructing mixed-income developments similarly assumes that middle-class neighbors will have a positive influence on the character of the poor. While acknowledging the impact of housing quality on economic and educational success and on psychological health, we should be careful not to assume that people living in certain types of housing are somehow morally inferior to others.

The relationship between housing security and quality of life is reflected in the way in which the lack of a secure home has, for most of history, defined Jewish self-identity. No sooner has humankind been created, according to the biblical account, than Adam and Eve are expelled from the Garden of Eden. Abraham begins his relationship with God by leaving home, and his grandson and great-grandchildren find themselves journeying down to Egypt. The central narrative of the Jewish people—the liberation from slavery and journey to the promised land—is a story of displacement and return. Since the destruction of the Second Temple in 70 CE, virtually every moment of Jewish life—from prayer services to life cycle events to holiday celebrations—has been punctuated by a reminder of the loss of this physical and theological center. Even after the establishment of the state of Israel, Jews continue to mourn the destruction of the Temple and to pray for a return to a rebuilt Jerusalem. Contemporary political fears about the tenuousness of the very existence of the state of Israel reflect the insecurity of place that has become so central to Jewish belief. Once homelessness has become so deeply rooted in our religious and national identity, even the attainment of a home cannot change our self-perception. Recognizing the ways in which the experience of homelessness remains rooted in our religious and national identities can help us to understand the experience of individuals whose own housing is insecure.

While the entire book of Lamentations focuses on the pain of losing the Jewish national home, one passage in particular describes the effect of displacement on communal life:

> Remember, God, what has befallen us; behold and see our disgrace. Our heritage has passed to aliens, our homes to strangers. We have become orphans, fatherless; our mothers are like widows. We must pay to drink our own water, obtain our own kindling at a price. We are hotly pursued; exhausted, we are given no rest.... Our skin glows like an oven, with the fear of famine. They have ravished women in Zion, maidens in the towns of Judah. Princes have been hanged by them; no respect has been shown to elders. Young men must carry millstones, and youths struggle under loads of wood. The old men are gone from the gate, the young men from their music. Gone is the joy of our hearts; our dancing has turned into mourning. (Lam. 5:1–16)

Without a secure home, normal social relations fall apart, and happiness becomes impossible. Homelessness brings with it fear, depression, and a loss of grounding. The book of Lamentations here compares homelessness to the loss of a parent or spouse. Like the loss of a protective family member, the lack of a secure home engenders feelings of loneliness and vulnerability. In contrast, the establishment of a permanent home promises lasting security. Thus, God's ultimate promise to the Jewish people, articulated first in God's covenant with Abraham, is the guarantee of a home. The equation between a home and a sense of security is perhaps best articulated by God's assurance that "I will establish a home for my people Israel and will plant them firm, so that they shall dwell secure and shall tremble no more" (2 Sam. 7:10). While the experience of national homelessness and the experience of individual housing insecurity differ in major ways, the memory of national exile and displacement offers us a lens through which to understand the sense of vulnerability that accompanies the experience of personal homelessness.[5]

In the contemporary world, homelessness, housing insecurity, and displacement lead to a host of related economic, psychological, physical, and societal problems. In some cases, housing problems even lead to societal dysfunction similar to that described by Lamentations. According to a study by John Hagedorn of the University of Illinois at Chicago, Chicago's high levels of violent crime—which remain far above those of other major U.S. cities—may be attributed, to some degree, to the city's ongoing displacement of public housing residents.[6] The deleterious effect of housing insecurity on children's academic performance and on the physical and mental health of children and adults has been well documented.[7]

Just as the uprooting of the Jewish people from their homeland in Jerusalem results in the general societal dysfunction described in Lamentations, the displacement of entire neighborhoods, often the result of local and national housing policy, results in the dissolution of the social structures that allow for the healthy functioning of communities.

Is Housing a Basic Human Right?

Jewish sources imply that housing is one of the basic necessities of life. A number of discussions of poverty seem to assume that even the poorest person would, at the very least, own a house. As we saw in Chapter

3, early rabbinic texts establish that a person who owns more than 200 *zuzim* may not take from the agricultural forms of *tzedakah*. This text then comments that "we do not force a person to sell his house [in order to acquire the 200 *zuzim* that would disqualify this person from taking *tzedakah*]" (Mishnah, *Pe'ah* 8:8).

In our contemporary context, it seems unlikely that a person who does not even have 200 *zuzim*—defined by most commentators as the cost of food, clothing, and perhaps a few other necessities[8]— would own a house. This assumption may reflect a reality in which poverty was a transient condition, resulting from a poor harvest, rather than a permanent or semi-permanent class. Alternatively, the text may emerge from a world in which, in contrast to our own reality, housing was cheap and food was expensive. Regardless of the social and economic conditions that produced it, the text classifies housing as such a basic need that a person should not be expected to sell his or her house in order to fulfill the mandate, present in other rabbinic sources, to do whatever possible to avoid taking *tzedakah*.[9]

In specifying that housing should not be counted as part of a person's assets for the purpose of determining eligibility for *tzedakah*, the Mishnah effectively classifies housing as such a basic need that people cannot possibly be expected to live without it. Elsewhere, the Rabbis enact laws to protect against *gozel 'aniyyim* (theft from the poor), the taking of *tzedakah* by those who are ineligible for such help. The Rabbis assume that *tzedakah* funds will always be limited and that a person who takes *tzedakah* deceitfully effectively deprives others of sustenance. Here, though, there is no evident concern that a person who could sell his or her house in order to buy food might be considered to be taking resources from others.

Much of the rabbinic discussion about giving *tzedakah* centers around the biblical verse commanding us to give *tzedakah* to a poor person "according to what he lacks" (*dei machsoro*) (Deut. 15:8). The Rabbis understand this category expansively: we are not obligated simply to provide for a person's immediate physical needs, but may be required to provide "even a slave and even a horse" if such is the need of the poor person (*Tosefta*, *Pe'ah* 4:10).

Several texts list examples of what the category of *dei machsoro* might include. Surprisingly, only three separate—though closely related—rabbinic sources specify housing as something that a poor person might lack. One *midrash* interprets *dei machsoro* as "food, drink, a place to sleep, and a loan."[10] In discussing the care of a poor orphan, one early text comments: "If an orphan wishes to get married, one must rent him a house, make him a bed, and afterwards find him a wife, as it says, '*dei machsoro*—even a slave and even a horse'" (*Tosefta, Ketubot* 6:5). A slightly altered form of this statement appears in a talmudic discussion of the needs of an orphan:

> The rabbis taught: if an orphan comes to get married, first rent him a house and prepare him a bed and vessels and afterwards marry him to a woman, as it says, "sufficient for his needs which are needed" (Deut. 15:8). "Sufficient for his needs" refers to the house; "which are necessary" refers to the bed and table; "to him" refers to the woman. (*Ketubot* 67b)

These texts define *dei machsoro* as referring to the domestic needs of the poor person. *Tzedakah*, according to these texts, should focus on providing each person with sufficient housing and furniture and a partner with whom to share it. There is no mention of food, perhaps because so many of the other laws of *tzedakah* center on the provision of food. Consistent with our contemporary reality, this talmudic exegesis identifies adequate housing as a primary need of the poor. It is significant, however, that in two out of three of these texts, the mention of housing as a need of the poor appears specifically within a discussion about the care of orphans. It is possible that the Rabbis do not conceive of anyone, other than an orphan wishing to start a new household, who would not already have a home.

A veiled reference to housing as a type of *tzedakah* reappears in Rambam's *Sefer haMitzvot*, an attempt to identify and elucidate the 613 commandments of the Torah:

> The command, without a doubt, is that we should feed the hungry, clothe the naked, and give a bed to those who have no bed, and coverings to those who have no coverings, and

> marry off the single who are not able to get married, and give
> a horse to ride to those who are accustomed to ride, as it is
> explained in the Talmud, that all of this is included in the
> phrase *dei machsoro*. (*Shoresh* 1)

Rambam here echoes and summarizes the talmudic discussions of *dei
machsoro*. In contrast, however, to the texts about the orphan, he
does not specify the obligation to build a poor person a house, but
mentions only the need to provide a bed—something *for* the house
that the person presumably already owns. We can, of course, understand the reference to a bed metonymically—just as, in English, we
say "a roof over your head" to indicate a house. Still, if homelessness
were as prevalent as it is today, we might expect Rambam more
clearly to refer to a house as an aspect of poverty relief.

Later halakhic works similarly fail to mention the house itself
as an object of *tzedakah*. In *Arba'ah Turim*, his fourteenth-century cod-
ification of talmudic law, Jacob ben Asher (the Tur) writes:

> How much do we give to the poor? "Sufficient for what he
> lacks, according to what he is lacking." How does one do
> this? If he is hungry, and needs food, you should feed him. If
> he is naked and needs clothing, you should clothe him. If he
> has no utensils, you should buy him utensils. If, when he was
> rich, it was his custom to ride on a horse with a servant run-
> ning in front of him, once he has become poor, you should
> buy him a horse on which to ride and a slave to run in front of
> him. Similarly, you should give each person according to his
> needs. (*Yoreh De'ah* 350:1)

Virtually the same language appears in the *Shulchan Arukh*, the
sixteenth-century code that Joseph Caro based on his commentary
on the *Tur*. Like Rambam before them, these two legal codes mention the need to provide articles for the house, without indicating
any obligation to give the poor person a house. While it is difficult to
construct an argument from silence, I would suggest two potential
explanations for this omission. Like the Talmud, these three legal
authorities may assume poverty to be a temporary condition, resulting

from a bad crop or other economic disaster. Such an interpretation would explain the emphasis on maintaining the lifestyle of a wealthy person who becomes poor. Alternatively, the legal codes may assume that the obligation to provide housing is a given, and for this reason, focus on a less obvious obligation, namely that of providing utensils. Such a reading, however, would not explain why these sources *do* mention the need to provide the poor with food, as the obligation for hunger relief is explicit in other texts. It is, of course, also possible that these codes do not consider the provision of housing to be among the obligations of *tzedakah*. However, the repeated insistence that *dei machsoro* includes anything the poor person needs makes it difficult to argue that housing, if needed, would not be among the items we must offer the poor.

The absence, in most of the sources cited, of a mention of housing may reflect a sense of housing as such a basic need that it should not need to be included within the category of *tzedakah*. That is, housing is something that every poor person should reasonably expect to have, and for that reason, nobody should need to receive it as *tzedakah*. In acknowledging the essential nature of housing, *halakhah* would then stand in contrast to American law, which does not define housing as an entitlement, but which does so for food stamps and Medicare. Even beyond simply demanding the provision of shelter, the texts that speak about supplying furniture and utensils remind us also that housing alone does not satisfy the needs of the poor. Adequate housing, according to these texts, must not only provide shelter, but must also allow for a dignified life.

Many have argued, with good reason, that the language of "rights" may not be applicable to Judaism at all.[11] Instead of speaking in the language of rights, Judaism speaks generally in the language of obligation. The practical difference in this choice of words is that the language of obligation shifts focus to those responsible for providing for the poor. If I speak of my "right" to something, it is not always clear who has the responsibility for ensuring that I enjoy this right. If, however, I speak of someone's "obligation" to provide me with something, then it is clear where the responsibility lies. By saying that housing is a basic human need, included in the category of *tzedakah*, we simultaneously say that individuals and the society as a whole are obligated to provide housing to those who need it.

What Is Adequate Housing?

Classical texts offer little guidance about the definition of a house, or about how to construct a house. A few categories of law, however, offer us some hints toward the definition of a house. In particular, we can infer some characteristics of appropriate housing from rabbinic discussions of the *sukkah*, a temporary home constructed for the weeklong holiday of Sukkot; of the *mezuzah*, a scroll placed on every doorpost of a Jewish home; and of the concepts of public and private space.

The most extensive of these rabbinic discussions about housing takes place in the context of establishing the laws of building a *sukkah*. From the regulations regarding the construction of this temporary home, we can infer, by contrast, how the Rabbis might describe a permanent home.

All rabbinic discussion about the *sukkah* is based on the distinction between what is *arai* (temporary) and what is *keva* (permanent). The *sukkah*, by definition, must be *arai*—that is, it cannot appear so sturdy that it might be confused for a permanent home. The Rabbis of the Talmud argue about whether this constraint against the *sukkah* appearing permanent constitutes a limit on the height of the *sukkah* or on the materials that may be used to construct it (*Sukkah* 2a). In either case, the point is the same: the *sukkah* should be a structure in which someone can live for a week, but not in which he or she can live permanently. In contrast, a permanent house, we can assume, is noticeably sturdy, either because of its size or because of the materials used to construct it. Similarly, the requirement that the roof of the *sukkah* be permeable, combined with the explicit permission to return to your home if rain threatens to ruin your *sukkah*, implies that a permanent house is expected *not* to have holes in the roof and should fully shield a person from the elements (Mishnah, *Sukkah* 2:9).

Though primarily defined as a temporary structure, the *sukkah* must also be sufficiently permanent to serve as a suitable dwelling for the weeklong holiday. The Rabbis comment, "For the seven days of Sukkot, a person makes his *sukkah* into a permanent residence and his house into a temporary residence" (Mishnah, *Sukkah* 2:9). You transform the *sukkah* into a permanent residence by eating and sleeping there and, significantly, by moving your best utensils into the *sukkah*. To convey a sense of permanence, it is not enough for the *sukkah* to be simply a place where you can survive for a week; rather, the *sukkah* must be a place in which you can live with relative dignity for the length of the holiday. To paraphrase the classic labor slogan, a *sukkah*—and even more so a permanent house—must be a place not only of bread, but also of roses.

A "permanent home" must, by definition, be permanent. The *sukkah* derives its significance from the contrast between it and the homes we live in during the rest of the year. If we did not have permanent homes to which we could return at the conclusion of the holiday, then the *sukkah* would lose its meaning. You could hardly expect a person living in a homeless shelter, or on the brink of losing his or her home, to appreciate the temporary impermanence of the *sukkah*. Appropriate yearlong housing, we might infer, should be guaranteed for a significant period of time, and should not feel to the resident as temporary and insecure as the *sukkah*.

While homelessness may be the most visible manifestation of the housing problem, high cost burden is a more pervasive indication of the depth of America's housing crisis. It is not only the homeless who live constantly with the sense of housing impermanence manifest in the *sukkah*. The more than 17 million Americans who spend more than 50 percent of their incomes on housing, and who may be just one or two paychecks away from eviction, can similarly never be fully secure in their housing.[12] For millions of people, the "temporary" experience of the *sukkah* has become a year-round reality. Conditions in many public housing units are so unsafe as to threaten the lives of inhabitants; this reality hit home for the Jewish community in August 2008, when a five-year-old Hasidic boy was killed when he fell down the shaft of a broken elevator in the public housing unit where his family lived.[13] At the same time, the demolition of public housing, without adequate plans for relocating people in the community, makes the insecurity even worse. Those paying unaffordable rents or mortgages, struggling to prevent their homes from entering foreclosure, or doubling up with relatives similarly cannot feel safe and secure in their homes. The lesson of the *sukkah* is that housing, in order to be considered permanent, must allow its residents to live with a sense of security, permanence, and dignity.

The Mezuzah

The traditional understanding of the biblical command to "write [these words] on the doorposts of your homes" (Deut. 6:9) understands the verse as an obligation for Jews to affix a *mezuzah* to each door of their home—a box containing this passage and the others that comprise the *Sh'ma* prayer.[14]

In the *Mishneh Torah*, Rambam defines the type of house that requires a *mezuzah*:

> There are ten conditions that a house must meet in order for the resident to be obligated to put up a *mezuzah*, and if it fails to meet any one of these conditions, [the resident] is not obligated to put up a *mezuzah*, and these are they: It must be at least four *amot* (cubits) by four *amot*. It must have two doorposts. It must have a lintel. It must have a roof. It must have doors. The gate must be ten *t'fachim* (handbreaths) or higher. It must be for ordinary purposes. It must be made as a place for people to live. It must be made as an honorable place. It must be made as a permanent place. (*Hilkhot Tefillin u'Mezuzah* 1:1)

We may understand these ten conditions as a concise description of what constitutes a permanent home. As in the case of the *sukkah*, permanent housing is defined, at least partially, by size. A house that is too small for a person to live there comfortably cannot be considered permanent. Per the rabbinic discussion about the minimum and maximum size of a *sukkah*, we might assume that a permanent house should be easily recognizable as such to a passer-by.

A permanent home, in Rambam's description, must have doors and a roof in order that the residents be protected from the elements and from other potential dangers, such as robbers. Finally, just as a *sukkah* should be constructed with the intention that it be temporary, a home must be constructed with the intention that it be a permanent dwelling place.[15] According to these requirements, it may be that transitional housing, FEMA trailers, shelters, and other nonpermanent or unsafe residences would not qualify as homes (and would not require the resident to put up a *mezuzah*).

Private and Public Space

Legal discussions of private and public space offer additional insight into rabbinic conceptions of the home. For the purpose of establishing the laws of carrying on Shabbat, the Talmud defines two primary types of space: the *r'shut hay'chid* (private property) and the *r'shut harabim* (public property).[16]

The Talmud and subsequent legal codes distinguish between the *r'shut hay'chid* and the *r'shut harabim* on the basis of both appearance and function. While the *r'shut hay'chid* is a personal dwelling place, the *r'shut harabim* may be a street, plaza, forest, or other space designated for public use. Whereas the *r'shut hay'chid* has walls of at least ten *t'fachim* (approximately between two and one-half and three feet) high, the *r'shut harabim* has no walls, or has walls that are periodically interrupted by gates or other openings.[17] Some further define the *r'shut hay'chid* as a place in which the doors are locked at night, in contrast to the *r'shut harabim*, where the doors are never locked.[18] A few commentators also require that the *r'shut harabim* be a place through which a large number of people pass every day.[19]

The distinction between the *r'shut hay'chid* and the *r'shut harabim* offers a few notes toward the definition of a house. Private space, the Rabbis tell us, should be protected both from the elements and from intruders. Within his or her house, a person can lock the doors and feel safe knowing that no one can enter uninvited. The *r'shut harabim*, on the other hand, is unprotected space defined by its accessibility to anyone who wishes to enter. As in the laws of the *sukkah*, appearance matters. A passer-by should be able to distinguish easily between private and public space.[20]

Therefore, as we consider the types of housing we consider appropriate for the lowest-income members of society, we should ask whether this housing offers sufficient physical and psychological protection to its residents, and whether this housing is easily recognizable as an appropriate place for people to live.

Housing Safety

Additional help in defining the nature and structure of a house comes from the biblical commandment to build a *ma'akeh* (guardrail) for the roof. This commandment, which appears in Deuteronomy 22:8, is one of a series of laws concerning respect for human life and for nature. Other laws recorded in this chapter include the obligation to shoo away a mother bird before taking her eggs or chicks so that she will not witness the abduction of her children; and the prohibition against attaching an ox and a donkey to the same plow, lest one or both suffer from being forced to work at the other's pace (Deut. 22:1–10). Similarly, the commandment to build a *ma'akeh*, which aims to prevent people from falling off the roof of a house, is based on compassion for humanity and on a commitment to the value of human life. Human life, according to the Bible, is so valuable that we are legally obligated to take extraordinary precautions to protect people from harm. Thus, a person who, in building a home, fails to consider the potential danger that this home may present is held liable for the death of any person who falls from the roof of the house.

The *mitzvah* of the *ma'akeh* teaches that a house must do more than just protect people from the basic elements. Rather, a house should protect people, to the greatest degree possible, from all potential danger. Concern for human life must, literally, be built into the fabric of the home.

Today, a literal interpretation of the commandment to build a *ma'akeh* might mandate the protection of residents by means of installing window bars and fire escapes; by fixing elevators and ventilation systems; and by removing asbestos, mold, lead paint, and potential allergens. However, a more expansive interpretation would suggest that homes must also protect inhabitants in other ways. A home, we might argue, should offer a safe place for children to play and should not be a place in which there is little protection against violence. In the past decades, we have seen the dangerous conditions created by large public housing units built without significant open space, well-lighted hallways, or other communal gathering points. A home that does not protect its residents against physical danger, we might say, is a home built without a *ma'akeh*.

Landlords and Tenants

Some of the fiercest housing disputes of the past decades have concerned conflicts between tenants and landlords. While few have gone to the extremes of the Upper East Side landlord who killed an elderly rent-control tenant[21] or of the Lower East Side landlord linked to the disappearance of two tenants who had complained about the lack of heat in their apartment,[22] there is no lack of stories of "slum" landlords who take advantage of tenants. My own landlord in Manhattan in the early 2000s, an observant Jew, told my neighbor that she didn't pay enough on her rent-stabilized apartment for him to close the holes that allowed mice and rats to run freely through her apartment. In numerous other cases, landlords simply abandon unwanted properties, leaving the tenants without needed repairs or utilities, or try to evict long-time tenants living in newly gentrifying areas.

Jewish law, anticipating and responding to the tensions between landlords and tenants, devotes much energy to legislating the relationship between the two. These laws focus on two major issues: the responsibilities of each party for the upkeep of the property and the ability of each party to break the lease.

A landlord, according to Jewish law, is responsible for providing the basic elements that make a home livable and that the tenant cannot reasonably be expected to provide. Rambam writes:

> One who rents a house to another is obligated to construct doors and to fix broken windows, to reinforce the ceiling, to fix broken beams, and to make a bolt and a lock and similar things which are produced by artisans and which are essential to dwelling in houses. The tenant is obligated to put up a *ma'akeh* and a *mezuzah.*"[23]

Most commentators understand the distinction between the obligations of landlords and tenants, both in Rambam and in the *gemara* on which he bases his ruling, as differentiating between items that must be produced by artisans and those that ordinary people can be expected to build.[24] While tenants may be expected to put some effort into making their homes livable, they are not required to invest money in hiring an artisan to make more significant home repairs.

Rambam's requirement that the tenant put up a *ma'akeh* appears to contradict the biblical text, which places the responsibility for the *ma'akeh* on the builder. Most of the commentators on Rambam explain this discrepancy by saying that the biblical text applies only to houses that are sold, and not to rental properties or to multifamily dwellings.[25] One thirteenth-century scholar suggests that the resident of the home is responsible for constructing the *ma'akeh* so that he or she does not become negligent in safety matters.[26] While the landlord must make the house habitable, the tenant reserves some responsibility for the safety of those who come to visit. From Rambam's description of the *ma'akeh* as something that can be built by anyone, and not only by an artisan, we can also assume that the *ma'akeh* that Rambam has in mind is easy to construct, and not something that the landlord or tenant would have to hire a professional to build. Perhaps the landlord would remain responsible for protective measures that only skilled craftspeople could build.

Some later halakhic authorities go even further than Rambam in holding the landlord responsible for making the home livable.

The Tur emphasizes that it is the tenant, and not the landlord, who determines what repairs the landlord is required to make. He requires the landlord to repair broken windows "if the tenant needs light" and further stipulates that "even if there is a lot of light, if there are windows that are stuck and whose latches won't open, the landlord must open these" (*Choshen Mishpat* 314:1). In his gloss on the *Shulchan Arukh*, the Rema specifies that the landlord is obligated to perform the necessary repairs even if the tenant sees and accepts the property as is. The landlord, according to Moshe Isserles, cannot claim that the tenant, in signing a lease, abandons the right to demand further repairs to the property (*Chosen Mishpat* 314:1). Significantly for our modern situation, one sixteenth-century authority, Rabbi Benjamin ben Mattathias, considers the landlord to be obligated to make the specified repairs regardless of whether the tenant is a Jew or non-Jew.[27]

It is significant that Rambam, while holding the landlord responsible for all repairs for which artisans must be engaged, specifically cites examples of infrastructure problems that threaten the safety of the tenants. Broken windows, doors, and locks all may facilitate burglary. Broken beams may lead to the collapse of the entire structure. Thus, in obligating the landlord to perform most property repairs, Jewish law holds the landlord liable for the safety of the tenant. A person who rents a home may not abdicate responsibility for what happens there; rather, the well-being of the tenants remains in the hands of the landlord for the duration of the lease.

In the contemporary world, the halakhic obligation on the landlord to maintain the physical condition of the rental property serves as a rebuke to slum landlords who often fail even to ensure that their tenants have heat and water. While the tenants' rights struggles of the 1960s produced many state laws mandating a "warranty of habitability"—a minimum set of standards that landlords must guarantee—the spotty enforcement of these laws enables landlords to continue to rent unsafe units. *Halakhah*, as we have seen, would prohibit such violations. In one contemporary application of the *halakhah* of landlord-tenant relations, the Boston Beit Din, in 1968, forced Israel, Joseph, and Raphael Mindick, three brothers known as slumlords, to make necessary repairs to their buildings, whose residents were primarily African American.[28] This willingness to hold a landlord to halakhic standards should serve as the example for *batei din* everywhere.

The rabbinic mandate to guarantee the safety of the tenants cannot be completely fulfilled by the physical upkeep of the building. Landlords must create homes that are safe and secure for the people who live there. This responsibility may include ridding the building of cockroaches or mold; constructing buildings whose design allows tenants easily to see what is going on in the area; and working with tenants to prevent gang activity in the neighborhood.

Other than laws regarding home repairs, most of the *halakhah* related to landlord-tenant issues concerns the duration of leases. At the root of these discussions about leases lies the concern that tenants not become homeless at the whim of the landlord. Thus, during the winter months, landlords are forbidden from evicting tenants because, according to the Talmud, homes were harder to find during the winter. During the summer months, when housing is more readily available, landlords must give tenants sufficient notice before terminating a lease (Talmud, *Bava Metzia* 101b). The varying availability of housing in different places leads to parallel laws that differentiate between urban and rural areas. Tenants are similarly required to give their landlords adequate notice before terminating a lease (*Bava Metzia* 101b).

While there is significant disagreement within the Talmud itself and among the commentators about what constitutes sufficient notice before an eviction, the assumption that underlies all of these discussions is that a lease should not be terminated if the tenant will have difficulty finding a new place to live. Landlords also may not raise the rent as a backhanded way of evicting a tenant during the winter (*Bava Metzia* 101b).

Rambam articulates the concern about evictions most clearly, saying that the landlord must give advance notice of a lease termination "so that [the tenant] can look for another place and will not be abandoned in the street."[29] If a tenant becomes homeless as the result of eviction, Rambam implies, the landlord can be held respon-sible. We might read Rambam here as a critic of cities such as Chicago, which, in the past few years, has demolished more than 16,000 units of public housing while building only 2,270 new units as of 2007. Homeless advocates in Chicago estimate that these evic-tions have already made hundreds of families homeless and may eventually double the homeless population of the city, currently approximated at 15,000 people.[30]

For their part, tenants living on an open-ended lease must give landlords thirty days' notice in a city, or twelve months' notice in a village.[31] The difference in standards between the city and the vil-lage reflects the ease of finding tenants in a big city versus the diffi-culty of finding tenants in a small village. The law assumes that the landlord relies on rent money for his or her income, and therefore attempts to ensure that the landlord will not be left unable to sup-port his or her household. If the tenant and the landlord make a lease for a certain time frame from the beginning, there is no need for additional warning.

Under a fixed lease, the landlord may not evict the tenant, even if the landlord becomes homeless, falls into poverty, or needs to sell the house to another.[32] A tenant who signs a lease for a certain time period can and should feel confident that his or her housing will be secure for the period of the lease. However, under an open-ended contract, the landlord may evict the tenant if the landlord's own home falls down, or if the landlord needs a home for a newly married child and is not able to notify the tenant ahead of time.[33]

In the ideal situation, the tenant will never be unexpectedly evicted and the landlord will never suddenly lose a tenant. Most of the relevant law, however, focuses on protecting the tenant, who usually has the most to lose. At least one contemporary *teshuvah* explicitly favors the tenant by exempting a tenant who breaks a lease without notice from compensating the landlord for the lost rent.[34]

The desire to protect tenants from homelessness is evident also in the requirement for a landlord to rebuild a house that has fallen down. According to one *mishnah*:

> If one rents a house to another and it falls down, the landlord is obligated to build the tenant a new house. If [the original house] was small, he may not build a big one. If it was big, he may not build a small one. If it was a single house, he may not build two houses. If it was two houses, he may not build one. The landlord should neither decrease nor add to the number of windows unless both of them agree [to this change]. (Mishnah, *Bava Metzia* 8:9)

This law, like the restrictions on evictions, is designed to guarantee tenants a place to live for the duration of their lease. Even a natural disaster, which presumably causes financial loss for the landlord, does not cancel the lease. For the period of the contract, the landlord is responsible for providing the tenant with a house of certain specifications, regardless of what happens to the original property. At the same time, the obligation to uphold the lease does not depend solely on the landlord's discretion; for example, the landlord is not permitted to move the tenant at will from one home of a certain size to another. The obligation of the landlord to provide alternate housing takes effect only if something happens to the original property.

The landlord must not only provide the tenant with a home for the duration of the lease, but must also ensure that this home meets certain specifications. A home smaller or of a different design than the one originally leased may not meet the needs of the tenant. A larger home may prove cumbersome or expensive to maintain. Furthermore, in prohibiting the landlord from forcing the tenant to accept a larger home or two homes instead of one, the *mishnah* eliminates the possibility that the landlord will attempt to use the increased size of the home as justification for demanding a higher rent.

The laws regarding the assumed duration of leases and the means of terminating a lease all stem from a desire to grant the tenant a sense of housing security. Tenants, Jewish law suggests, should not have to worry that they might suddenly find themselves homeless. This concern about housing stability assumes new relevance at a time in which more and more families find themselves only a paycheck away from homelessness. In the United States today, approximately 3.5 million people, including 1.35 million children, experience homelessness in a given year,[35] an estimated 1.3 million families entered foreclosure in 2007 alone, and another 3.5 million families risk foreclosure by 2011.[36] As Jewish law understands, providing immediate shelter does not fully ease the housing burden. Adequate housing must provide a sense of dignity and must also be sufficiently secure that a single crisis will not drive residents into homelessness.

The Role of the Federal Government

In discussing public housing, subsidized housing, and other welfare issues, conservatives often speak of the need for "personal responsibility." The argument, in short, is that welfare and other assistance programs only reinforce dependence on public aid, and that those who work hard enough will eventually succeed in lifting themselves out of poverty.

Judaism, too, demands taking responsibility for our actions. Indeed, many of the fundamental principles of Judaism, including the concepts of mitzvah, chiyyuv (obligation), teshuvah (repentance), s'khar (reward), and onesh (punishment) are predicated on a belief that human beings are responsible for their actions. Individuals have the option of doing right or wrong and of fulfilling or abdicating their responsibilities, but they then must accept the consequences of these choices. Those who make the wrong choice are expected to do teshuvah—to admit their wrongdoings and, to the extent possible, repair the damage.

The housing policies of the federal government over the last half century have, in large part, created today's affordable housing crisis. I would argue, then, that the federal government therefore has a responsibility to do teshuvah, to repent and make amends, for the contemporary housing struggles of low-income families. These policies represent one of the most important, least often told, stories about wealth and poverty in the United States.

Since the 1930s, the federal government has pursued a housing policy that explicitly or implicitly favors suburbs over urban areas, whites over minorities, and middle-class homeowners over low-income tenants. A series of federal policies have led directly to the increasingly segregated and overwhelmingly suburban nature of American housing today.

The history of contemporary federal housing policy begins in 1933 with the establishment of the Home Owners Loan Corporation (HOLC), a New Deal program formed to refinance mortgages in danger of default and to grant low-interest loans to help owners recover homes that had been forcibly sold. The establishment of long-term mortgages with uniform payments spread over the life of the debt allowed more middle-income Americans to purchase their own homes. The following year, the National Housing Act created the Federal Housing Administration (FHA), which insures long-term mortgages made by private lenders. This act virtually eliminated the risk associated with loans for home purchase or construction, encouraging banks to lower mortgage rates. These lower interest rates permitted more families to own homes and, in fact, often made it cheaper to buy than to rent. By supporting new developments outside of core cities, favoring single-family housing programs, and preferring the construction of new homes to the remodeling of existing ones, FHA projects encouraged middle-income families to move to the suburbs.[37] According to Robert Fishman, "A white home-owner who wished to stay in his old neighborhood had to seek old-style conventional mortgages with high rates and short terms. The same purchaser who opted for a new suburban house could get an FHA-insured mortgage with lower interest rates, longer terms, a lower down payment, and a lower monthly payment."[38] Federal funding for highways further quickened the rate of suburbanization.

The return of 16 million soldiers from World War II prompted a national housing shortage. While the Veteran Administration (VA) Housing Program, introduced in 1944 as part of the G.I. Bill, allowed veterans to buy a home without a down payment, the lack of available housing made it difficult to take advantage of this provision. In 1949 the government passed a new housing act that guaranteed increased profits for banks and construction companies involved in new housing developments. During the 1950s, one-third of all new private housing was financed with FHA or VA assistance.[39] Virtually all of this housing was constructed in the suburbs.

One of the most influential provisions of the Housing Act of 1949, combined with the Urban Renewal Act of 1954, permitted municipalities to raze areas in which 20 percent of the buildings were classified as "blighted" and to receive federal funds for the redevelopment of these areas. These two federal acts offered local governments leeway to destroy many minority neighborhoods that, although low-income, were thriving and healthy communities. In one study of Boston's West End, an immigrant neighborhood classified as "blighted," sociologist Herbert Gans found homes that appeared run-down on the outside, but whose interiors were meticulously maintained.[40] While the municipalities used the newly cleared land to develop luxury apartment buildings, convention centers, and office buildings, the displaced communities scrambled to find affordable housing elsewhere. On the basis of these two laws, between 1949 and 1968, local governments demolished more than 425,000 units of housing, mostly occupied by minority tenants. In the same period, only 125,000 new units were constructed, more than half of which were unaffordable for the displaced residents.

New highway construction only increased the number of demolitions. While the federal government provided most of the funding for the construction of the interstate highway system, local authorities designed the routes, often using urban expressways to carry out their own segregation agendas.[41] Between 1956 and 1972, the combination of urban renewal and highway construction displaced approximately 3.8 million people.[42]

Official and unofficial segregation measures further reduced the supply of housing for minorities. HOLC instituted a color-coded system based on the races, ethnicities, occupations, and incomes of residents of each neighborhood and on the age, quality, and price of the housing stock. Thus, those living in "redlined" African American neighborhoods found it increasingly difficult to secure the mortgages that made home ownership possible. The greater availability of mortgages in all-white areas encouraged white homeowners to move out of more ethnically diverse areas.[43]

Until 1968, the FHA explicitly encouraged neighborhood segregation and respected restrictive covenants, unwritten agreements, and neighborhood "traditions" of segregation. According to a 1947 FHA manual, "If a mixture of user groups is found to exist, it must be determined whether the mixture will render the neighborhood less desirable to present and prospective occupants. Protective covenants are essential to the sound development of proposed residential areas, since they regulate the use of land and provide a basis for the development of harmonious, attractive neighborhoods."[44] While more white families than ever bought their own homes during the 1940s and 1950s, African Americans purchased less than 2 percent of the FHA- and VA-financed housing acquired between 1946 and 1959.

While the 1968 Fair Housing Act made such overt discrimination illegal, neither U.S. Department of Housing and Urban Development (HUD) nor local authorities had the power to enforce this law, but could only refer cases to the Department of Justice. Without an effective means of enforcement, this law failed to have an immediate effect on the availability of housing.

Even today, the bulk of government housing subsidies go to the wealthy and to homeowners. Homeowner tax breaks, instituted in 1912 to help family farmers, now provide more than $119.3 billion a year in subsidies, compared with approximately $37 billion/year for low-income housing.[45] In 2004, the wealthiest fifth of the population, with average incomes of $148,138 per year, received 36.6 percent of government housing subsidies, while the poorest fifth, with average incomes of $10,295, received only 20 percent of housing subsidies.[46] In contrast to common perceptions, most poor people do not live in subsidized housing, but most wealthy people do.

While some federal money did finance the development of urban public housing, the number of new housing units constructed could not match the number of homes demolished through urban renewal. The public housing constructed in the 1950s also reinforced existing patterns of racial segregation. The new high rises often served as physical boundaries between white and black parts of the city, and most public housing was constructed in predominantly black neighborhoods. Some cities, such as Chicago, actually maintained two lists of potential public housing tenants—one of whites and the other of blacks—in order to ensure the racial segregation of each housing project.[47]

In the 1960s and 1970s, the federal government made some strides toward reversing the discriminatory effects of earlier housing legislation and providing more affordable housing for low-income and minority tenants. The Housing and Urban Development Act of 1968 authorized the construction, over a ten-year period, of 26 million housing units, including 6 million units for low- and moderate-income families.[48] The six-year period from 1976 to 1982 saw the construction of more than 1 million federally subsidized units.

Beginning with the Reagan administration, however, the federal government began cutting back on housing construction. Since 1982, fewer than 25,000 federally subsidized units have been built annually. The burden of creating affordable housing has shifted to state and local governments, with mixed results. The growing "hands-off" attitude of the federal government toward affordable housing only reinforces the dominant corporate culture: if affordable housing proves profitable, low-income people will have decent places to live. If private builders cannot profit from the construction of affordable housing—and so far, they have not—the housing crisis will continue to grow.

If the federal government continues to ignore the need for affordable housing, generations to come will pay the price. If we continue to demolish public housing without replacing it, rely on builders to create affordable housing, and subsidize homes for the rich while cutting aid to the poor, we condemn hundreds of thousands of

Americans to insufficient or insecure housing, or to wandering in search of a permanent place to live. This housing instability is likely to contribute to increased violence, to widen the gap between rich and poor, and to weaken low-income communities.

A Jewish approach to housing, as I have suggested here, begins with the assumption that even the poorest people should expect to have housing. A house is defined as a place that is secure and permanent, and that offers its inhabitants both protection and dignity. In the case of rental properties, the obligation to make housing safe lies primarily on the landlord; in the case of properties for sale, the obligation is divided between the builder and the owner. The resident of a house, too, bears responsibility for making the home safe for others who enter it.

Finally, in the case of the U.S. government's approach to housing, the concept of *teshuvah* is instructive. We do not usually talk about institutions or governments doing *teshuvah*; the laws of repentance generally apply to individuals, and specifically to Jews, who have hurt other individuals or who have broken divine commandments. But from the laws of *teshuvah* we can learn much about the appropriate way to remedy mistakes. In his *Hilkhot Teshuvah* (*Laws of Repentance*) in the *Mishneh Torah*, Rambam emphasizes that a person has not fully done *teshuvah* until returning to an identical position and resisting the previous mistake (2:1). Today, the United States again faces a housing crisis perhaps even more severe than the crises of the 1940s. In order to do real *teshuvah* for the policies of the 1950s and 1960s, the United States will have to craft a new housing policy that reverses some of the segregationist trends of the last half century, and that helps ensure affordable housing for the poorest segments of society, rather than simply offering additional subsidies to the wealthy.

The ways in which a society houses its residents serve as powerful visual symbols of its attitude toward its most vulnerable members. One *midrash* provides an especially stark example of the ways in which the quality of housing might provide a glimpse into the values of a society:

Rabbi Yehoshua ben Levi reports, "When I went to Rome, I saw pillars of marble that were covered with blankets so that they would not crack from the heat or freeze from the cold. I also saw a poor person with only a thin reed mat below him and a thin reed mat on top of him."[49]

For the Rabbis, the Roman Empire is the prime example of an evil society that cares little for its residents. In the ideal society, buildings will never be considered more important than people, and no individual will find himself or herself shivering under a thin mat, with nowhere safe and warm to go.

7

I Will Remove Illness from Within Your Midst

The Provision of Health Care

The issue of health care encompasses many issues, including the question of who bears responsibility for providing health care, whether and how much doctors and other health care workers should be paid, and what responsibility patients must take in their own care. Beyond these questions are even more detailed ones about how to balance competing needs for health care, which treatments the government should underwrite, and what decisions to make in certain medical situations. In this chapter we will tackle the central question of where the responsibility for providing medical care lies. Our answer to this question sets the groundwork for analyses of specific policies and situations.[1]

To begin this discussion, we should first consider the Jewish approach to human life. The biblical story of Creation twice asserts that human beings are created *b'tzelem elohim*—in the image of God. While the Bible itself certainly describes God often in anthropomorphic terms, rabbinic and later interpretations understand the concept of creation *b'tzelem elohim* not as a description of the physical likeness between humanity and God, but rather as evidence of the divinity inherent in each human being. Thus, procreation perpetuates the divine presence, and injury to a human being diminishes God's presence.[2] One rabbinic text offers a particularly vivid portrayal of this idea:

> Rabbi Meir said, "When a person suffers, what language does God use? My head is too heavy! My arm is too heavy!"[3]

Accordingly, another *mishnah* in the same tractate mandates that witnesses in capital cases be reminded of the value of human life:

> How are the witnesses intimidated in capital cases? Witnesses in capital cases are brought in and intimidated [in this way]: "Perhaps you are only repeating hearsay or what another witness said, or what a trustworthy person said. Perhaps you don't know that we will check your testimony by inquiry and cross-examination. You should know that capital cases are not like civil cases. In civil cases, [the witness] can make atonement [for false testimony] through payment. In capital cases, the witness is held responsible for the blood [of the convicted] and of his [potential] descendents until the end of time. We find this in the case of Cain, who killed his brother. The Torah teaches [that God says to Cain]: "the bloods of your brother cry unto me." It doesn't say "the blood of your brother," but rather "the bloods of your brother." That is to say, "his blood and the blood of his [potential] descendants." ...
>
> For this reason was the human being created alone, to teach you that whoever destroys a single soul, Scripture holds guilty as though this person had destroyed a complete world; and whosoever preserves a single soul, Scripture credits this person with having saved a complete world. (Sanhedrin 4:5)

If human pain directly causes an injury to God, then the death of a human being—especially someone innocent of any crime—even more greatly diminishes the divine image. In deciding whether to give incriminating testimony in a capital case, witnesses need to take into account the potential ramifications of causing the death of another person. A witness who abets the execution of an innocent person is held responsible not only for the death of this individual but also for the loss of all the children and grandchildren he or she might have had—and by implication, of any other contributions he or she might have made to the world.

The consequences for murdering, harming, or contributing to the death of a human being are severe indeed. As we will see, this premium on human life translates also into the establishment of positive obligations to save life, even at the expense of other commandments.

The Obligation to Heal

The assertion that human beings are created in the image of God serves as the theological foundation for the obligation to save life. If the destruction of life is viewed as a desecration of God, then the preservation of life can be understood as strengthening the divine presence by maintaining one more instance of God's image in the world.

Each rabbinic law translates an abstract, theological "value concept" into a concrete behavioral requirement, as the twentieth-century thinker Max Kadushin has argued.[4] If we believe that humans are created in the image of God, this concept may inspire us to value human life. To integrate this value into Jewish practice, we need a law. When we enshrine the principle as a law, the act of saving a life turns from a good idea or a moral principle into a legal obligation. In this specific case, two biblical laws result. First, the prohibition, "Do not stand on the blood of your neighbor" (Lev. 19:16), which the Rabbis understand as an obligation to prevent the blood of another from being shed. The Talmud comments, "How do we know that one who sees one's neighbor drowning in the river, or being dragged by a wild beast, or being attacked by robbers, is obligated to save this person? The Torah says, 'Do not stand by the blood of your neighbor'" (*Sanhedrin* 73a). Second, some read the obligation to return a lost object to extend to returning a person's life to him or her (Deut. 22:1–3). Rambam, himself a physician, explains, "This verse includes [returning] a person's body, for if one sees him dying and can save him, one should save him, whether physically or with money or with knowledge."[5] With this comment, Rambam extends the obligation to save life beyond those with medical skill to those who can contribute financially to the treatment of a sick person.

To the modern mind, there does not seem to be much reason to argue about whether doctors or others should attempt to save life. Western society has a generally positive view of doctors, and American Jews regularly joke about the parental fantasy of a child becoming (or marrying) a doctor. The Jewish community has no strong faction that advocates avoiding doctors and leaving healing to God.

But two reservations give the Rabbis pause in formulating laws that mandate healing. First, since some rabbinic traditions describe God alone as holding the keys to life, perhaps human beings should not interfere with divine actions.[6] Second, any medical treatment introduces new dangers. There is fear that a doctor may try to heal a sick person only to exacerbate the illness or even kill the patient. These concerns still ring true today, and would have been even more true hundreds or thousands of years ago, before the extraordinary advances of modern medicine.

Few Jewish authorities seriously pursue the possibility that all healing should be left in the hands of God. Beginning in the Bible, God is credited as the ultimate healer but divine healing often relies on human intervention. When Moses prays for a cure for his sister Miriam, who has been struck by a skin disease, God responds by dictating a process of quarantine and reintegration (Num. 12:1–16). When the prophet Elisha brings a young boy back to life, it is clear that God is the one restoring life but notable that God chooses to work through a human being rather than through more direct means (2 Kings 4:8–37). But once the prophetic era has ended, Jewish authorities become suspicious of anyone who claims that God is speaking or working directly through him or her. This suspicion leads a few rabbis to contend that illness constitutes a divine punishment or test, and to advise against treating any illness not caused by human misbehavior. In his commentary on the Torah, Abraham Ibn

Ezra (Spain, 1092–1167) limits doctors to healing external injuries caused by human agency, and not to curing internal maladies, which, according to Ibn Ezra, only God is authorized to heal.[7] Ibn Ezra bases his argument on two biblical commands. On the one hand, the Torah specifies that "if a person strikes another with his fist or a rock ... [the guilty party] should thoroughly heal [the injured party]" (Exod. 21:19). On the other hand, the book of Job describes God as the one who "inflicts pain and gives relief; wounds and makes whole" (Job 5:18). The contrast between these two verses leads Ibn Ezra to argue that God maintains exclusive authority over the healing of diseases not caused by human hands, and that the authority of doctors extends only to healing wounds that one person brings on another.

The weight of Jewish legal tradition rejects this view, instead permitting and even obligating doctors to address every sort of illness. One midrashic parable, written years before Ibn Ezra issued his legal ruling, imagines a sick person begging two rabbis for healing:

Once, Rabbi Yishmael and Rabbi Akiva were walking in the outskirts of Jerusalem, and a sick man confronted them.

He said, "My rabbis, tell me how I can be cured."

They said to him, "Take these medicines until you are cured."

He said to them, "But who brought this disease upon me?"

They said to him, "The Blessed Holy One."

He said to them, "And you have stuck your head into a matter not your own. God struck and you dare to heal? Are you not violating God's will?"

They said to him, "What is your occupation?"

He said to them, "I till the soil; here is my sickle."

They said to him, "And who created the field and the vineyard?"

He said to them, "The Blessed Holy One."

They said to him, "And you stick your head into something which does not concern you? God has created the field and you pick its fruits?!?"

He said to them, "Don't you see the sickle in my hand? If I did not plow and clear and fertilize the field, it would not bring forth anything."

They said to him, "Just as the tree will die if you don't weed and fertilize the field, so also the human body. Medicines can be compared to weeding and fertilizing and the physician to the farmer." (*Midrash Shmuel* ch. 4)

This story points to a long tradition that suggests a partnership between God and humanity, in which God creates basic elements with the expectation that human beings will transform these elements into the materials needed to sustain life. For example, one *midrash* tells a story of a king who gives his two servants wheat and flax for safekeeping. One servant transforms the wheat and flax into bread and clothing, while the other lovingly preserves the raw materials (*Eliyahu Zuta* ch. 2). The king, of course, prefers the creativity of the first. The *midrash* itself is meant as a parable for the study of Torah—God is pleased that the Jews have interpreted, reinterpreted, and derived laws from Torah, rather than preserving it as a museum piece. But the example used within the *midrash* also suggests that God, like the king, prefers humanity to improve upon the raw materials of Creation.

The *midrash* about the sick man and the rabbis both continues and expands on this tradition of divine-human partnership. If we take the *midrash* seriously, then we conclude that God purposely created human beings as imperfect medical specimens, the preservation of whose life depends on humanly created and administered medicine. Beyond simply giving physicians permission to heal, or even obligating physicians to heal, this *midrash* suggests that human life is actually unsustainable without medicine. Through providing medical care, human beings actualize the promise of creation in the divine image—like God, human beings hold the keys to life and death. Placing healing powers in the hands of rabbis further casts medicine as a religious duty, and not simply as a profession like any other.

Other rabbinic stories emphasize the need to visit and care for the sick in order to expedite the healing process. As in the *midrash* quoted above, the rabbinic assumption is that God may ultimately control healing, but human beings can and should influence the process. In one set of talmudic stories, a series of rabbis fall ill and Rabbi Yochanan heals each in turn. When Rabbi Yochanan himself becomes ill, another rabbi provides the cure. Quite logically, the Talmud asks, "Why doesn't Rabbi Yochanan save himself?" The answer: "A prisoner cannot free himself from prison" (*B'rakhot* 5b). Again, the healer is celebrated, and there is no expectation that the patient must appeal to God, atone for his sins, or otherwise find a way to heal himself without assistance from outside experts.

Perhaps the most vociferous defender of the power of physicians is Moses Maimonides (Rambam), not only a rabbinic scholar but also a doctor who wrote many volumes of medical advice. In the introduction to his treatise on asthma, Rambam rails against those who refuse treatment out of fear of medical mistakes, saying:

> I know that you could say: "The conclusion to be drawn from your words is to abandon medicine because all one's efforts and toil in this profession all seem to be for naught." I will dispel the doubt for you.... Know that medicine is an absolutely essential science for man at all times and in all places, not only during times of illness but even during times of health to the point where I firmly believe that one should never be separated from medicine.[8]

With this exhortation, Rambam echoes the talmudic ruling that a Torah scholar may not live in a city that does not have a doctor, as well as certain instruments of hygiene or good health such as a bathroom, a bathhouse, and perhaps even certain kinds of healthy fruit (*Sanhedrin* 17b). In the section of the *Mishneh Torah* concerned with the preservation of life, Rambam further lists dozens of biblical and rabbinic laws aimed at protecting human life. These include prohibitions against ingesting food or drink likely to endanger your health; a requirement to construct guardrails on the roofs of your home; and the obligation for a society to build cities of refuge to protect those accused of manslaughter from death at the hands of the victims' relatives.[9] In the twentieth century, Rabbi Moshe Feinstein, an influential

American legal authority, went even further in ruling that young couples considering marriage should be screened for Tay-Sachs disease,
as such screening is likely to prevent the birth of a child with a
painful and incurable disease.[10] In Feinstein's view, doctors and
patients are obligated not only to care for existing conditions, but
also to pursue preventive treatment.

One medieval authority effectively splits the difference
between those who would leave healing to God and those who
charge doctors with the obligation to heal. According to Ramban
(Spain, 1194–1270), God reserved exclusive rights to heal during
the prophetic period. Now that the prophetic period has ended,
God has granted doctors the means to heal through natural means.
He writes:

> The verses, "for I am God your healer" and "I will remove ill-
> ness from your midst" promise that the Jewish people will not
> require a physician and that illness will not come upon them
> under ordinary circumstances. Indeed, this was the situation
> for the righteous during the age of prophecy.... Since many
> do not rely on heavenly healing and are accustomed to turn
> to a physician for a medical cure, the Torah granted the physi-
> cian the right to heal. And God left the sick person to the
> workings of nature so that natural remedies would be effec-
> tive for him. Thus, the physician should not refrain from heal-
> ing the sick, neither because of a fear lest they die at his hand,
> nor because he may say that God alone is the healer of all
> flesh. Rather, the physician should heal because the sick have
> become accustomed to turning to physicians.[11]

While Ramban does not go as far as the *midrash* of the sick man and
the rabbis in embracing the human obligation to heal, he does
accept medicine as a less-than-perfect accommodation to the world
as it is. In a perfect world, according to Ramban, God would provide
all healing, and people would always be righteous enough to merit
such healing. In our world, however, God does not act as a personal
physician, but rather creates natural remedies that human beings
can and should use in the practice of medicine.

Another serious objection to healing by doctors concerns the fear of malpractice or accidental death. If these issues remain concerns even in the twenty-first century, how much more so were the Rabbis concerned in a time when doctors relied on natural herbs and bloodletting, which often had no effect, worsened the patient's condition, or even brought about death. The Rabbis of the Talmud thus declared that "even the best of doctors are bound for *gehinnom* (hell)" (Mishnah, *Kiddushin* 4:14).

Jewish law addresses these concerns by restricting medical practice to those who are certified as qualified, and then exempting these qualified physicians from liability for unintentional mistakes that lead to injury or death. In the *Shulchan Arukh*, Joseph Caro writes:

> The Torah gave permission to the physician to heal; moreover, this is a religious precept and is included in the category of saving life, and if the physician withholds services, it is considered as shedding blood.... However, one should not practice medicine unless one is an expert and unless there is no greater expert present, for one who practices medicine not under these conditions is considered as one who sheds blood. And one who practices medicine without the permission of the court owes a fine, even if this person is an expert. And one who practiced medicine with the permission of the court and made a mistake and caused harm, is not liable [for punishment by] the human court, but is liable [for punishment by] the divine court. And one who kills someone by mistake should seek refuge. (*Yoreh De'ah* 336:1)

Like most other legal authorities, Caro rules that doctors are not only permitted but also obligated to practice: to refuse is to violate the law against shedding blood. The religious court retains the authority to certify physicians, and physicians who have obtained this communal permission to heal are obligated to practice their trade without fear of causing harm accidentally. Caro may frighten a few doctors by placing those who cause accidental death in the category of those who commit manslaughter, who, according to the

Bible, should flee to a "city of refuge," where they will be protected from the vengeful family of the deceased. One commentator on the *Shulchan Arukh* seeks to reassure those who might be put off from practicing medicine by the fear of causing death. Shabbetai ben Meir haKohen (known as the Siftei Kohen or Shakh; Lithuania/Moravia, ca. 1621–1662) writes, "In any case, there is no need to refrain [from attempting to heal another person] because of the fear of mistake, for it is a *mitzvah* [to heal]."[12]

In our discussion we have moved from a prohibition against causing harm, to an obligation to save life, to a more general obligation for doctors to provide medical services. The texts we have examined generally take a reactive approach to healing: the obligation kicks in once a person sees his or her neighbor drowning, or once a doctor encounters a sick patient. In the next few pages, we will consider attempts to institutionalize medical care within the communal infrastructure and address the question of preventive care.

Payment for Medical Services

If the provision of medical care is a *mitzvah*, then a person should no more be paid for healing than for lighting Shabbat candles or for holding a Passover seder. Or—to take a more pertinent example—you do not rescue a drowning person only if that person's family first promises a reward. Should doctors, then, offer their services to the community for free, and earn their living in other ways?

Ancient and medieval Jewish writings suggest that doctors most often had other primary professions and practiced medicine only on the side. Thus some Rabbis allowed doctors to receive compensation only for the time lost from their other professions. Ramban writes:

> Concerning physicians' compensation, it appears to me that he is allowed to accept payment for his loss of time and for his trouble, but may not receive payment for teaching [the patient about the illness] since it is a matter of the loss of the patient's body, about which the Torah says, "You shall restore

it to him." And in regard to the fulfillment of mitzvot, we apply the principle that "Just as [God] act[s] gratuitously, so too you should act gratuitously" (Talmud, *B'khorot* 29a). Therefore, it is forbidden to receive payment for one's medical knowledge or instruction.[13]

In this comment, Ramban refers to the talmudic prohibition against judges earning money for their duties, lest their judgments be clouded by the promise of reward. Instead, judges should be compensated only according to the work that they are forgoing to devote time to judgment.

When a judge or a doctor has no other career, and devotes his or her entire career to judging or doctoring, the rules change. In response to the same passage to which Ramban refers, the Tosefot, medieval talmudic commentators, note:

One should not be surprised that the judges in Jerusalem received a salary from the Temple treasury that was not based on the concept of the salary of an idle worker, for since judging was their entire work, and they did not have any other trade, it was necessary to support them. Similarly, in terms of the custom today to teach Torah for a salary when one has no other job—this is permitted.[14]

Most modern authorities extend this principle to establishing regular salaries for doctors, whom we no longer expect to have full-time jobs beyond providing medical care. Rabbi Yitzchak Zilberstein, the chief rabbi of the Israeli community of Ramat Elchanan, writes, "The rabbis worried about paying judges an appropriate salary, lest they fall into taking bribes—similarly, in the case of doctors, of course they worry about paying them an honorable salary in order to maintain their energy for healing."[15] One commentator on the Talmud even worries that a volunteer doctor might not prove reliable: when a person injures another, the guilty party is liable to pay for medical treatment, yet according to Rabbenu Asher (the Rosh), a thirteenth-century legal authority, the injurer may not skirt this obligation by offering free medical care:

If the injurer says, "I have a close friend who will heal you for free," the injured can say, "If the doctor does not receive payment, his heart and mind will not be focusing on the needs of the sick person, since he is not anticipating receiving a fee."[16]

For their part, doctors and other health care providers may not charge such exorbitant prices that patients forgo treatment. Joseph Caro rules:

> If one has medicine that a sick person needs, it is forbidden to charge more than the appropriate price for this medicine. Furthermore, even if the sick person agreed to a high price out of urgent need, as the medicine is nowhere else to be found, one can still only accept the appropriate price. (*Shulchan Arukh, Yoreh De'ah* 336:3)

Allowing salaries for doctors, like requiring affordable prices for drugs, seeks to create a system in which doctors are fully able to carry out their obligations toward patients, and in which patients are easily able to secure the medical care and drugs that they need. We might read these texts in the context of our discussion of *tikkun olam* in Chapter 2. There, we learned about prohibitions against redeeming captives for exorbitant amounts of money for fear of encouraging kidnappings, against allowing men to annul divorce documents in ways that might leave women unsure about their marital status, and against paying more than the going rate for *mezuzot* and other sacred documents. All of these rulings aim to create a functional society in which kidnappings are rare and the community does not bear an unreasonable burden of ransom costs, in which women can be sure of their marital status, and in which Jews can afford to buy ritual items. Similarly, the laws regulating the payment of doctors and the price of medicine attempt to establish a health care system in which doctors and other potential lifesavers feel motivated to operate at their highest capacity, and in which patients can expect to be able to afford their treatments.

These texts are especially troubling to read in contemporary America, where an inefficient and profit-driven health care system simultaneously makes it difficult for doctors to treat uninsured patients without risking their own livelihoods and prevents many patients from being able to afford needed medical care and medicine. Doctors often cannot afford to see more than a few Medicaid, Medicare, or charitable care patients, and often feel forced to see an overwhelming number of patients during the course of the day in order to earn enough money from insurance companies. Patients who lack insurance avoid seeking health care until an emergency develops, and then can find themselves bankrupted by high bills. Hospitals are crowded, understaffed, and short on funds. In this system, health care deteriorates and virtually everyone, from doctors to patients to hospital administrators, suffers.

Until now, we have examined health care through the lens of doctor-patient relations. But today's system presents us with many more players than the doctor, the patient, and the immediate community. The expectation that a patient and the doctor will individually work out a mutually acceptable system of compensation is inconsistent with a system of health care in which large insurance companies make decisions about doctors' compensation and, often, about patient care.

Communal Care for the Sick

In addition to requiring doctors to heal, Jewish legal texts impose on the community an obligation to provide financial and other resources for the ill. The *Shulchan Arukh* prioritizes using communal funds for the care of the sick over other obligations, such as the construction of a synagogue (*Yoreh De'ah* 249:16). One twentieth-century Israeli legal authority, Rabbi Eliezer Waldenberg, quotes an earlier medical authority, Rabbi Rafael Mordechai Malchi, in commenting:

> It has been enacted that in every place in which Jews live, the community sets aside a fund for care of the sick. When poor people are ill and cannot afford medical expenses, the community sends them a doctor to visit them, and the medicine is paid for by the communal fund. The community gives them

food appropriate for the ill, day by day, according to the
directions of the doctor. (*Tzitz Eliezer* 5:4)

Jewish law not only mandates the establishment of funds for the
sick, but also fiercely opposes any attempts to reappropriate these
funds for any other purposes. In one opinion, Rabbi Nissim ben
Reuven of Gerona (known as the Ran; Barcelona, 1320–1380) forbids money designated for the sick from being used to support
needy students. In addition to asserting that dedicated health care
funds may not be used for other purposes, the Ran also notes that
health care funds are specifically designated for the "poor of the
world" and not only for the "poor of the city."[17] In caring for the
sick, a given community must go beyond the needs of its own members. This is a direct contrast to the laws of *tzedakah*, which generally
prioritize the poor residents of our own city over the residents of
another city. In the case of health care, the Ran implies that every
person's health is everyone else's responsibility. With this comment,
he anticipates the current situation, in which the health care of
every individual in the United States—and arguably in the world—
really is dependent on that of everyone else. Individual, communal,
corporate, and governmental decisions about when to provide or
seek certain types of care, which drugs to fund, whether to immu-
nize, and how to distribute health care funds can have an impact far
beyond the immediate result of the decision.

In the absence of a national government prepared to care for the
health of the populace, Jewish communities throughout history set up
communal health care funds and funds for the provision of food, shelter, and other necessities for the sick. Until the creation of the modern state of Israel, there was no reason for Jewish law to spend much
time considering the obligations of the government toward the health
of the citizens. Instead, Jewish legal authorities insisted on the Jewish
communal responsibility toward the ill. Just as crafts guilds would set
up funds for the care of sick members, individual Jewish communities
would set up funds for the care of their own sick.

Beginning in thirteenth-century Europe, Jews moved beyond
simply setting up communal funds to establishing hospitals, used

mostly for the care of the destitute ill. (Wealthier patients received care in their own homes.) From this point on, Jews established hospitals in virtually every place in which they made their homes. The first such institution in the United States was New York's Mount Sinai Hospital, founded in 1852 as "Jews' Hospital." In Israel (then Palestine), the first hospital was built in 1854 with a gift from Meyer de Rothschild. In 1918 this hospital became known as Hadassah Hospital, which remains one of the most important medical institutions in the state of Israel.

The early American Jewish hospitals served a number of functions for the Jewish community. Most obviously, these hospitals cared for the Jewish poor, who could not always gain admission to Christian hospitals. For the most part, these hospitals served the Jewish community exclusively and unapologetically. Mount Sinai Hospital named as its founding purpose the care of "indigent Hebrews" and, with the exception of accident victims, admitted only Jewish patients.[18] The original bylaws of New York's Montefiore Hospital, founded in 1885 to care for patients too sick to be admitted to Mount Sinai, defined the institution's purpose as follows:

> To afford permanent shelter in sickness and to relieve invalids residents [*sic*] of the City of New York belonging to the Hebrew faith, who by reason of the incurable character of the disease from which they may be suffering are unable to procure permanent medical treatment in any of the Hospitals or Homes."[19]

Mount Sinai, like many hospitals in the late nineteenth century, did not accept patients with contagious diseases. Hospitals such as Montefiore met the growing need for refuge for patients suffering from communicable diseases such as tuberculosis, stigmatized as a Jewish or tailors' disease. Only three years after its founding, Montefiore removed the phrase "belonging to the Hebrew faith" from their bylaws, while still specifying that "all religious ceremonies practiced in the Home must be in accordance with the Jewish faith. This shall not, however, preclude the attendance of a clergyman of any other faith at the solicitation of a patient."[20] Still, Montefiore and other

Jewish hospitals and sanatoria that arose in the late nineteenth and early twentieth centuries maintained a focus on caring for tuberculosis patients and others who could not gain access to traditional hospitals.

These hospitals were also made necessary by forms of anti-Semitism that sometimes prevented Jewish patients from receiving the care they needed at Christian or secular facilities. In their history of Newark's Beth Israel hospital, Alan Kraut and Deborah Kraut described such situations:

> Non-Jewish physicians' cultural insensitivity could shape their diagnoses. Physicians who were not conversant in Yiddish or informed as to the customs and problems of Eastern European Jewish immigrants sometimes diagnosed neurasthenic symptoms presented by these patients as a uniquely Jewish ailment that they dubbed "Hebraic Debility." Those so diagnosed were said to be highly nervous and having difficulty adjusting to life in the United States.[21]

This description brings to mind the struggles of contemporary immigrants to secure hospital translation services, and of immigrants and other minorities to receive culturally sensitive treatments. Study after study has found that minorities, including immigrants as well as African Americans and women, routinely receive worse health care: sometimes because they do not live near the best hospitals, sometimes because they lack private health insurance, and sometimes because their complaints are taken less seriously than those of white, male, and/or English-speaking Americans.[22] While some states, such as New York, now mandate that hospitals provide translation services, immigrants in other states still rely on their children to translate sensitive medical information, or struggle to communicate with health care professionals in stilted English.

Two additional forms of discrimination prompted the creation of Jewish hospitals. First, hospital wards often became battlegrounds for Christian clergy intent on securing deathbed conversions. Jewish hospitals protected patients from such advances. Second, and perhaps just as important, Jewish hospitals employed Jewish physicians when many other hospitals and residency programs would not. According to Kraut and Kraut, "Jewish medical students were often met with hostility, subjected to admissions quotas in medical schools, denied residencies in non-Jewish hospitals, and, after graduation even refused hospital privileges. U.S. Jewish hospitals were thus portals for many young Jewish immigrants who sought careers in medicine."[23] Hospitals such as Mount Sinai became training grounds for the best and the brightest Jewish doctors. One history of Mount Sinai reports:

> There was the sense at Mount Sinai of being a member of an elite group of physicians, carefully selected and trained, nurtured with additional training abroad, and then moved up the ranks. Also, there was the relentless anti-Semitism that kept some from pursuing residencies at other hospitals. It was clear that if one were a young Jewish physician with high ambitions, the wards of Mount Sinai were the place to be.[24]

The early Jewish hospitals continued the tradition of providing communal support to the ill, and also took on the challenge of treating even the most ostracized sick and dying as creations in the divine image. The creation of a system of hospitals, medical schools, and placements for doctors also helped to establish a medical system that would eventually come to care for the needs of Americans of all faiths and ethnicities.

The Responsibility for Providing Health Care

As detailed above, most Jewish communities throughout history have provided basic care for the sick. In some cases, this care has consisted of little more than the provision of food and other basic necessities; in other cases, communities have built hospitals, medical schools, nursing homes, and other significant communal structures. Without political authority, Jewish communities could care for their own members, but they had little influence over health care policies in the states in which they lived.

The establishment of the state of Israel in 1948 gave Jews the chance to craft law for a sovereign state. The socialist leanings of the founders of the state, combined with a general sense of responsibility for the Jewish community, gave Israel a universal, if imperfect, health care system run by a quasi-governmental agency. While Israeli civil law does not, for the most part, consciously follow *halakhah*, the establishment of a Jewish state inspired many Jewish religious authorities to consider the ways in which Jewish civil law might inform the running of a modern state.

In an influential opinion concerning doctors' strikes, Rabbi Shlomo Goren, then the chief Ashkenazi rabbi of Israel, argues that the government ultimately bears responsibility for the health of the populace. For this argument, he draws on the talmudic ruling that the leaders of a community are responsible for fixing roads and other parts of the communal infrastructure. If the leaders fail to meet this responsibility, the Talmud says that "any blood that is spilled there is counted as though they spilled it" (*Moed Katar* 5a). Based on this, Goren concludes, "the responsibility of the *beit din* or the communal leadership is not limited to bodily harm that they cause directly." In the case of doctors, Goren declares the state responsible for the health of the citizens, then comments, "The government may not excuse itself from its responsibility toward the sick since the government is responsible for the health of the people, not the doctors, since the doctors have no responsibility toward the sick or toward their employers the moment they quit their jobs."[25] While Goren ultimately does not permit doctors to strike to the point of refusing to provide patient care, he does allow doctors to set conditions for their return to work, and he implores the government to meet these demands.

Earlier, we considered Jewish legal texts that defined the health care fund as an obligation incumbent upon the community, rather than as an optional resource that a community might choose to establish. The priority placed on this fund underscores the belief that the entire community bears responsibility for the health and well-being of each individual member of the community. In his ruling on doctors' strikes, Goren effectively extends this communal responsibility to the state as a whole. Even more to the point, Rabbi Chaim David Halevy (1924–1998), the Sephardic Chief Rabbi of

Tel Aviv/Jaffa, commented that "every advanced nation" should provide health care to its residents.[26]

In most other Western countries, as in Israel, the government does assume responsibility for health care, although the quality and extent of this care may vary widely. The United States is unique among developed, industrialized nations in providing health care only for the elderly and for certain very low-income people. Sixty percent of Americans receive health care through their jobs, 27 percent are covered through government programs, and an estimated 16 percent—47 million people in all—have no coverage whatsoever. Those who cannot afford health care and are ineligible for government programs often forgo regular medical care. They rely instead on emergency room care or go to clinics only when their illnesses become acute. This situation has negative repercussions for just about everyone involved. Those who take advantage of regular primary care are less likely to get sick, and they are more likely to discover illnesses before these become emergencies. Uninsured patients who use emergency rooms for treatment often find themselves saddled with thousands of dollars of medical debt, much of which goes unpaid. The United States spends more than $40 billion a year on uncompensated medical care for the uninsured, and taxpayers bear the brunt of these costs.[27] Crowded emergency rooms leave doctors frazzled and hospitals unable to provide the best possible care. Increasing access to primary care would lessen the burden in all of these areas.

Most Americans receive health care as a benefit from their employers. Judaism offers no direct precedent for linking health care to employment, but it does mandate that employers adhere to the "custom of the land" in regard to all work conditions—including wages, hours, and benefits such as the provision of food. Within America, we might say that it has become the "custom of the land" for employers to provide health care and, on this basis, might require all employers to provide such health care. One text does require employers to treat employees as "the poor of their household," and therefore to provide employees with food, shelter, and other items necessary for their well-being, presumably including health care.[28]

Ultimately, however, Judaism seems to prefer a system in which the community sets up overarching structures to provide for the medical care of individuals, rather than a system in which individual employers or others become responsible for the medical care of the ill.

Within a contemporary American context, we might say that cities, states, and the federal government assume the role of the communal authority that is obligated to provide a communal health care structure to meet the medical needs of all members of that community. From a Jewish perspective, then, a major problem with the American health care system is the lack of community oversight over the distribution of funds, the staffing of hospitals and other care facilities, and the appropriate treatment of patients. While we may understand the government to be the modern equivalent of the community described in Jewish legal texts, insurance companies do not easily fall into this paradigm. Unlike communities or governments, insurance companies do not answer to the community of people dependent on them, and do not rely on taxes or other monies collected from the community in an equitable way.

The first step in creating a new American health care system should involve restoring community—in this case, government—control over the system. In this way, the health care system will be supported by, and accountable to the residents of the society, just as the *kuppah* was once collected from and administered by the individual community. Per our discussion, this new health care system must treat all individuals as creations in the divine image, care even for those who are ostracized because of their illness or ethnicity, pay doctors enough to avoid a shortage of health care providers, and offer preventive care. Such a system has the potential to save lives, reduce differences in life expectancy among people of different economic classes, and produce a functional and equitable system for the long term.

8

The City and the Garden
Environmental Sustainability for the Twenty-first Century

The environment is likely to be the defining issue of the twenty-first century. Over the last few years, we have begun to come to terms with the impact of human actions on the ecosystem. On a macro level, we know that human actions have contributed to global warming, driven many species to extinction, and altered the interactions of plants and animals that allow the ecosystem to flourish. On a micro level, we see children suffering from asthma, fishers unable to earn a livelihood because the fish have disappeared, and adults in polluted areas developing cancer in unprecedented numbers.

One of the challenges of the environmental movement has been the gap between those working on conservationist issues, such as the protection of endangered species and the fight against global warming, and those working on environmental justice issues, such as the politics of waste disposal and the location of chemical plants and other polluting bodies. A comprehensive response to the environmental challenge will require an ideological and practical partnership between those working on global environmental issues and those focused on local issues regarding the distribution of resources and burdens.

Some have described this bridge as "just sustainability,"[1] defined as the attempt to distribute natural resources and environmental burdens equitably while also creating an ecosystem that will be sustainable for the long term. This concept can unite both managerial thinkers and local organizers in powerful work that takes into account both the immediate needs of human beings and the long-term needs of our world. Such coalitions seek, for example, to develop affordable housing that is energy efficient and close to public transportation, to create living wage jobs by expanding recycling services, and to involve community members in preventing or removing toxic waste.

Humanity and Nature in Jewish Tradition

The just sustainability discourse serves as a useful corrective to the more common, binary model that artificially separates concern for humanity from concern for nature. In the Jewish tradition, these two spheres are intrinsically and inseparably linked: virtually every major Jewish holiday celebrates both a historical event and a natural one. Passover commemorates the exodus from Egypt, but it also begins the barley harvest season that culminates with Shavuot. Shavuot not only marks the harvest, but also celebrates the divine revelation on Mount Sinai. The double significance of each holiday testifies to a worldview in which natural and historical events make up a single coherent story.

In Jewish tradition, the physical world plays a starring role in the process of redemption and revelation. Liberation relies, in part, on the suspension and then the resumption of the natural laws that dictate the current of the Red Sea. The transformation of the Israelites from slaves to free people takes place in the natural wonder and solitude of the desert wilderness. Even Moses's primary encounter with God takes place on a mountain that, according to rabbinic tradition, God momentarily suspends over the heads of the people in order to persuade them to accept the Torah (Talmud, *Shabbat* 88b).

On the other hand, at least one *midrash* assumes the stability of the physical world to be contingent on human action. This rabbinic tradition tells us that God created the world on the condition that the Jewish people would accept the Torah at Mount Sinai. For hundreds of years between Creation and the Exodus from Egypt, the physical world waited, uncertain of its fate. Finally, the Jewish people stood at the base of Mount Sinai, ready to receive the revelation. According to the Rabbis (*Shabbat* 88a), at that moment the earth trembled, and it quieted only when the people proclaimed, *"na'aseh v'nishma"*—"we will do and we will hear" (Exod. 24:7).

Even while holding human beings responsible for the viability of the world, Jewish sources maintain an anthropocentric view of Creation. The *midrash* asks why God calls the sixth day, on which humanity is created, *tov m'od* (very good) rather than simply calling the day *tov* (good) as God does on other days of Creation (Gen. 1:31). One of the midrashic answers notices that the Hebrew word *m'od* (consisting of the letters *mem-alef-daled*) is an anagram of the word Adam (*alef-daled-mem*) and understands God to be asserting that the world is created for the benefit of humanity (*B'reishit Rabbah* 8:5). Even more explicitly, another *midrash* comments:

> Rav Chuna said in the name of Rav Ayvu: God created humanity with deliberation, for God created humanity's food needs, and only then created humanity. The ministering angels said to God, "Master of the universe: 'What is man that you are mindful of him, and the son of man that you think of him?' (Psalms 8:5). Why did you create this trouble?"
>
> God said to them, "If so, 'all flocks and herds' (ibid. v. 8)—why were they created? 'Birds of the sky and fish of the sea' (ibid. v. 9)—why were they created? This is compared to a king who had a tower full of all good things, but had no guests. What enjoyment does the king have from all of these things?" They said to him, "Master of the universe, 'Adonai, our God, how majestic is your name in all the earth' (ibid. v. 10). Do what pleases you." (*B'reishit Rabbah* 8:5)

According to this text, God creates the entire world for the pleasure and well-being of humanity, and creates humanity as a companion and partner for Godself. In contrast to philosopher and professor of bioethics at Princeton University Peter Singer's critique of "speciesism" and his equal concern for the suffering of all species, Jewish tradition unapologetically privileges humanity, created in the image of God and as a partner for God, over the rest of the natural world. The formation of humanity is the culmination of the divine process of Creation, and God remains willing to destroy all of Creation if the Jewish people break the covenant through which they and God are bound together.

A classic environmentalist critique of Western religion suggests that Judaism and Christianity bear responsibility for the hubris that allows human beings to wreak technological havoc on nature.[2] Such critiques contrast an idealized notion of a nature-loving society with a Jewish and Christian belief that the natural world is created for the sole purpose of satisfying human need and comfort.

Responses to this critique tend to emphasize the ecological concerns of the Hebrew Bible and of later Judaism and Christianity. Jewish and Christian environmental thinkers point to the biblical flood that nearly wiped out the earth as divine punishment for the human destruction of the earth, to the Jewish principles of *bal tashchit*, "do not waste" (Deut. 20:19–20) and of offering blessings for food and other aspects of Creation, as well as to the Christian emphasis on realizing the harmonious Kingdom of God.[3] These responses quite correctly point out the deep concern for the natural world inherent in both Judaism and Christianity, but they sometimes seem reluctant to assert that mainstream Judaism and Christianity do value human life above all else. The human responsibility for environmental stewardship ultimately stems from a concern for the sustainability of human society. God brings the flood, the Rabbis suggest, not simply because human beings are engaging in wanton destruction, but also because individuals prove themselves incapable of sharing the earth's resources (*B'reishit Rabbah* 31:5). In one of the most drastic statements of the interdependence of humanity and the natural world, God cautions that a rejection of the commandments will result in the land refusing to yield produce and eventually evicting its inhabitants (Lev. 26). This warning immediately follows a set of laws regarding the *sh'mitah* (sabbatical) year, which simultaneously provides for a respite for the earth and the relief of the debt that can make escape from poverty almost impossible. Disregard for laws governing relationships among God, humanity, and nature disrupts the delicate balance of the world. Eventually, this breakdown results in an upheaval that distances humanity from nature.

Regardless of which is designed to serve the other, Judaism makes clear that the health of humanity and of the natural world depend deeply on one another. It makes little sense, then, to speak of conservation without considering questions of human health and equality. Neither can we count the human repercussions of environmental damage without thinking about the long-term consequences for the natural world. Whereas the conservationist might ask only how we reduce waste, and the environmental justice advocate might consider the distribution of waste among privileged and vulnerable neighborhoods, a just sustainability perspective will ask how we can reduce waste *and* ensure that each community is bearing its share of the burden for disposal. In the next few pages, we will explore more in depth the contours of a Jewish just sustainability practice.

Rural Life and Urban Life

Is the ideal Jewish life lived in a peaceful rural setting or amid the hustle and bustle of the city? The Bible seems to hedge its bets. Immediately after creating the first human being, God places this person in the Garden of Eden, a lush setting whose produce should fulfill humanity's every need. But we all know how the story ends: Adam and Eve disobey the only command that God has given them, and they find themselves permanently banished from the garden and forced to toil for their own food. In later Jewish thought, the term *gan eden* (Garden of Eden) becomes synonymous with the paradise to which we will return only at death or in the messianic age. Perhaps, then, the Jewish ideal is a life lived in a rural setting, in close relationship with nature.

On the other hand, the rest of the Bible heads more and more surely toward an urban life. The Israelites leave slavery in Egypt on the promise of establishing their own community in the promised land. When the people reach the land of Israel, Joshua—acting on divine instruction—divides the land among the tribes. Each area of land centers around one or more cities and their suburbs. As time goes on, one city—Jerusalem—increasingly becomes the center of attention. King David conquers this city and makes it the center of his kingdom, and David's son Solomon builds a Temple there. After the conquest of the ten northern tribes of Israel, the territory under Jewish control shrinks, and the long-term preeminence of Jerusalem is guaranteed. Until the destruction of the Second Temple in 70 CE, Jewish religious life centers on Jerusalem. Sacrifices are offered only there, and Jews living elsewhere make pilgrimages to Jerusalem three times a year, on Passover, Shavuot, and Sukkot.

After the destruction of the Temple, Judaism reconstitutes itself in the Diaspora, and new modes of practice emerge. Even so, Jerusalem retains a primary place in the liturgy and practice of this diasporic religion. Until today, Jews continue to pray daily for the restoration of Jerusalem, in its ideal form, as the center of Jewish life. The messianic age, according to rabbinic texts, will be heralded by an ingathering of the scattered Jewish people to a rebuilt Jerusalem.

In the most simplistic reading, we might say that the weight of tradition leans toward idealizing the city over the garden. While *gan eden* may be equated with paradise, Jews pray for a return to Jerusalem, and not for a return to *gan eden*. Even the wedding *sheva b'rakhot* (seven blessings), which collapse past and present so as to equate the new couple with Adam and Eve, pray for a future in which the sounds of happiness and joy will be heard in the streets of Jerusalem, even while comparing this joy to that experienced in Eden. The rabbinic assumption that Adam and Eve spent less than an hour in the garden before their expulsion suggests a belief that living in harmony with the natural world is fundamentally unsustainable (*Vayikra Rabbah* 29:1).

At the same time, the Rabbis were intimately aware of the dangers of city life. The first major city described in the Torah ends in rubble after the inhabitants have the hubris to attempt to build a tower to reach God (Gen. 11:1–9). Later in the book of Genesis, God destroys the cities of Sodom and Gomorrah, whose residents have united in evil, and especially in cruelty to strangers (Gen. 19). The rabbinic instruction to pray for your safety upon entering a city reflects a real fear of the violence and chaos possible when large numbers of people live together in a small space (Talmud, *B'rakhot* 60a).

Instead of arguing that Judaism idealizes either the pastoral existence of the Garden of Eden or the rich spiritual possibilities of the city, we might say instead that Jewish law and tradition honors both life among people and life in harmony with nature. In fact, Jewish texts attempt to legislate the establishment of a community that cares both for its members and for the natural world.

Do No Harm

One of the basic principles that governs communal life in the halakhic tradition is the demand that individuals refrain from any activities that may cause harm to their immediate neighbors or to the community as a whole. This principle is encapsulated in a series of laws that hold a person who digs a pit on public property liable for any damages that ensue. The digger of the pit accepts permanent responsibility for this pit. If someone digs a pit, covers it to prevent damage, and then notices that the cover has come off, this person is responsible for covering the pit again, and he or she will be held liable for death or injury to any animals or people who fall into the uncovered pit (Talmud, *Bava Kamma* 49b–50a). This set of laws prevents a person from claiming ignorance of the potential consequences of his or her actions, or from abdicating responsibility for a structure that he or she has built but no longer needs. In contemporary times, we might extend this category of a pit to the construction of factories that dump hazardous chemicals in the water or in the air; mountaintop removal that leaves residents of a coal mining town in danger of being flooded by toxic muck; and lax enforcement of building codes aimed at protecting residents from mold and other irritants.

Just as a person may not leave an open pit in the public domain, you may not otherwise cause harm to your neighbors, even through making improvements to your own property. The resident of the bottom half of a two-story, two-family home may not, for example, install an oven unless the ceiling is sufficiently thick to ensure that the smoke will not enter the upstairs residence (*Tur, Choshen Mishpat* 155). Similarly, you may not install a threshing floor so close to another's property that the chaff is likely to land on and damage the neighbor's crops, nor plant a tree so close to another person's field that the roots will cause damage (Mishnah, *Bava Batra* ch. 2). Neighbors whose homes open onto a shared courtyard may also prevent stores or workshops from opening in the courtyard on the grounds that the noise of customers coming and going, or that of hammering and grinding, will make sleeping impossible.[4] Especially foul-smelling institutions, such as graveyards, tanneries, or dumping grounds for carcasses, must remain outside of a city, and not in the direction of the wind.[5]

This set of laws brings to mind the *midrash* mentioned in Chapter 1, in which a passenger on a boat drills a hole under his own seat, seemingly unaware of the effect that his actions will have on his fellow passengers. Jewish laws governing neighborly relations attempt to balance individual economic and quality-of-life needs with the comfort of our neighbors. Thus, neighbors may prevent a particularly foul-smelling or loud business from opening, but they may not ban all businesses or refuse to allow a school within their domain. In the United States, we speak often of NIMBYism (Not In My Backyard), which usually manifests as an attempt by wealthy neighborhoods to keep undesirable elements such as homeless shelters, affordable housing, waste processing plants, and factories out of their neighborhood.

Jewish law allows for a certain amount of NIMBYism only when the element to be introduced will make life virtually impossible for the residents of a neighborhood. It may be reasonable, for instance, to prevent a factory that will release dangerous chemicals from opening too close to human habitation, or to prohibit loud vehicles from passing through a neighborhood at night. Such restrictions should not, however, severely limit the quality of life of other people, for instance by increasing the prevalence of homelessness, making it impossible for others to earn a living, or transferring burdens to other communities. When the rabbis demand that tanneries sit far outside of the inhabited areas of a town, they do not mean to place the tannery in *another*, perhaps poorer or non-Jewish town. Rather, they mean that tanneries and other agents of pollution should remain far from *any* human habitation.

The laws governing the placement of polluting businesses also remind us that responsibility extends to the consequences of our actions. Within Jewish law, there is a category called *p'sik reisha*—literally "cutting the head off." This category emerges from the prohibition against killing an animal on Shabbat. A person may not claim to have intended *only* to cut the head off of a chicken in order to use the head, and not to kill it, as the latter is a necessary consequence of the former. Within the laws of Shabbat, actions that will necessarily result in a violation of Shabbat, even if indirectly, are generally forbidden. For instance, a person may not wash his or her hands over the lawn, as watering the lawn is not permitted on Shabbat.[6]

We might extend this category to environmental regulations and demand that individuals take responsibility for the results of their actions if those actions will necessarily cause collateral harm to others. But how far should we extend this category? It is one thing to demand that a person take responsibility for a smoking habit that disturbs the neighbors across the hall, or for excessive use of water that results in increased costs for all members of a cooperative apartment building. Should a person also take responsibility for what happens to a plastic bag that he or she discards, or for the amount of electricity that he or she uses? And how do we take into account the fact that individual human actions only contribute to a small part of the massive environmental crisis in which we now find ourselves?

The simple answer may be that individuals are certainly responsible for the consequences of their actions, and that the principle of *bal tashchit* (do not waste) further cautions against the squandering of any resources. Striving for an entirely no-impact lifestyle—in which you recycle or compost all of your waste, and replace any natural resources that you use—may be laudable, but universal success would seem an unlikely expectation. Given the disinclination in Jewish law to enact laws that the community will not be able to follow, we might encourage the reduction of our carbon footprint without expecting anyone to take total responsibility for all of his or her actions. For guidance on more reasonable expectations about taking responsibility for the more immediate results of our actions, we turn now to rabbinic discussions about the responsibility to our community.

Communal Responsibilities

As we have seen in our discussion of poverty and *tzedakah*, Jewish law makes certain demands on residents of a community to support the poor residents of the city and to avoid causing direct damage to our neighbors. Additionally, residents of a community may be expected to contribute to the physical infrastructure of the community by giving money for the repair of city walls, for the construction of protective structures such as gates or defense walls, and for building a synagogue or purchasing religious books for communal use.[7] Residents of a shared courtyard may further compel one another to construct walls aimed at protecting individual privacy or doors that separate the entire group of homes from the public domain (Talmud, *Bava Batra* 71). This set of regulations reinforces the sense that individuals have responsibility for the good of the whole. An individual cannot simply put a lock on his or her own door or declare himself or herself unconcerned about peeping toms and, on such a basis, refuse to contribute to the upkeep of shared infrastructure. Rather, each person bears responsibility for the privacy and security of the community of neighbors.

In addition to contributing financially to communal infrastructure, each resident may expect to benefit from communal resources. For example, any manure—valuable as fertilizer—left in a shared courtyard should be divided among the residents of the courtyard (*Bava Batra* 11b). As we have seen, members of a community also benefit equally from the construction of city walls or other infrastructure, and from the purchase of communal books. In these provisions for community members both to contribute to communal infrastructure and to benefit equally from such infrastructure, we may find some guidance for contemporary environmental justice struggles, which generally focus on the division of both resources and burden.

Over the past several years, residents of New York City have been battling over questions of garbage disposal, including the placement of waste transfer stations. In New York, as in many other cities, the poorest neighborhoods generally bear the brunt of waste disposal plants and transfer stations, bus depots, and other public works projects that generate significant pollution, noise, or traffic. Residents of wealthy neighborhoods, who wield significant political power, have generally succeeded in keeping waste transfer stations out of their neighborhoods. Residents of less wealthy areas, most of whom do not have political connections, find themselves bearing the brunt of the waste disposal problem. Elsewhere in the country, residents of low-income neighborhoods find themselves living in the shadow of chemical plants, nuclear testing facilities, and factories that dump waste into the water.[8]

The basic rabbinic answer to the question of waste disposal is to suggest dumping garbage outside of the city. From a biblical verse that mandates disposing human excrement outside of the Israelite camp during the years of wandering in the desert, the Rabbis derive an obligation to designate a place outside of the city for the disposal of waste.[9] From this law, we must conclude that the solution to questions of solid waste disposal should be to find a dumping ground in an uninhabited area. In fact, many cities—notably New York—have tried to find relatively deserted places to leave their garbage.[10] But in today's world, where few truly uninhabited places remain—and where pollution even in a sparsely populated place will ultimately harm a much larger ecosystem—this solution is not generally a realistic one. Instead, the areas whose residents are least likely to complain, or the towns most in need of the money earned from accepting urban waste, become the depositories for more than their share of waste products and pollutants. But the Jewish teachings regarding the separation of waste from human habitation may demand that we find ways to ensure that individual communities will not have to suffer excessively from the smell or noise associated with waste disposal.

Without a real option for disposing of waste in a way that will not disturb anyone or deprive future generations of natural resources, we might look instead to the rabbinic requirement, described above, that each member of society accept his or her share of responsibility for communal burdens, while also reaping an equal share of the benefits of a functional infrastructure. Assuming that a no-impact lifestyle is unrealistic, communities, cities, and countries should find ways to distribute both environmental burdens and benefits equitably, without regard for the relative power or wealth of affected communities. Ideally, the principle of *bal tashchit* and the divine warnings about not abusing the land will also compel us to reduce the production of waste and the use of natural resources.

Over the past few years, the environmental movement has drawn new attention to individual choices. Throughout the country, households are installing compact fluorescent bulbs, bringing reusable bags to the grocery store, and carpooling to work. These individual changes are important and laudable, but will not ultimately be sufficient to reverse or slow the environmental crisis. In the end, the choices of large corporations and of nations will determine the future of the global environment. While Jewish law does not primarily concern itself with the governing of states or of global corporations, the insistence on individual responsibility for communal action is instructive in guiding our understanding of current environmental issues. Individuals must take responsibility for their own actions, but the community must also maintain overall responsibility for the well-being of its inhabitants. As we have seen, individuals must contribute to the *tzedakah* fund, to the health care fund, and to the infrastructure of the area, but the communal government administers and collects these funds. Each individual retains responsibility for the actions of the community, and the community maintains ultimate responsibility for the health and welfare of the inhabitants. In the case of the environment, we might say that each individual citizen is accountable for the actions of the community as a whole—in this case, the city, state, or federal government—and that the government ultimately bears responsibility for ensuring the sustainability of life within the community.

The environmental issue challenges us to balance concern for humanity with concern for the natural world. The Jewish texts that we have examined concern themselves primarily with the well-being of humanity, but they also insist on the protection of the natural world. The challenge for the environmental movement of the twenty-first century will be to bring together the conservationist impulse with environmental justice concerns, and to create a plan for the future that leads to greater equality and shared responsibility among people, while also preserving the natural world for generations to come.

9

When Your Brother Is Flogged
Crime, Punishment, and Rehabilitation

At first glance, it seems more difficult to apply Jewish law to the American criminal justice system than it has been to consider issues such as landlord-tenant relations and employer-employee relations within the context of Jewish law and tradition. After all, the classic Jewish legal system looks nothing like the American legal system. Jewish law traditionally allowed for only a few forms of punishment, including capital punishment, banishment from the community, and fines. Long-term imprisonment, by far the most common punishment in America, is virtually absent from the Jewish legal system before the fourteenth century.

Rather than force a direct comparison between Jewish criminal law and the contemporary American justice system, I will consider three questions that underlie any criminal justice system: What is a crime? What is the responsibility of a society vis-à-vis its citizens, whether these citizens keep or break the laws? Is rehabilitation possible?

The United States imprisons more people than any other Western nation. In the United States, those convicted of crimes go to prison more often, and serve longer sentences, than criminals in other Western countries. As of 2008, almost 2.3 million Americans—more than one out of every hundred adults—were in state or federal prison or in local jails,[1] nearly a three-fold increase in the prison population since the 1970s.

The simplest explanation for the increasing number of prisoners would be that crime is increasing. However, crime rates have fallen 25 percent, even as prisons have grown. We might, then, assume that stricter sentencing guidelines have contributed to a decrease in crime. The logical conclusion would be that we have succeeded in locking up most of the criminals and have therefore created a more law-abiding society. But as Harvard sociologist Bruce Western has demonstrated, there is virtually no correlation between crime rates and incarceration rates. The rate of incarceration in the United States has risen steadily since 1970, while crime rates have risen and fallen repeatedly throughout that period.[2] Marie Gottschalk, professor of political science at the University of Pennsylvania, writes, "There is some relationship between the crime rate and the incarceration rate, but it is slight. Analysts using a variety of methodologies have found that the deterrent and incapacitation effects of incarceration in bringing down the crime rate are small, and that offenses avoided through greater use of prisons tend to be nonviolent rather than violent crimes."[3]

America's high imprisonment rate is not the result of a high crime rate. Instead, it results from a confluence of factors. Some of these factors reflect changes in public opinion: the conservative political trend of the 1970s and 1980s, harsh drug policies, a growing victims' rights movement, and a liberal backlash against the radical prisoners' movements of the 1960s and 1970s have all contributed to public support for leaders who are "tough on crime." Sentencing and policing practices have also resulted in a growing number of prisoners. New policing practices focus on uncovering low-level crime in low-income urban neighborhoods, and stricter sentencing guidelines mean that people who are convicted are likely to spend more time in prison, and often are likely to return to prison as a result of parole violations. Economic need has brought about strong support for prisons in struggling rural communities.[4]

We can hardly talk about criminal justice in America without talking about race. Today, an African American man has a one in three chance of spending time in prison. Despite evidence that most drug users are white, African Americans are ten times more likely to be imprisoned for drug-related offenses. This discrepancy reflects policing policies, differences in sentencing, and drug policies that impose harsher penalties for crack cocaine than for drugs used primarily by whites.[5]

The criminal justice system—and the prison industry in particular—lies at the nexus of social and economic ills afflicting both urban and rural communities today. Almost no issue, from housing to labor to urban planning policy to representative democracy itself, is untouched by it. Yet this emotional and crucial issue remains far from the national agenda. Jewish communities rarely take on criminal justice as a major focus of our social justice work: the issue can feel too big to address, and we remain reluctant to admit that members of our own community also experience arrest and imprisonment. When Jewish communities do work on criminal justice issues, we tend to focus on death penalty reform and on specific death penalty cases. It is easier, from a Jewish point of view, to talk about questions of life or death than to talk about the messiness of long-term punishment. Even though the death penalty is an important topic, fewer than 3,500 people currently sit on death row—this is a far cry from the more than 2 million in prison.[6] In my examination of criminal justice, I hope to push the Jewish community toward taking this issue on as our own.

What Is a Crime?

Jewish legal terminology offers no single term for crime. Rather, crimes are divided into *dinei n'fashot* (capital crimes) and *dinei mamonot* (property crimes or disputes involving money). The thirty-six crimes classified as *dinei n'fashot* fall more or less into the three most serious categories of sin within Jewish law: bloodshed, idolatry, and sexual deviance. We can describe all of these crimes as ones that do violence to the divine presence in some way. Murder reduces by one the manifestation of God in the world; idolatry and the related crimes of sorcery, public violation of Shabbat, and blasphemy all represent an insult to God's authority; and improper sexual behavior such as incest is understood as a violation of the human responsibility to replicate the divine presence. All of these *dinei n'fashot* represent both crimes against God and threats to the civic and moral fiber of Jewish society. These crimes are to be tried by a court of twenty-three and may be punished through capital punishment. With the dissolution of the Sanhedrin (high court) after the destruction of the Second Temple in 70 CE, Jewish legal authorities lost the mandate to carry out capital punishment, but maintained an ability to administer lashes or excommunication from the community. Although Jewish law unequivocally prescribes capital punishment as the fitting response to a diminishment of the divine presence, it establishes strict protections against the unintentional execution of an innocent person.[7]

Dinei mamonot (or what we might call civil cases) include theft, damage to property or person, and disputes over loans, sales, or other financial dealings. These cases, which are judged by a court of three, are generally punished through fines or monetary restitution for the loss. Courts that judge *dinei mamonot* neither impose physical punishment nor enforce removal from the community. Unlike American law, which lumps together violent crimes and property crimes within a single criminal justice system, Jewish law treats property crimes as something more akin to a business dispute than to a murder. Today, roughly half of America's prisoners are incarcerated for nonviolent crimes, and approximately one-fifth of prisoners are serving time for drug-related offenses.[8] More than two-thirds of these drug offenders are serving time for low-level crimes such as possession, small-scale selling, or serving as lookouts for drug dealers.[9] The classification of drug use as a crime, rather than as a public health issue, has resulted in the imprisonment of more than a million people at any given time; the breakup of millions of families; the loss of untold numbers of chances for treatment and rehabilitation; and an economic and social crisis occasioned by the reentry into the community each year of hundreds of thousands of former convicts, a substantial number of whom struggle with addiction, mental illness, or physical disabilities.[10] Instead, we might recognize drug abuse as a disease, as most medical literature does, and focus on treating the underlying addiction, rather than locking up people over and over for drug-induced property or violent crimes.[11] In many cases, it is appropriate and necessary to treat addiction in controlled inpatient environments. But the focus on the disease, rather than the crime, will help to ensure that addicts are treated like patients and guided toward a cure, rather than simply punished as criminals and eventually put back on the street.

In distinguishing between *dinei n'fashot* and *dinei mamonot*, Jewish law stresses that not all crimes are created equal. For *dinei mamonot*, the primary goal of the sentencing system is restitution for the injured party, and not the removal of the offender from the community. Only those who show themselves willing to murder or otherwise to disrupt the fabric of society are punished by death or excommunication. For those guilty of property crimes, the goal is restitution and rehabilitation rather than removal.

Concern for the Victim

Moses, the first Jewish communal leader, spends a significant portion of his time judging disputes, until his father-in-law persuades him to appoint judges to take up some of this burden. Accordingly, Jewish rabbinic law would later consider courts to be essential to the creation of a society that protects the health and welfare of its citizens. Indeed, the Rabbis listed the appointment of judges among the seven commandments that God is said to have given to Noah and his sons at the end of the great flood, and that, according to *halakhah*, remain incumbent on all non-Jews (Talmud, *Sanhedrin* 56b).

The Rabbis also discuss the dangers of traveling through cities, and in doing so distinguish between the safety of a city with a functional criminal justice system and one without such a system. This talmudic discussion includes blessings to say when entering and leaving a city, establishing that a person should pray for protection on the way into a city and offer thanks when leaving a city safely.

These prescribed prayers testify to the dangers associated with cities: inside a city, an anonymous stranger might be robbed, beaten, or killed without anyone coming to his or her aid.

One talmudic rabbi elaborates on this general instruction to pray on the way in and out of a city:

> Rav Matt'na said: This applies only to a city in which criminals are not tried and sentenced, but in a city where criminals are tried and sentenced, this is unnecessary. Some report: Rav Matt'na said: Even in a city where criminals are tried and sentenced, for sometimes one may happen not to find anyone who can plead in one's defense. (*B'rakhot* 60a)

According to either version of Rav Matt'na's statement, a city becomes dangerous in the absence of a system that protects citizens and strangers from victimization by local criminals. Without any court system, victims have no recourse other than taking revenge into their own hands, and those who wish to take advantage of vulnerable strangers can feel free to do so. Similarly, in a place without a means to provide legal support to both sides, or without a culture that values witness testimony, an outsider cannot expect to receive a fair trial. The ensuing anarchy makes the city so dangerous that visitors must pray for their lives on their way into the city, and offer a prayer of thanks when leaving safely.

Whatever the correct version of Rav Matt'na's statement may be, he does not simply distinguish between cities with many criminals and cities without many criminals. Rather, he places responsibility for protecting visitors either on the legal system as a whole, or also on every resident capable of protecting or legally defending the most vulnerable. This formulation is reminiscent of urbanist Jane Jacobs's assertion that what keeps cities safe are "eyes on the street"—ordinary residents who keep an eye out for unusual activity and who feel accountable for the well-being of those who live in or visit the area.

This ideal, in which the community takes responsibility for the safety of residents and strangers alike, is central also to the biblical law regarding the case in which the body of a traveler is found between the boundaries of two towns. The elders of the closest town break the neck of a heifer as a means of atoning for the death, and publicly declare their innocence in shedding the victim's blood (Deut. 21:1–9). The Talmud explains that this public declaration and atonement serve two purposes. First, the public nature of the ritual alerts people in the nearby town to the death and may entice witnesses to come forward with information about the murderer. Second, the elders atone for the fact that the townspeople failed to protect the stranger by accompanying him on his way out of town (*Sotah* 45a–46b). Rather than focusing on finding and punishing the perpetrator of the crime, the law of the *eglah arufah* (the broken-necked heifer) holds the community responsible for the well-being of visitors.

The Humanity of the Perpetrator

But society's responsibilities do not only extend to victims and potential victims. The biblical mandate to establish cities of refuge for those who have committed manslaughter hints at a communal responsibility also toward those who have perpetrated crimes. A person who has accidentally killed another is not subject to the penalty of capital punishment but is in danger of being killed by a revenge-seeking member of the victim's family. In order to stem a potential cycle of revenge, God instructs the people to set up cities of refuge immediately upon entering the land of Israel. Manslaughterers, along with their families, could flee to these cities in order to escape the wrath of potential avengers, who would not be allowed to carry out revenge within the city. These cities of refuge are intended both to protect the general population from those who have previously shown sufficient bad judgment or carelessness as to cause the death of another, and to enable those guilty of manslaughter to live in dignity, accompanied by their families, in a place where they are protected both from stigma and from revenge. As in the case of the *eglah arufah*, the community as a whole, and not a professional legal body alone, takes responsibility for the establishment of these cities of refuge.

In the United States, the system of punishment remains largely hidden from the view of the general population. The most sensational cases occupy space in the newspaper and on the airwaves, but few of us think often about the daily experience of those undergoing trial and serving time for more run-of-the-mill crimes. Most prisons are situated far from major cities, and outside of the communities from which the greatest numbers of prisoners are taken. In some communities, the criminal justice system is deeply felt, as hundreds or thousands of parents, children, partners, and friends are missing from their families' lives. For those who are lucky enough not to have loved ones in prison, it is tempting to ignore the justice system except when called for jury duty every few years.

In contrast, much of the Jewish legal system is set up in such a way as to force the community to come face-to-face with both criminals and victims, as well as with the consequences of decisions in criminal cases. In cases of *dinei n'fashot*, rabbinic law establishes an elaborate system of evaluating witness testimony, trying the case in front of a court of twenty-three judges, and permitting capital punishment when there is no room for doubting the guilt of the defendant. The person sentenced to capital punishment is then paraded some distance from the courthouse to the site of the execution. This public journey offers the opportunity for new witnesses to come forward to offer evidence of the defendant's innocence, or even for the defendant himself or herself to offer new evidence. Any evidence on the defendant's behalf halts the execution. In most cases, the witnesses carry out the death sentence themselves, and in some cases, other members of the community may be involved as well (Mishnah, *Sanhedrin* 5–6). This public execution ensures that the community will understand the full implication of the court's decision. Seeing the convict brought out for execution should inspire anyone with knowledge of this person's innocence to volunteer the information, and will certainly make witnesses and others think long and hard about offering evidence to convict.

Some have suggested that the United States look to community justice models as a means of lessening the reliance on prisons, and of reducing the negative impact of mass incarceration on low-income communities.[12] In such a model, community volunteers work with local police to prevent crime, mediate small claims issues, judge those accused of crime, mandate reparations and community service, and run programs aimed at reintegrating the guilty into the community in a responsible way. Such a model has the potential to go some ways toward creating the communal responsibility for both victims and perpetrators that Jewish texts imagine.

There is a long-standing historical and ideological debate about whether any Jewish community ever practiced capital punishment as outlined in rabbinic law, and about whether the Rabbis supported the institution of capital punishment even in theory, or whether they attempted to legislate it out of existence by making it virtually impossible for any court to prove guilt sufficiently to warrant execution. I will not enter into this debate here, both because so much has been written about the question of capital punishment in Judaism and because, as mentioned, the small number of death row prisoners in America already attract a disproportionate amount of attention both in the general and in the Jewish community.[13] Certainly, the success of endeavors such as the Innocence Project in freeing erroneously convicted death row prisoners should give pause to even the most ardent proponent of supporting capital punishment through reference to Jewish text. But I offer examples of the public nature of capital punishment in talmudic text primarily as evidence of the rabbinic conviction that both judgment and punishment should take place in public, in order to ensure that the witnesses will take full responsibility for the consequences of their testimony, and that members of the community at large will also understand themselves to be accountable for the court's decision.

A number of rabbinic texts insist on the basic humanity of even the most reviled criminal. The Mishnaic text most often cited in discussions of Judaism and social justice declares, "If one destroys a single soul, it is as if that person destroyed the entire world; if one saves a single soul, it is as if one saved the entire world" (*Sanhedrin* 4:5). In Chapter 7, we considered the text that supports this bold statement. As we said there, this statement appears within a text that depicts God holding Cain responsible not only for Abel's death, but also for the death, as it were, of all of Abel's potential descendants. While this text is striking in and of itself, the context in which it appears is even more striking. The Mishnah has been engaged in a description of the process for bringing a person to trial for a crime punishable by execution. The discussion of the value of human life constitutes the warning given to witnesses for the prosecution. Before making the decision to offer testimony that may result in an execution, witnesses should understand that they will be held responsible not only for the death of the defendant, but also for the loss of any children or grandchildren that might otherwise be born to the defendant in the future. In this spirit, Rambam also insists that only a person who has children is qualified to serve as a judge, "in order that he will be merciful."[14] While we may no longer wish to restrict judgeships to parents, we learn from Rambam the necessity for a judge—or perhaps anyone involved in the criminal justice system—to be able to imagine even the most difficult defendant as someone's beloved child, and to approach this defendant in the way that we would hope others would approach our own child.

A discussion of the process of the punishment of lashes further insists on the basic dignity even of the convicted criminal. According to the biblical text that establishes the precedent for lashes as a form of punishment, "If the guilty one is to be flogged, the magistrate shall have him lie down and be given lashes in his presence, by count, as his guilt warrants. He may be given up to forty lashes, but not more, lest being flogged further, to excess, your brother be degraded before your eyes" (Deut. 25:2–3). The Rabbis, who considered every word of the Torah to convey meaning, wondered why the verse begins by referring to the person in question as a *rasha*—a guilty or wicked person—and ends by referring to this person as "your brother." One *midrash* on this verse comments, "All day, the text calls him 'wicked,' as it says 'if the wicked person is subject to lashes' (Deut. 25:2). But from the time that he is flogged, the text calls him 'your brother,' as it says, 'your brother is flogged'" (*Sifrei*,

Tetze Piska 76). Without exempting the guilty party from punishment, this text insists that observers view this person as a "brother" exactly at the moment of this person's degradation.

The shame associated with criminals and imprisonment can lead us to minimize the dignity of those involved in crime. In America, most prisons sit far from major population centers and out of the sight of most U.S. residents. The powerful victims' rights movement, active since the 1970s, has brought us face-to-face with those who have suffered from rape, assault, and the murders of loved ones. Those who have suffered needlessly from violent crime certainly deserve sympathy and support. But concern for victims can sometimes lead us too quickly to a desire for revenge that ignores the humanity of the accused. Most of us identify much more readily with victims than with perpetrators. We have trouble imagining ourselves committing a serious crime, but worry often about our own safety and that of those close to us. Well-publicized images of unrepentant criminals robbing, raping, and murdering unsuspecting citizens lead us to the erroneous assumption that violent crime is increasing. Our anger and fear can translate too easily to a desire for stricter and stricter punishment. In the United States, the "tough on crime" movement of the past thirty years has produced longer sentences and has given license for prison administrators to make frequent use of solitary confinement, restraints, and even chain gangs.[15]

The call to view the guilty as "your brother" asks us to think about how we would want our own family members to be treated by the criminal justice system. What considerations would we hope would be granted to friends and relatives struggling with mental illness or addiction? How often would we want to see these friends and relatives? What relationships would we hope that imprisoned parents might have with their children? How would we want our family members protected from prison abuse and rape? For those of us who have experienced the incarceration of friends or family members, these questions are anything but theoretical. For those of us who have not had personal experiences with the prison system, these questions challenge us to see the humanity of perpetrators as well as victims.

When Is Prison Necessary?

In biblical and most of rabbinic law, the only available punishments for crime are capital punishment, banishment, fines, or *lex talionis* (an eye for an eye).[16] In the Bible, imprisonment serves primarily as a means of detaining the accused until the completion of the trial. In two biblical cases, one involving a blasphemer and the other involving a violator of Shabbat, the accused is placed in a *mishmar*—a holding place—until God dictates the appropriate punishment. A few prophets also find themselves in prison after angering the king with their prophecies, but the Bible hardly condones the imprisonment of prophets.[17]

For the most part, the Bible presents imprisonment as a punishment used by non-Jews. Joseph spends time in prison after being falsely accused of seducing the wife of one of Pharaoh's servants, and the Philistines imprison Samson after Delilah has tricked him into revealing the source of his strength.[18] When granting Ezra the scribe permission to reestablish Jewish authority in Jerusalem, the Persian king authorizes the Jewish rulers to impose punishments including death, banishment, confiscation of property, and imprisonment (Ezra 7:26). This text does not necessarily endorse imprisonment as punishment, but mentions it as a possibility at least within the eyes of a non-Jewish king.

The Rabbis of the Talmud are also familiar with prisons, but generally speak of these as places run by non-Jewish governments in which Jews sometimes find themselves. Several Rabbis spend time in Roman prisons on religious charges, and dungeons full of implements of torture make periodic appearances in midrashic texts. The Rabbis appreciate the dangers of imprisonment, and they consider the release from prison an almost miraculous event, worthy of blessing. In fact, those newly released from prison are among the three categories of people—along with those who have recovered from an illness and those who have survived a dangerous journey—who recite the *Gomel* blessing to give thanks to God for saving their lives (*B'rakhot* 54b).

The closest early rabbinic equivalent to prison is the institution known as the *kippah*, which the Talmud describes as a cell just tall enough for a person to stand inside.[19] Two categories of offenders might find themselves in the *kippah*. First, *kippah* may be imposed on those who have been punished three times (or four, according to one opinion) for a crime for which the punishment is *karet*—excommunication from the Jewish people and presumed eventual death at the hands of the divine court. Second, those whom the (earthly) court believes to be guilty of murder, but who cannot be executed for formal or procedural reasons, may also be subjected to *kippah*.

According to the earliest sources, the punishment of *kippah* constituted a slow torture leading to inevitable death. The Mishnah explains, "If one who has been punished by lashes repeats the crime, the court places him into the *kippah* and feeds him barley until his stomach bursts. If one killed someone not in front of witnesses, he is placed in the *kippah* and fed minimal bread and water" (*Sanhedrin* 9:5). A parallel early source offers an only somewhat gentler picture of this punishment:

> He is warned once and is silent; he is warned again and indicates consent. If he is warned a first, then a second time, the third time, he is placed in the *kippah*. Abba Shaul says, "even the third time, we warn him, and the fourth time, he is placed in the *kippah*." And we feed him minimal bread and water.
>
> This is the rule for those who are liable for lashes and who repeat the crime: We give them lashes a first, then a second time; the third time, they are placed in the *kippah*. Abba Shaul says, "also the third time, we give them lashes, and the fourth time, they are placed in the *kippah*." And we feed him barley until his stomach bursts. (*Tosefta, Sanhedrin* 12:7)

The punishment of *kippah*, according to these sources, is effectively a death sentence, and perhaps feels even crueler to the incarcerated than a quick execution would be. Not surprisingly, the brutality of this sentence gives pause even to some of the first interpreters of the

Mishnah. The Rabbis of the Talmud look at the Mishnah's instruction to impose *kippah* on someone who has already been punished by lashes and ask, incredulously, "Because he was lashed and repeated the crime, we place him in the *kippah*?!" The Talmud's response narrows the instances in which *kippah* can be inflicted: "According to Rabbi Yermiyah, according to Rabbi Shimon Ben Lakish: this refers to lashes of *karet* (excommunication), as he is liable for death" (*Sanhedrin* 81b). The Rabbis thus limit the punishment of *kippah* to cases in which a person has been punished two or three times for a crime worthy of excommunication, for which it is assumed that God will carry out a death penalty. Medieval writers further restrict *kippah* to cases in which the offender has been warned of the consequences of his crime immediately prior to each offense.[20]

In the Middle Ages, Rambam expanded the punishment of imprisonment to those who have killed someone indirectly, through a hired assassin or through placing a deadly obstacle in the way of another. These murderers are technically exempt from capital punishment, but should not, according to Rambam, be allowed to go free. In these cases, prison serves both as a punishment and as a deterrent to other would-be murderers:

> The court is obligated, in any case, to punish them with a serious punishment, close to death, and to confine them in a small and narrow place for many years, and to afflict them with all sorts of afflictions in order to instill fear in other wicked people, so that the incident will not become an obstacle or a stumbling block, such that another person will say, "I will bring about the death of my enemy as so-and-so did, and I will go free."[21]

The type of imprisonment that Rambam describes here is similar to *kippah*, in that it constitutes a small, dark, and miserable living space. Unlike *kippah*, however, this type of imprisonment does not necessarily seem intended to kill the inhabitant.

There is nothing pleasant about the punishment of imprisonment, according to these early texts. Conditions inside the *kippah*, or inside the space that Rambam describes, are barely livable. Because of its brutality, and because the institution of *kippah* is generally understood to be outside of the categories of punishment specified by biblical law, early texts restrict imprisonment to a small number of offenders, who have either publicly indicated their disregard for the authority of the courts, or who have murdered in such a way as to avoid ordinary forms of punishment.

By the Middle Ages, many of the Jewish debates about crime and punishment had become entirely hypothetical. Halakhic sources understood the court to have lost the authority to carry out capital punishment beginning with the exile of the Sanhedrin, forty years before the destruction of the Second Temple in 70 CE.[22] On a more practical level, individual Jewish communities had varying degrees of legal autonomy, depending on the whims of the non-Jewish governing powers.

Beginning in the fourteenth century, imprisonment became an increasingly common punishment in the general world, as well as within Jewish communities. In a number of the places where Jews lived, the non-Jewish authorities granted Jewish communities the authority to establish their own prisons and to sentence criminals to imprisonment. Individual Jewish communities established *takkanot* (communal agreements) permitting imprisonment for offenses ranging from murder and adultery to theft, assault, and gambling. In some cases, the imprisonment might last for as little as a day or a week; in other cases, imprisonment might last for several years.[23]

Legal authorities remain conscious that imprisonment is not among the punishments dictated by the Bible or other early sources. A number of legal positions describe imprisonment as *l'tzorech sha'ah*—a response to the needs of the moment.[24] This description suggests that imprisonment might not be ideal, but that it is the punishment most readily available to the courts for serious offenses, or for compelling a person to comply with fines or other penalties imposed by the court. Rather than present prisons as the first-choice punishment for criminal offenders, these texts imply that prisons are, instead, a punishment of last resort when the courts have few other options for maintaining order.

Prison: Temporary or Permanent?

The general discomfort with prisons as a form of punishment surfaces in a debate about whether to affix a *mezuzah* to a prison cell. The *mezuzah* represents the fulfillment of the commandment to place the words of the Torah "on the doorposts of your home" (Deut. 6:9) and consists of a case holding a parchment on which the relevant biblical passage is written. In general, a *mezuzah* is placed only on a permanent home, and not on an impermanent home, such as a *sukkah* (outdoor shelter built for the holiday of Sukkot) or a tent pitched for a few nights. The debate about whether to place a *mezuzah* on a prison cell thus hinges on the question of whether a prison cell is a permanent home. One twentieth-century rabbi, Rabbi Isaac Jacob Weiss of Poland, ruled that a prison cell was a temporary dwelling, and therefore exempt from a *mezuzah*.[25]

In contrast, Rabbi Ben-Zion Meir Chai Uziel argued for placing a *mezuzah* on a prison cell even though the cell is only intended to be a person's home for a short period of time. In describing life in prison, Uziel comments, "The entire time that one dwells in the prison, both the prisoner and the administrator of the prison wait for the moment when the prisoner will be released and the cell will be vacated; therefore, it is thought of as a home that is not established as a permanent dwelling, similar to homes on ships."[26] Still, he says, the prison does become a person's home for a set period of time, just as a ship may become a home for the period of the voyage. In both cases, according to Uziel, a *mezuzah* should be hung to indicate that the place, while impermanent, serves as a home. In the state of Israel, Uziel adds, the state should hang mezuzot in prison cells. Even though these cells will not permanently serve as the homes of individual people, and the inhabitants may change, the cells will be used continuously as dwelling places.

Notably, both sides of this debate about whether to hang a *mezuzah* in a prison cell assume that the cell will be only a temporary home for the person incarcerated there. Each convict will serve his or her time, and then return home after no more than a few years.

The only question open for debate is whether the prison itself takes on the status of a permanent dwelling, since *someone* is almost always living there.

Other than the limited case of the *kippah*, used only for prisoners who would otherwise be condemned to death for murder or similarly serious crimes, prison is assumed to be a short-term punishment of last resort. In this spirit, the twentieth-century Polish-Israeli legal authority Meshulam Rath commented:

> In general, I am hesitant about the agreement of the rabbis regarding imprisonment of five or three years as punishment for sin, for nothing like this is present in our *halakhah*—rather, we have only temporary imprisonment in order to force compliance, or to hold a person [until the trial is completed.] ... or placement in the *kippah* for a murderer.[27]

In sum, prisons have a complicated history in *halakhah*. Traditional law limits the use of confinement to cases of a person who committed a crime punishable by excommunication three times, even after being warned; a murderer who can not be penalized according to the ordinary means; or to a person kept in administrative detention until the completion of a trial, or until the person agreed to comply with a fine dictated by the court. The restriction of imprisonment to a small number of serious crimes contrasts with the current situation in the United States, in which close to 50 percent of federal and state inmates are serving time for nonviolent crimes, including property offenses, drug possession and sales, and parole violations.[28]

As Jewish communities began to use imprisonment for a wider range of cases, legal writings simultaneously expressed some hesitance over this form of punishment and acknowledged that it was the only means of maintaining social order available to most Jewish courts. Thirteenth-century Rabbi Jacob ben Asher (the Tur) perhaps best sums up the overall feeling about imprisonment when he comments that courts may use this method of punishment "as long as their intention is only to pursue justice and truth, without any other additional intention."[29] This caution challenges us to ask whether our own society uses imprisonment only as a means toward the pursuit of justice and truth, or whether other considerations, such as politics and economics, cloud our decisions about when and whether to imprison the convicted.

Is Rehabilitation Possible?

The movement to rehabilitate offenders has gotten a bad rap in the United States. The tough-on-crime movement of the 1970s and 1980s and the failures of some rehabilitative programs have all contributed to a general pessimism about the possibility of integrating the incarcerated back into society.[30] Many policymakers and citizens have simply thrown up their hands and supported ever harsher punishments, rather than risk any attempts at rehabilitation.

Teshuvah, generally translated as repentance or return, plays a central role in Jewish ideology and practice. In his laws of *teshuvah*, Rambam defines as one of the essential principles of Judaism the belief that human beings have free will, intrinsic to which is the ability to change their behavior.[31] Close to two months of the Jewish calendar are devoted to the practice of *teshuvah*. The month of Elul, leading up to the holiday of Rosh Hashanah, is meant to be an opportunity for personal reflection, for asking forgiveness, and for making commitments to change our behavior. The process of *teshuvah* intensifies during the ten days between Rosh Hashanah and Yom Kippur, when God is said to seal each person's fate. The following week between Yom Kippur and Hoshanah Rabbah offers yet one more chance to do *teshuvah* and to change our direction for the coming year.

This multistep approach to *teshuvah* offers a glimpse into the rabbinic belief that *teshuvah* is virtually always possible. Each autumn offers multiple new chances to do *teshuvah*: someone who is distracted during the month of Elul may become inspired to do *teshuvah* in the week between Rosh Hashanah and Yom Kippur. A person who has managed to ignore the call for *teshuvah* through the end of

Yom Kippur has a final chance in the time between Yom Kippur and Hoshanah Rabbah. Even those who do not do *teshuvah* by this final date are not out of luck, as "the gates of *teshuvah* are always open."[32]

This belief in the enduring possibility of *teshuvah* is reflected in a number of rabbinic stories in which even the most hardened sinners do *teshuvah* and become productive members of society. Most famous among these characters is Resh Lakish, a brigand who abandons the life of crime to study Torah and become one of the most important Rabbis of the Talmud.[33] In another talmudic story, Beruriah sees her husband, Rabbi Meir, praying for the death of two youths who are tormenting him. Through a clever interpretation of a biblical verse, Beruriah persuades her husband to pray instead that the youths will do *teshuvah*. Rabbi Meir's prayer is answered, and his tormenters abandon their previous ways.[34]

Even a moment of repentance may be enough to excuse a lifetime of sin. According to Rambam, a person who sins throughout his or her entire life may do *teshuvah* at the last moment and be forgiven on his or her deathbed. In the talmudic story of the martyrdom of Rabbi Chananya ben T'radion, the Rabbi's executioner does *teshuvah* in the very last moment and, as a result, receives the promise of life in the world to come.[35] Another rabbinic text imagines Wisdom and Prophecy, personified, being asked how a sinner should be punished. Each responds with dire predictions about the evil and death that will reward a sinner. God, in contrast, responds, "Let the sinner do *teshuvah* and be forgiven."

The belief in the ever-present possibility and power of *teshuvah* leads to prohibitions against reminding sinners of their past, as well as to positive calls to encourage *teshuvah*. It is forbidden, for example, to accept compensation from a thief or usurer who does *teshuvah*, lest the thought of paying back what he or she has stolen sway such a person from pursuing *teshuvah*. While a person may be sentenced to a fine for a property crime, someone who voluntarily and wholeheartedly repents is not held liable for this fine.

In support of this principle, the Talmud tells the story of a thief who decides to do *teshuvah*. His wife becomes angry with him, saying

"Idiot! If you do *teshuvah*, you will not even have a belt to your name!" Faced with the prospect of losing everything he has, the criminal abandons his intentions of *teshuvah*.[36] Similarly, in the thirteenth century, Rabbi Yom Tov ben Abraham Ishbili (Ritba) ruled leniently in the case of a young man who had been sentenced to a five-year banishment as punishment for breaking into the synagogue and attempting to steal the ornaments from the Torah. In his response, Ritba expresses concern that if the young man actually has done *teshuvah*, then an overly harsh punishment may drive him to a lifetime of bad behavior. He therefore recommends lifting some of the harshest elements of the punishment in order to encourage the offender to maintain his commitment to *teshuvah*.[37] Another thirteenth-century rabbi, Rabbi Shlomo ben Aderet (known as Rashba; Barcelona, 1235–1310), counsels treating criminals gently after first and second offenses, "for perhaps they will return from their wicked ways."[38]

One of the basic principles of *teshuvah* is that a person who has done real *teshuvah* is no longer considered guilty of the sin. According to Rambam, a person who has done *teshuvah* can even look back on an earlier version of himself or herself and say, "I am not the person who did those deeds."[39] In most cases, a person who has done *teshuvah* can even return to leadership positions. A *Kohen* (person descended from the priestly class) who has committed heresy and who has then done *teshuvah* may once again be honored with the first Torah reading, and may again bless the people through the ritual of *n'siyat kapayim* (raising the hands).[40] Some legal authorities do forbid murderers from returning to communal leadership, and people guilty of other serious crimes from returning to positions such as the head of the court.[41] In distinguishing between murderers and other offenders, and among different kinds of communal service, these texts balance a belief in *teshuvah* with a reluctance to honor those who have committed the most heinous of crimes.[42]

In the United States, people often find themselves punished for crimes long after they have finished their sentences. Eleven states prohibit at least some ex-felons from voting; this means that a person who has finished serving a prison sentence, and who is considered fit to reenter society, remains permanently denied one of the basic rights of citizenship. Currently, 2.1 million ex-offenders are disenfranchised.[43] In California, the "three strikes law" means that people who have previously served time for two felonies may, many years later, find themselves sentenced to life for offenses as minor as shoplifting. In Jewish language, we might say that this person has done *teshuvah* for the serious crime that first landed him or her in the criminal justice system, but is still liable for slipups on less serious crimes. Federal and state laws bar some ex-offenders from holding driver's licenses, receiving student loans, or accessing public assistance.[44] Even more devastating for many ex-offenders is the near impossibility of finding work after being released from prison. Few employers are willing to hire a person with a criminal record, and few government programs ease this transition. Rather than encourage and believe in *teshuvah,* our current system seems designed to make *teshuvah* virtually impossible.

Jewish law does not take crime lightly. The Rabbis consider certain serious crimes—especially murder—deserving of the most severe of punishments, at least in theory. While much of Jewish criminal-law discussion centers on the modes and implementation of capital punishment, there is little evidence that Jewish courts ever actually executed anyone. The combination of the fear of killing an innocent person, the sense of powerlessness following the expulsion from Jerusalem and the concomitant dissolution of the Sanhedrin, and the lack of real political power all led Jewish courts to seek modes of punishment outside of those prescribed by the Torah. In the United States, the government certainly has the power to institute virtually any sort of punishment that it wishes. From the hesitancy of Jewish sources to impose punishments, we can learn to place checks on the criminal justice enforcement by a society for whom power is not the question.

While instituting severe punishments for certain crimes, Jewish law generally places property crimes, such as stealing and cheating, in a different category altogether. For these crimes, monetary fines usually suffice as punishment, and offenders who do real *teshuvah* may escape punishment altogether. From this separation, we can learn to think about nonviolent crime in America not as a subsection of violent crime, but as a separate category of behavior that does not necessarily lead to violence. Separating out nonviolent crime may lead us to identify instances of treatable addiction, possibilities for educational and career enrichment, or people who have simply fallen through the cracks.

In contrast to American law, Jewish law tends to see prison as the last resort, rather than the first. Prison is considered to be a less-than-perfect response to the societal needs of the moment, and it is reserved for incorrigible offenders or others who have committed crimes serious enough to warrant separation from the community. There is an assumption that prison will be a temporary home, rather than a permanent residence. For the most part, prison serves as a means of compelling a person to appear in court or to obey the decision of the court. When prison does constitute a punishment, the offender serves only up to a few years and then returns to his or her community.

Perhaps most importantly, Jewish law assumes that the society as a whole bears responsibility both for protecting citizens from crime and for caring for the criminal. Members of society help to facilitate *teshuvah* by refusing compensation from a thief who has repented, by treating a person who has already been punished as a "brother," and by protecting the safety of those who might be the targets of revenge killings. In the United States, prisons tend to be built away from major population centers, and few of us have access to the inside of a prison; it is therefore easy to avoid thinking about what happens there. In contrast, Jewish law challenges us to understand those who have committed crimes as members of our communities—and to accept the responsibility that accompanies this redefinition.

Judaism in the Public Sphere

I began this book by talking about my own journey toward integrating my Jewish life with my commitments to creating a better America. Over the course of this book, I have created a conversation among Judaism, public policy, and lived experience. My intention through these chapters has been to deepen our understanding of all three of these areas, as well as to create a template for Jewish engagement in public life.

In the next few pages, I will suggest three principles that emerge from our discussions of specific issues, and I will lay out a vision for Jewish participation in the American public sphere.

Essential Principles

Three essential principles emerge from our examination of specific issues: the fundamental dignity of human life; the commitment to lessening disparities of money or power; and the mutual responsibility between the community and the individual.

First, Jewish text insists on the dignity of human life. Human beings, according to the Torah, are not only created in the divine image, but also represent manifestations of the divine presence. For this reason, as we saw in our discussion of health care, an injury to a human being is an injury to God. In the realm of poverty relief, the insistence on the divine nature of each person leads to a concern for maintaining the dignity of even the poorest member of society. When the rabbis speak about *tzedakah*, work, and criminal justice, they use phrases such as "your brother" as a reminder that those in need or those undergoing punishment must be treated as family members, rather than as people who are wholly other.

Second, Judaism recognizes the inherent disparity in power among people of various economic and social classes. Few texts idealize an equal redistribution of wealth and power—perhaps because such a solution has historically exceeded the Jewish community's power to enforce. Rather, *halakhah* aims to mitigate inequality so as to prevent one person from exploiting or degrading another. It tends to favor and protect the more vulnerable party, while still looking out for the well-being of the more powerful one. Thus, the law prevents selling needed medicines for more than the going rate, while also allowing doctors to accept money for their work; permits workers to leave in the middle of the day, while also limiting this permission when the labor market is tight and the crops are in danger of spoiling; and prevents a landlord from evicting a tenant suddenly, while also allowing the lease to be broken if the landlord loses his or her own home. When the balance tilts too far to one side, the principle of *tikkun olam* (in its early rabbinic manifestation) allows for adjustments to the legal system such that society functions more equitably.

Finally, Jewish law insists that the individual has a responsibility to the community, and that the community, in turn, has a responsibility to the individual. Almost as soon as a person moves into a new community, he or she begins contributing to the *tzedakah* fund; someone who establishes permanent residence in a town begins to contribute to the infrastructure of that place. The individual, in return, can feel confident that the community will support him or her in times of need, as *tzedakah* and health care funds are available to all members of the community. In the environmental arena, individuals share not only the benefit of the community's natural resources, but also the burden for the responsible disposal of waste and harmful substances. Every individual is charged with considering the consequences of his or her actions for the community as a whole. In turn, urban planning guidelines take into account the health and comfort of each individual within the community. In the context of criminal justice, the community takes responsibility for the punishment, rehabilitation, and reintegration of the convict. With this support, each individual is expected to abstain from crime and to pursue *teshuvah*. In the cases in which the community decides to kill or permanently banish the convicted, the community as a whole takes responsibility for the gravity of this decision.

When considering how Judaism might inform additional public policy debates, we ought to begin by first applying these three principles. Let's take, for example, the question of immigration. As I write this conclusion, the United States is embroiled in a debate about the future of immigration into the country. Some believe that borders must, for moral reasons, be entirely open. Others believe that in practical terms the United States cannot absorb any additional immigrants. Some believe that immigrants are essential to the economic health of the country. Others believe that immigrants are taking jobs from native-born Americans. Some value the diversity that immigrants bring into the United States. Others fear the loss of a common language and culture.

Jewish law has little specific advice on the question of allowing immigration, since historically the Jewish community has been on the immigrant side of the ledger, seeking refuge rather than inhabiting the stable community that others seek to join. The few discussions of immigration policy from a Jewish point of view so far have tended to invoke the character of the biblical *ger* (stranger, or sojourner), whom the dominant community is obligated to protect. While the biblical *ger*, who is never able to own land or to become a full member of the community, is not a perfect parallel for the contemporary immigrant, the emotional pull of the *ger* experience still guides the way that many of us think about immigration. The narrative—or *aggadah*—of the Jewish experience of immigration to America is a powerful rallying cry for Jewish support for immigration. This story should certainly be part of the communal conversation about immigration, and, as I have suggested, *aggadah* should certainly influence our reading of *halakhah*.

But simply invoking the historical story of immigration only goes so far toward guiding policy conversations. Different families have different immigration narratives and different memories of these stories. Further, narrative itself does not give us specific guidance on how to translate it into policy positions. By relying on narrative alone, we can easily find ourselves adrift among competing stories, without the tools to weigh various policies.

Instead, we might apply our three principles, beginning by asking how well certain policies or practices maintain the dignity of individuals. Then we might ask which policies shift the balance of power in such a way as to minimize exploitation. Finally, texts about communal responsibilities lead us to consider the boundaries of our community and to define our responsibility toward those who occupy various places inside and outside of that community, as well as what we might ask of those people.

The Public Sphere

In the introduction to this book, I remarked that I do not believe that the United States or any other country should run according to *halakhah*. How then can we presume to bring Judaism and Jewish law to bear on secular social and economic issues?

The beauty of America is the opportunity for citizens of varying ethnic, religious, and ideological backgrounds to bring their own beliefs and experiences into the public debate. Ideally, the conversation around public policy issues will become richer as a result of this diversity of opinion, and the resulting public policy will be more successful.

Yet Jews sometimes hesitate to speak as Jews in the public sphere. In contemporary America, public religious space has largely been claimed by the Christian right. Those who speak from a religious standpoint are assumed to care most about banning abortion and limiting the rights of gays and lesbians. In the past decade, the Christian left has grown, as organizations such as Call to Renewal and Evangelicals for Social Action have attempted to redefine Christian politics as a dedication, first and foremost, to poverty relief. Still, many progressives worry that speaking from our own religious tradition will lead to a debate about which religion has the better claim to truth, or will unwittingly legitimize others who claim to know God's political preferences. Others worry that strong Jewish voices in the political sphere will lead to increased anti-Semitism. We are conscious of the large numbers of Jews who play public roles in the U.S. government, and we have seen instances in which this public profile has led to scapegoating and resentment of Jews as a group.

The Jewish community has long been among the strongest voices for the separation of church and state. Jewish communal organizations and individuals have successfully opposed school prayer, the public display of religious symbols, and religious prose-lytizing in the military. This focus on preventing religious coercion has led many of us to believe that the Constitution calls only for a strict separation between religion and public life. But in addition to limiting the government's ability to provide any favoritism to one religion over another, the First Amendment also guarantees the rights of citizens to express their religious beliefs freely. No single set of religious beliefs should dominate public discourse, but religious beliefs can and should be brought into the public domain, just as any other ideologies, experiences, and insights would. As the theologian Abraham Joshua Heschel commented when explaining his own involvement in justice issues, "We *affirm* the principle of separation of church and state. We *reject* the separation of religion and the human situation."[1]

In the nineteenth century, the poet Judah Leib Gordon coined the phrase, "Be a Jew in the home and a man in the street,"[2] which became the rallying cry for the *Haskalah* (Enlightenment) movement that sought to integrate Jews into secular society, and to bring contemporary scholarship to bear on Judaism. For the *maskilim* (Enlightenment Jews), this meant dressing in modern clothing, studying secular subject matter, and otherwise publicly assimilating into European society, while retaining Jewish practices at home.

Today, most Jews are fully integrated into American society. Outside of the *Haredi* (ultra-Orthodox) community, few Jews question whether it is permissible to study secular subjects, wear modern clothing, or participate in American popular culture. Leib's distinction between the old-fashioned "Jew" and the modern "man" [*sic*] no longer rings true. The question for this generation is not how to become an "American in the street," but how or whether it is possible to be an American Jew in the street, as well as in the home. The answer to this question may determine how Jews can bring Jewish law and tradition into the public square in such a way as to enrich the debate, rather than lead to a head-to-head collision with people of other faiths over the question of how God might vote.

Much of the American conversation about religion in the public square revolves around visible manifestations of religion, such as crèches and Christmas trees on public property, or prayer and Bible study in school. The Jewish community expends significant resources on responding to these incidents, either by demanding the strict banishment of religion from public life or by promoting the inclusion of Hanukkah menorahs and other symbols of our own. It is important to protect the boundary between church and state in order for people of all religions to feel comfortable in public space, and in order to ensure that public displays of Christianity do not become coercive. At the same time, such displays of religion are ultimately symbolic, and they are less important than decisions about policies that affect the economic and social welfare of individual citizens and communities.

Many individual Jews play prominent roles in public life, as community organizers, public policy experts, legislators, and government officials. Some of these individuals speak proudly of their Jewish commitments and inspirations; others keep their Judaism private. Some of these individuals have found a place in a Jewish community; others believe that their own commitments are incompatible with those of most Jewish communities. At the same time, many Jewish organizations are deeply engaged in policy debates at local, state, national, and international levels. In some cases, this involvement focuses on specifically "Jewish" issues, such as Israel, separation of church and state, and private school funding. But many Jewish organizations—including local social justice groups, synagogues, and national bodies—devote themselves to issues as varied as reproductive choice, immigration, and international human rights. Many, or even most, of these organizations strive to speak about these issues with a Jewish voice. Most reference the Jewish experience of oppression, quote relevant biblical verses, and ask prominent rabbis to give sermons and write articles that link Jewish thought to particular issues. Some publish materials aimed at helping individuals, synagogues, and schools to study issues from a Jewish perspective.

What is missing in much of this work is a real public discussion about how Jewish law and tradition might address contemporary policy questions. Those on either side of an issue often quote texts to support their points, but they do so in a way that does not invite debate or discussion. Instead, when Jews engage in the public discourse as Jews, we should bring Jewish law and principles into the conversation in such a way as to enrich, rather than shut down, the discourse. We should also bring into this dialogue Jews and others who are engaged in public life; the conversation among rabbis, public policy experts, grassroots activists, and Jewish communal professionals should generate a nuanced understanding of how the Jewish community might approach individual issues.

This approach precludes quoting a simplified version of Jewish law or text in order to prove a point, or asserting that Jewish law unequivocally demands a certain approach to an issue. Rather, Jewish sources should help us to see various sides of an issue, challenge our assumptions, and enable us to formulate a response that takes multiple factors into account. The commitment to living our Judaism publicly should then push us to take public action on these principles, both as individuals and as a community.

If we succeed in facilitating this rich conversation, we will create a new kind of Jewish politics in America. Rather than trade sound bites, we will continue the talmudic tradition of dialogue, in which various questioners and commentators engage in an often messy conversation that eventually leads to a fuller understanding of the situation at hand. Jews who now exercise their commitments to public life outside of the Jewish community will find a place within this community, as they contribute their own wisdom and observations to the conversation. Individual Jews and Jewish institutions will strengthen their commitment to public life, as the question of how to address current issues becomes part of the general Jewish conversation, rather than something separate from it or as an add-on to discussion of Shabbat, *kashrut*, and other aspects of Jewish practice. We will witness the emergence of a Judaism that views ritual observance, study, and engagement in the world as an integrated whole, rather than as separate and distinct practices. The Jewish community's deepened involvement in public life will change the face of religious politics in America, as other communities will recognize the Jewish community as an important and authentic religious voice in the public square of America. Finally, the integration of religion, legal discussion, and participation in public life will instill in the Jewish community the power to have a major impact on the ideologies and policies of the United States.

NOTES

Foreword

1. Elliot N. Dorff, *For the Love of God and People: A Philosophy of Jewish Law* (Philadelphia: Jewish Publication Society, 2007), especially Chapter 6.

2. For example, Jeremiah 9:23; Micah 6:8; Psalms 1; 34:13–15; 112; Proverbs 31.

3. Isaiah 49:6; see also 42:1–4 and 51:4–5.

4. Leviticus 19:2.

5. M. *Avot* 2:5 (2:6 in *Sim Shalom*).

6. B. *Bava Metzia* 30b.

7. Nahmanides, *Perush La-Torah*, comment on Deuteronomy 6:18.

8. B. *Bava Metzia* 35a. The same law may apply to creditors and debtors; see B. *Bava Metzia* 16b–17a, also on the basis of Deuteronomy 6:18.

9. B. *Bava Metzia* 108a–108b.

10. B. *Eruvin* 49a; B. *Ketubbot* 103a; B. *Bava Batra* 12b, 59a, 168a. See M. *Avot* 5:10, where this is portrayed as the attitude of ordinary person— "Mine is mine, and yours is yours"—but which clearly is not the exemplary behavior that the Rabbis wanted us to exhibit.

11. M. *Bava Metzia* 4:1 (44a).

12. T. *Bava Metzia* 3:7; B. *Bava Metzia* 48a. In line with this, the Talmud actually legislated two rules on the basis of the duty "to do the right and the good in the eyes of God." In one, if a person holding an object for another loses the object deposited with him, pays the owner for the loss, and then finds the lost object, he may with no deadline return the object to the owner and get his money back. In the other, people who own land adjacent to another piece of land that becomes available have first rights to buy the adjacent piece and even to evict someone who already paid the land tax and took possession of it. In these examples, a broad rabbinic ethical principle is strong enough to support new and binding laws.

13. M. *Bava Batra* 8:5 (133b).

14. T. *Shevi'it* 8:12; B. *Bava Kamma* 94b.

15. B. *Shabbat* 121b.

16. M. *Shevi'it* 10:9; B. *Kiddushin* 17–18a.

17. B. *Kiddushin* 59a.

18. B. *Shabbat* 120a.

19. B. *Hullin* 130b; see also B. *Bava Metzia* 52b.

20. For example, M. *Avot* 2:2; 3:5; 6:6. In Rabbi Elazar ben Azariah's comment, "No Torah, no *derekh eretz*, No *derekh eretz*, no Torah" (3:17; 3:21 in some editions), the term may mean gainful employment, but it may mean ethics.

21. T. *Sotah* 7:13; see B. *Sotah* 44a. Other examples of *derekh eretz* meaning proper behavior include B. *Berakhot* 22a, 35a, 61a; B. *Shabbat* 114a; B. *Eruvin* 100b; B. *Yoma* 4b, 75a; B. *Betzah* 25a–25b. For a general discussion of Jewish law and morals outside and within the law, see Elliot N. Dorff, "The Interaction of Jewish Law with Morality," *Judaism* 26.4 (Fall, 1977), pp. 455–466; and Elliot N. Dorff, *For the Love of God and People: A Philosophy of Jewish Law* (Philadelphia: Jewish Publication Society, 2007), Chapter 6.

22. *Genesis Rabbah*, Lekh Lekha 44:1; see also *Leviticus Rabbah*, Shemini 13:3 and *Midrash Tanhuma*, Shemini (ed. Buber, 15b).

Introduction: The Search for an Integrated Judaism

1. The ceding of religious authority for issues of personal status has not been without controversy. The fact that the Orthodox establishment has a monopoly on these matters means that as of 2009, there is no civil marriage in Israel—a Jew may marry a Jew in a religious ceremony, a Muslim may marry a Muslim, and a Christian may marry a Christian, but a couple of mixed (or no) religious background may not legally marry. Weddings, conversions, and divorces performed by non-Orthodox rabbis are similarly not recognized by the state. Since Israel does accept civil marriages performed in other countries, many couples obtain civil marriages elsewhere rather than submit to the authority of the state rabbinate. While this issue is beyond the scope of this book, the reader should be aware of the complications inherent in the current division of religious and civil authority in Israel.

2. Robert Cover, "Violence and the Word," in *Narrative, Violence, and the Law: The Essays of Robert Cover*, Martha Minow, Michael Ryan, and Austin Sarat, eds. (Ann Arbor: University of Michigan, 1995), 203–238.

3. Martha Minow, "Stories in Law," in *Law's Stories: Narrative and Rhetoric in the Law*, Peter Brooks and Paul Gewirtz, eds. (New Haven: Yale, 1996), 36.

1. A Vision of Economic Justice

1. Comment to Deuteronomy 15, Ramban's commentary on the Torah.
2. See, for example, Leviticus 25:23 and ff.
3. Solomon Schechter, *Aspects of Rabbinic Theology* (Woodstock, VT: Jewish Lights, 1993), 114.

2. Essential Terms: *Tikkun Olam, Tzedek*, and Prophetic Judaism

1. There is significant rabbinic discussion about whether Christianity and Islam, in particular, constitute idol worship. A number of significant religious authorities, including the Tosefot (medieval Talmud commentators) and fourteenth-century Rabbi Menachem Meiri, conclude that these religions are not, in fact, idol worship and that prohibitions against relations with idol worshippers do not apply to adherents of these religions. (See Tosefot on Talmud, *Avodah Zarah* 2a and Menachem Meiri, *Beit Hab'chirah, Avodah Zarah* 53.)
2. *Seder T'fillot Rosh Hashanah, Dibbur haMatchil "Al ken."*
3. Contemporary Jewish legal thinkers have devised numerous methods of ensuring that women do not get stuck with husbands who refuse them divorce. Conservative rabbis generally solve the problem in one of two ways: either the couple signs a prenuptial agreement specifying that the marriage is conditional on the husband's agreeing to grant a *get* if his wife desires one; or the *ketubah* (marriage contract) includes the "Lieberman clause," which grants a Conservative rabbinic court the power to adjudicate divorce disagreements. Within the Orthodox world, the problem of *agunot* (literally "chained women," women unable to secure a divorce) continues to be a problem. Orthodox rabbis address this problem in numerous ways, including applying social and economic pressure on husbands who refuse to grant their wives a *get*; asking couples to sign a prenuptial agreement in which the husband agrees to support his wife until he grants her a *get*; and, in Israel, allowing specially trained women advocates to plead the case of the *agunah* before the rabbinical court.
4. Though most often translated as "bastard," the status of *mamzer* should be distinguished from the connotation of the English word "bastard," which refers to a child born out of wedlock. The term *mamzer* refers

only to a child whom a married woman has with a man who is not her husband. For reasons of practicality and compassion, contemporary rabbis have tried to eliminate the category of the *mamzer*, most often by refusing to believe information that suggests that a child has been born out of an affair.

5. Lawrence Fine, *Physician of the Soul, Healer of the Cosmos: Isaac Luria and His Kabbalistic Fellowship* (Palo Alto: Stanford, 2003), 206.

6. Clinton's quote appears in Ben Harris, "Candidates, Surrogates Appear at New Hampshire Shul's '08 Forum," Jewish Telegraphic Agency, January 7, 2008. Obama's quote appears in his speech to the American Israel Public Affairs Committee, June 4, 2008.

7. Arnold Jacob Wolf, "Repairing Tikkun Olam—Current Theological Writing," *Judaism* 50:4 (Fall 2001): 479–82.

8. G. Johannes Botterweck, Helmer Ringgren, and Heinz-Josef Fabry, *Theological Dictionary of the Old Testament*, Vol. 12 (Grand Rapids, MI: Wm. B. Erdmans, 1978), 27–41.

9. See, for example, Psalms 37:12–15, where "righteous" and "poor" seem to be used in parallel.

10. Moshe Weinfeld, *Social Justice in Ancient Israel and in the Ancient Near East* (Minneapolis: Fortress Press, 1995), 35.

11. E. R. Achtemeier, "The Gospel of Righteousness: A Study of the Meaning of Ṣdk and Its Derivatives in the OT" (PhD diss., Columbia University, 1959).

12. Walter Jacob, "Prophetic Judaism: The History of a Term," *Journal of Reform Judaism* (previously the *CCAR Journal*) 26:2 (Spring 1979): 36–37.

13. Abraham Joshua Heschel, *The Prophets* (New York: Harper Perennial Classics, 2001), 398.

3. Defining Poverty and the Poor

1. See, for example, Rashi on Deuteronomy 15:4.

2. G. Johannes Botterweck, *Theological Dictionary of the Old Testament*, Vol. 1, (Wm. B. Eerdmans, 1974), 239–263.

3. There is not, however, a one-to-one correspondence between *evyon* and *tzaddik*—that is, there is no assumption that every poor person is righteous, and no suspicion that a wealthy person might not be righteous. In fact, many of the Rabbis describe themselves or their

colleagues as wealthy, and even propose that Moses became wealthy immediately upon assuming leadership.

4. Arvid Schou Kapelrud, *Central Ideas in Amos* (Oslo, Norway: Oslo University Press, 1961), 203.

5. See, for example, Exodus 3:7 ("I have seen the suffering of my people") and 2 Samuel 22:28 ("You will save the afflicted people").

6. See, for example, Talmud, *Ketubot* 67b.

7. See, for example, John Cassidy, "Relatively Deprived," *New Yorker*, April 3, 2006: 42–47.

8. *Eliyahu Zuta 5, Dibbur haMatchil "Vayomer."*

9. *P'sikta d'Rav Kahana* 28.

10. See, for example, *Leviticus Rabbah* 5:4. See also Richard Kalmin's distinction between the attitudes of Babylonian and Palestinian Rabbis on the question of whether and how to accept support from nonrabbinic Jews in Kalmin, *The Sage in Jewish Society of Late Antiquity* (New York: Routledge), 27–50.

11. Moses Maimonides, *Mishneh Torah, Matanot l'Aniyim* 10:2.

12. *The War Against the Poor: The Underclass and Antipoverty Policy* (New York: Basic Books, 1996).

13. Michael Katz, *The Undeserving Poor: From the War on Poverty to the War on Welfare* (New York: Pantheon, 1989), 12.

14. Oscar Lewis, *La Vida: A Puerto Rican Family in the Culture of Poverty—San Juan and New York* (New York: Random House, 1966), quoted in Katz, *The Undeserving Poor*, 19.

15. Ibid.

16. Martin Gilens, *Why Americans Hate Welfare: Race, Media, and the Politics of Antipoverty Policy* (Chicago: University of Chicago, 2000).

17. See, for example, the discussion of *gozel 'aniyyim* in the *Beit Yosef* on *Yoreh De'ah* 253:1.

18. See, for example, *Sefer Or Zarua* I, *Hilkhot Tzedakah* 14 (*Dibbur haMatchil "Sha'al Rabbi Kalonymous"*), and *Teshuvot haRashba* I:871. The *Tur, Yoreh De'ah* 253, without comment, applies the laws of *leket*, etc. to *tzedakah*. Commenting on this section, the *Beit Yosef* says, "Even though the Mishnah only says that one [who has 200 *zuzim*] should not take *leket*, *shikh'chah, pe'ah* and *ma'aser 'ani*, our rabbi [the Tur] wrote, 'One should not take any *tzedakah*,' for one who does not take these things should not take any kind of *tzedakah*.' This is in accordance with the

Mordekhai's commentary on the first chapter of *Bava Batra* (500), which he attributes to Rabbenu Ephraim and to the Or Zarua."

19. Later commentators specifically forbid a creditor from collecting *tzedakah* money, as the giver of the *tzedakah* intends for it to go to the recipient and not to the creditor. (See, for example, Rabbi David ben Solomon ibn Avi Zimra, *Teshuvot Radbaz* 4:159).

20. *Yerushalmi, Pe'ah* 8:8 (21a–b). This opinion, cited in the name of Rabbi Chanina, is challenged by others, who consider one garment to be sufficient. In the end, the *gemara* appears to accept the opinion of Rabbi Chanina.

21. The *Bavli* here suggests that one of these texts applies to the situation of a person who has not yet taken *tzedakah*, and that the other applies to the situation of a person who has already taken *tzedakah*. It is not clear which text the *Bavli* applies to which situation. Rashi understands the *gemara* to apply Mishnaic text to the situation of someone who has not yet taken *tzedakah*, and the *Tosefta*'s text to the situation of someone who has already taken *tzedakah*. According to this reading, a poor person is not forced to sell his or her vessels in order to take *tzedakah*. However, if a wealthy person fraudulently takes from the agricultural forms of *tzedakah*, the court may seize and sell his expensive dishes in order to regain the worth of the produce this person has stolen. Rabbenu Tam (Jacob ben Meir Tam; France, 1100–1171) takes the opposite approach, applying the *Tosefta* to the case of a person who has not taken *tzedakah*, and the Mishnah to the case of someone who has already taken *tzedakah*. According to Rabbenu Tam, a person who owns expensive dishes is forced to sell these before taking *tzedakah*. However, if a person has already taken *tzedakah* and then comes into possession of expensive dishes, we do not force him or her to sell these. The Rosh (Rabbi Asher ben Yechiel; Germany/Spain, 1250–1328) takes a third approach, suggesting that a person who takes *tzedakah* in private is not forced to sell his or her dishes, but that someone who must begin accepting *tzedakah* publicly, from the *tzedakah* collector, is forced to sell expensive dishes. Presumably, the Rosh is concerned that a community will stop giving *tzedakah* if it seems that the *tzedakah* is going to the wealthy.

22. *Yerushalmi, Pe'ah* 8:7; cf. *Yerushalmi, Sotah* 3:4; and the commentary of the *P'nai Moshe* on both passages.

23. The limits on any particular program are, of course, determined by the government that administers them. As such, we might argue that

governmental programs are less limited than the *kuppah*, whose size depended on the wealth of the individuals in a particular community.

24. Perhaps more permissively, Rabbi Moshe Isserles (the Rema) considers a person's house and utensils to be outside of the purview of wealth calculations for the purpose of *tzedakah*. He writes: "In any case in which there is an enactment that prohibits giving *tzedakah* to those who have a certain amount, we do not count one's house or utensils" (*Yoreh De'ah* 253:1). From the absence of any qualification of "utensils" we may assume that the Rema would not distinguish between fancy vessels and plain ones.

25. From what is known about prices and monetary values in other parts of the Roman Empire, some have tried to determine the value of money in Palestine during this time. See, for example, Gildas Hamel, *Poverty and Charity in Roman Palestine* (Berkeley: University of California Press, 1990) and Richard P. Duncan-Jones *Structure and Scale in the Roman Economy* (Cambridge, England: Cambridge University Press, 1990). Hamel suggests that during much of this period, one day's worth of bread (two loaves) cost 1/12 *dinar* (39). At this rate, 200 *zuzim* would buy bread for 1,200 days—more than three years. However, the economic differences between Palestine and other parts of the Roman Empire make it impossible to come to any definitive conclusions about the real value of a *zuz*. Despite his attempts to determine the value of Palestinian currency during this period, Hamel admits that "one cannot rely upon [the figure of 200 *zuzim* as the poverty line], if only because the value of the *zuz* varied during the period (especially during the third century CE)" (218). I would like to thank Dr. Seth Schwartz for his guidance and cautions on this matter.

26. On *Yerushalmi, Pe'ah* 8:7 (20d).

27. *Hilkhot Tzedakah* 14; cf. *Teshuvot haRashba* I: 572.

28. *Hilkot Tzedakah* 14; cf. *Teshuvot Ba'alei haTosefot* 32, *Dibbur haMatchil* "*u'Mah she'Amarta.*" Like most rabbinic and later halakhic sources, the *Ba'alei haTosefot*, a collection of *teshuvot* by thirty-nine Rabbis who lived in the Rhine valley in the eleventh through thirteenth centuries, assumes that poverty is a temporary, rather than a permanent condition. Consistent with talmudic sources, theses medieval authorities insists that a poor person be helped to maintain the same lifestyle that this person had before becoming poor.

29. *Yoreh De'ah* 252:2; cf. *Sm'ak* 146.

30. Rabbi Mordechai Ya'akov Breisch (1896–1970) considers and rejects the possibility that interest may constitute the *revach* mentioned by the Tur (*Chelkat Ya'akov, Yoreh De'ah* 137 [4:1]). If this were the case, anyone not able to live for a year off of his or her interest would be considered eligible for *tzedakah*! Instead, Breisch says, we should simply include the value of the interest earned in the calculation of a person's assets. Breisch, citing the Tur, stresses that 200 *zuzim* should be understood as the amount of money necessary to live for an entire year.

31. *Teshuvot Avkat Rokhel* 2, *Dibbur haMatchil "Teshuva im."*

32. Rabbi Yair Chaim ben Moses Samson Bachrach, *Chavvot Yair* 186.

33. Danilo Pelletiere, Keith E. Wardrip, and Sheila Crowley, *Out of Reach 2007–2008* (Washington, DC: National Low Income Housing Coalition, 2008), http://nlihc.org/oor/oor2008/.

34. See, for example, Deuteronomy 15:9 and 24:15.

4. Sufficient for One's Needs: The Collection and Allocation of *Tzedakah*

1. Rambam, *Mishneh Torah, Matanot l'Aniyim* 10:12.

2. James Andreoni, "Impure Altruism and Donations to Public Goods: A Theory of Warm Glow Giving," *The Economic Journal* 100:401 (1990): 464–477.

3. See, for example, Rashi on Deuteronomy 15:10.

4. *Orchot Chayyim, Skha'ar Han'divut.*

5. *Kedushah Sh'niah, Dibbur haMatchil "v'Hineh."*

6. See, for example, Giving USA Foundation, *Giving USA 2007* (Glenview, IL: Giving USA Foundation, 2007); The Center on Philanthropy at Indiana University, "Average and Median Amounts of Household Giving and Volunteering in 2002 from the Center on Philanthropy Panel Study (COPPS) 2003 Wave" (Indianapolis: The Center on Philanthropy, 2006); and Independent Sector, *Giving and Volunteering in the United States* (Washington, DC: Independent Sector, 2001).

7. See, for example, Russell N. James III and Keely S. Jones, "Tithing and Religious Charitable Giving in America" (Paper presented at the annual conference of the Association for Research on Nonprofit Organizations and Voluntary Action, Atlanta, GA, November 2007) and Arthur C. Brooks, *Who Really Cares: The Surprising Truth about Compassionate Conservatism* (New York: Basic Books, 2006).

8. *Shulchan Arukh, Yoreh De'ah* 251:12.

9. Talmud, *Ketubot* 50a. This hard and fast rule of maximizing giving at 20 percent may not apply to the super wealthy, who are unlikely to become dependent on *tzedakah*, even if they give away much more than 20 percent of their income. In 2006 Warren Buffett made headlines by announcing his plans to give away 85 percent of his wealth to charitable causes (Carol J. Loomis, "Warren Buffet Gives Away His Fortune," *Fortune Magazine*, June 25, 2006, *money.cnn.com/2006/06/25/magazines/fortune/charity1.fortune/*). The 15 percent remaining will certainly keep Buffett and his three children among the wealthiest people in the world; we need hardly worry about a member of his family becoming dependent on handouts from others.

10. Rambam, *Mishneh Torah, Matanot l'Aniyim* 9:3.

11. Yechiel Epstein, *Arukh haShulchan, Yoreh De'ah* 247.

12. Rambam, *Mishneh Torah, Hilkhot M'lachim* 10:12.

13. See, for example, Rambam, *Mishneh Torah, Matanot l'Aniyim* 10:16

14. Rabbi Moshe Sofer, *She'elot and Teshuvot of the Chatam Sofer* 2:231.

15. *Mishneh Torah, Hilkhot Matanot l'Aniyim* 10:7

16. Rabbi Eliezer Waldenberg, *She'elot and Teshuvot of Tzitz Eliezer* 9:1.

17. Ya'akov Ariel, "Olam Chesed Yibaneh: Chevrah Yisraelit Idialit," *Tzohar* 19 (Fall 2003): 23–33.

5. Servants to Servants or Servants to God: Workers, Employers, and Unions

1. *P'sachim* 113a; cf. *Bava Batra* 110a.

2. Human Rights Watch, *Unfair Advantage: Workers' Freedom of Association in the United States under International Human Rights Standards* (New York: HRW, 2000), 11.

3. *Sh'mot Rabbah* 1:27; cf. 1:11.

4. Paterson-area clergy meeting convened by UNITE (Union of Needletrades, Industrial and Textile Employees), Paterson, NJ, July 2001.

5. The discussion of public disgrace in chapter 8 of Talmud, *Bava Kamma* suggests that a person is liable for disgracing another even when the object of the disgrace is not aware of the insult. See, in particular, the discussion of insulting a sleeping person who then dies without awakening (86b).

6. Human Rights Watch, *Unfair Advantage.* Human Rights Watch finds several similar instances of employer surveillance. In an organizing campaign at the Villa Maria nursing home in Miami, "a supervisor infiltrated a union meeting by signing a union card with a false name to spy on workers and report attendance back to management" (79). Similarly, when workers in a North Carolina pork processing plant tried to organize a union, management employed a number of obstructive tactics, including issuing warnings against union supporters, interrogating workers about their attitudes toward unions and about the feelings of other workers, spying on union supporters, and asking workers to spy on co-workers.

7. For this section, I rely on my own observations as well as discussions with Paterson-area clergy members.

8. *Bamidbar Rabbah* 15:20. *Perach* and *ferach* are the same word. In Hebrew, a single letter represents both the "p" and the "f" sound; pronunciation varies depending on the placement of this letter in a word.

9. *Nickel and Dimed: On (Not) Getting by in America* (New York: Metropolitan Books, 2001), 144–145.

10. Interview with Denis Johnston, director of communications for SEIU 32 BJ, December 2001.

11. Mass firings such as these are anything but unique. A 1994 study prepared by Professor Richard Hurd of Cornell University for the U.S. Department of Labor finds:

    • Adjusted for the number of certification elections and union voters, the incidence of unlawful firing of workers exercising the right to organize increased from one in every twenty elections adversely affecting one in seven hundred union supporters [in the early 1950s] to one in every four elections victimizing one in fifty union supporters [by the late 1980s].

    • Most unlawfully fired workers do not take advantage of their right to reinstatement on the job, and most who are reinstated are gone within a year.

    • In a national poll 59 percent of workers said it was likely they would lose favor with their employer if they supported an organizing drive. And 79 percent agreed that it was "very" or "somewhat" likely that "nonunion workers will get fired if they try to organize a union."

Furthermore, Human Rights Watch, citing a 1997 study by the Secretariat of the North American Commission for Labor Cooperation, reports that "employers threaten to close the workplace in half of the organizing campaigns undertaken by workers in the United States, but rarely in Canada or Mexico. Such threats are used even more intensively in U.S. industries where workers feel most vulnerable to shutdowns and relocations. Employers threatened closings in nearly two-thirds of organizing efforts in manufacturing facilities and warehouses." Human Rights Watch, *Unfair Advantage: Workers' Freedom of Association in the United States Under International Human Rights Standards* (New York: HRW, 2000),11.

12. For example, see Exodus 22:20 and 23:9, Leviticus 19:24 and 25:23, and Deuteronomy 10:19.

13. Ben-Tzion Meir Chai Uziel, *Mishpetei Uziel, Choshen Mishpat* 52:1.

14. Talmud, *Bava Kamma* 117b; cf. *Bava Metzia* 10a.

15. Andrew Blankstein and Bob Pool, "Three Jailed in Alleged Smuggling of Fake Taekwondo Athletes," *Los Angeles Times*, April 4, 2008; *money.cnn.com/2006/06/25/magazines/fortune/charity1.fortune/*. The U.S. Department of Justice estimates that 50,000 people are trafficked to or through the United States each year. The precise number, of course, is impossible to determine. U.S. State Department, *Trafficking in Persons Report* (Washington, DC, June 2008).

16. See, for example David Schnall, *By the Sweat of Your Brow: Reflections on Work and the Workplace in Classic Jewish Thought* (New York: Ktav, 2001); Meir Tamari, *With All Your Possessions: Jewish Ethics and Economic Life* (New York: Free Press, 1987); and Aaron Levine, *Moral Issues of the Marketplace in Jewish Law* (New York: Yashar, 2005), and *Economic Public Policy and Jewish Law* (New York: Ktav, 1993).

17. Robin D. G. Kelley, *Race Rebels: Culture, Politics and the Black Working Class* (New York: Free Press, 1994), 1–13.

18. See, for example, Exodus 22:20–23.

19. The *gerim* (sojourners, or strangers) mentioned in the Bible are not precisely analogous to contemporary non-Jews. Rather, *gerim* appear to be people who live within the Jewish community and who are bound by the *mitzvot lo ta'aseh* (commandments *not to do* something), if not by the *mitzvot aseh* (commandments *to do* something). These *gerim*, who are unable to own land and who never become full members of the community, are, according to the Bible, in need of special protections.

A category of *gerim* as such no longer exists. However, the biblical extension of workers' protections to one group of people who are not fully Jewish sets a precedent to extend employment laws to other groups of non-Jews, especially those who are in need of special protection.

20. *Dibbur haMatchil "Hishamer Militza'er."*

21. *Sefer haYirah, Dibbur hamatchil "Hishamer militza'er."*

22. Chaim David HaLevy, *Aseh L'cha Rav* 5:23.

23. America's Second Harvest (Now: Feeding America), *Hunger in America 2006* (America's Second Harvest: Chicago, 2006), www.hungerinamerica.org/.

24. Talmud, *Bava Metzia* 86b, cf. Rambam, *Mishneh Torah, Hilkhot Skhirut* 9:4; *Shulchan Arukh, Choshen Mishpat* 333:3.

25. Warhaftig, *Dinei Avodah b'Mishpat ha'Ivri* (Jerusalem: Hebrew University, 1964), Vols. 1, 2.

26. Chaim David HaLevy, *Aseh L'cha Rav* (Tel Aviv: *Ha'va'adah L'hotza'at Kitvei Ha'ga'on Rabbi C. D. Halevy,* 1975/6), 2:64.

27. Moshe Feinstein seems to interpret the statement that "two or three" may not make a binding stipulation as giving permission to the majority to make such a stipulation in *Igg'rot Moshe, Choshen Mishpat* 59.

28. Comment to *Bava Batra* 9a

29. See *Arba'ah Turim, Choshen Mishpat* 331:28, and Rabbi Joseph ben Rabbi Meir HaLevy ibn Migash (R'i Migash) (Spain, 1077–1141), quoted in Beit Yosef 331:28.

30. Opposition against living-wage legislation is often expressed as a concern that raising wages will result in the loss of jobs. Every major real-life study of the effects of living-wage legislation has concluded that cities where it is implemented experience no significant job loss and, in some cases, even gain jobs. A 1999 report on the effects of the nation's first living-wage law, passed in Baltimore in 1994, found that the living-wage law had no serious detrimental effect on either the rate of employment or on costs to the city. Instead, "the aggregate cost increase to the city amounted to 1.2 percent, less than the rate of inflation. The real cost to the city of these contracts, then, actually declined slightly despite the increase in wage rates." Reports on the effect of the living wage in Detroit, Los Angeles, and Miami-Dade reached similar conclusions. (Christopher Niedt, Greg Ruiters, Dana Wise, and Erica Schoenberger, "The Effects of the Living Wage in Baltimore" [Baltimore: Johns Hopkins University/the Economic Policy

Institute, 1999] and David Reynolds, Rachel Pearson, and Jean Vortkempt,, "Impact of the Detroit Living Wage Ordinance" [Detroit: Wayne State University, 1999]).

The authors of a study on the effects of a living wage in Los Angeles offer some explanation for this lack of job loss, commenting, "Labor turnover has declined as a result of the ordinance. Current rates of turnover at living wage firms average 32 percent, compared to 49 percent at comparable non-living wage firms. These turnover reductions represent a cost savings for the average firm that is 16 percent of the cost of the wage increase, based on various estimates of the cost of replacing a low-wage worker" (David Fairris, David Runsten, Carolina Briones, and Jessica Goodheart, "Examining the Evidence: The Impact of the Los Angeles Living Wage ordinance on Workers and Businesses" [Los Angeles: UCLA, 2005]). Rather than eliminate jobs, employers find other ways to cut costs or, in some cases, raise prices, and are rewarded with increased workforce stability. In most cases, paying a living wage has a minimal effect on a company's overall costs. A 2004 study by a University of Massachusetts economist found that in most companies, the cost of paying a living wage accounts for only 1–2 percent of the overall operating costs (Mark Brenner, "The Economic Impact of Living Wage Ordinances" [Amherst, MA: University of Massachusetts, Political Research Economy Institute, 2004]. Also see Jeff Chapman, "Employment and the Minimum Wage: Evidence from Recent State Labor Market Trends" [Washington, D.C.: Economic Policy Institute, May 2004]).

The lack of job loss can also be partially explained by the nature of low-wage jobs in America. At this point, virtually all manufacturing jobs that can be outsourced have been sent overseas. The low-wage jobs that remain are either manufacturing jobs that cannot be outsourced (such as certain types of food production or clothing manufacturing that require fast turnaround) or—more commonly— service jobs such as retail sales, food preparation, or cleaning. Employers cannot send these jobs abroad, and generally cannot reduce the number of employees necessary to run these businesses. Therefore, employers generally find some other way to pay for higher salaries. Presumably, there is some wage level at which employers would be forced to lay off workers; however, as studies such as those cited above have demonstrated, wages of $12 or $13 per hour do not reach this level.

31. The best indications of the actual, bare-bones costs of living in various metropolitan areas are the self-sufficiency indexes developed by Diana Pearce for Wider Opportunities for Women and the Economic Policy Institute. These indexes consider the basic costs of housing, transportation, food, health care, child care, and other essentials for families of various sizes living in various counties in each state. These reports are available at http://www.wowonline.org/ourprograms/fess/sss.asp or www.epi.org/content.cfm/issueguides_poverty_budgetsbystate. For "housing wage," which reflects the amount that a person would need to earn in order to spend 30 percent of his or her salary to rent a two-bedroom apartment at the fair market rate in a given area, see http://nlihc.org/oor/oor2008/.

32. Rambam, *Mishneh Torah, Hilkhot Skhirut* 13:7; cf. *Shulchan Arukh, Choshen Mishpat* 337:20.

33. *Tosefta, Bava Metzia* 8:2, cf. Rabbi Isaac Alfasi (Rif), *Bava Metzia* 52b, and Rambam, *Mishneh Torah, Hilkhot Skhirut* 13:6.

34. *Tosefta, Bava Metzia* 8:2, cf. *Shulchan Arukh, Choshen Mishpat* 337:19.

35. Bureau of Labor Statistics, *Multiple Job Holding in States 2006* (Washington, DC: Bureau of Labor Statistics, 2006), www.bls.gov.

36. Stephen C. Betts, *Multiple Job Research Project* (online research project, Wayne, NJ: William Paterson University), http://euphrates.wpunj.edu/faculty/bettss/academic.htm.

37. Bobbi Murray, "Living Wage Comes of Age," *Nation*, July 12, 2001: 24–28.

38. Health Professionals and Allied Employees Speakout, a session in which people tell their own stories, June 2001.

39. The question of whether the principle of *pikuah nefesh* can impose obligations also applies to this case, in which we might argue that the denial of benefits constitutes a threat to workers' lives.

40. Schall, *By the Sweat of Your Brow*, 141. Schnall's statement assumes an acceptance of the general principle *haminhag m'vatel et hahalakhah* ("the custom overrides the law") suggested by Rav Hoshea in *Yerushalmi, Bava Metzia* 7:1. The question of the general applicability of this principle is a matter of much debate. The Or Zarua understands this principle to apply only to an accepted *minhag*, certified by a recognized authority (2:393). Similarly, Masekhet Sofrim permits only a *minhag vatikin* ("custom of the elders") to override *halakhah* (14:16). The Rashba softens the necessity for earlier precedent, requiring only

an "agreed-upon *minhag*" (*She'elot u'Teshuvot* 2:43). Joseph Caro, however, seems to accept the principle *haminhag m'vatel et hahalakhah* as a general rule (*Beit Yosef* and *Shulchan Arukh, Choshen Mishpat* 232:19).

41. Ibid., 130. I find extremely problematic Schnall's assumption that certain employers—notably school systems—can justify paying low wages by assuming that employees, especially teachers, will take on part-time work.

42. Ibid., 127–43. As Schnall notes, the statistic that teachers are among the most likely to take on supplementary jobs corresponds with the fact that most halakhic discussion around multiple employment has concerned teachers. There has been a general halakhic tendency to prohibit teachers from working after hours.

43. The definition of "full time," of course, changes according to the time and place. The Rabbis understand the biblical definition of "full time" to be dawn to dusk, though by talmudic times, the workday appears to be shorter than this (*Bava Metzia* 83a). In America, we can define full time as approximately forty hours per week, with an appropriate number of sick days and vacation days. In other countries, this definition may be different.

44. Bureau of Labor Statistics, www.bls.gov.

45. *She'elot u'Teshuvot of the Tzitz Eliezer* 2:23.

46. *Mishneh Torah, Hilkhot Sanhedrin* 2:12.

47. Oral statement by Rav Kook, recorded in Rabbi Kazriel Tkhursh, "*Dinei Shevitot b'halakhah*," *Shanah b'Shanah*, 1963; Chaim David Halevy, *Aseh L'cha Rav* 5:23; Rafael Katznelbogen, *HaMa'ayan* Tishrei 5725: 9–14.

48. *Igg'rot Moshe, Choshen Mishpat* 58.

49. Quoted in Tzvi Yaron, *Mishnato shel HaRav Kook* (Jerusalem: Moreshet Press, 1986), 164.

6. They Shall Tremble No More: Housing and Homelessness

1. Millenial Housing Commission, *Meeting Our Nation's Housing Challenges* (Washington, DC: Millenial Housing Commission, 2002) www.mchc.gov.

2. Ibid., 11.

3. E.R.L. Gould, "The Housing Problem in Great Cities," *Quarterly Journal of Economics* 14 (May 1900): 378–389, quoted in Robert B. Fairbanks, "From Better Dwellings to Better Neighborhoods," in *From Tenements to the Taylor Homes: In Search of an Urban Housing Policy in Twentieth-Century*

America, John Bauman, Roger Biles, and Kristin Szylvian, eds.
(University Park, PA: Pennsylvania: Pennsylvania State, 2000), 25.

4. Gwendolyn Wright, *Building the Dream: A Social History of Housing in America* (Cambridge, MA: MIT, 1983), 255.

5. The experience of national homelessness certainly differs in some fundamental ways from that of personal homelessness. Judaism has not always viewed the experience of exile as an entirely negative state of being: according to the midrashic tradition, the *Shekhina*, the accessible manifestation of God's presence, followed the Jews into exile and cared for them there; *Chasidism* (a Jewish movement that originated in eighteenth-century Eastern Europe that emphasizes the ecstatic experience of religion)views exile as a means to enlightenment; and contemporary Jewish life in America shares little with the diasporic experience described by the Lamentations passage.

6. John Hagedorn, "Variations in Urban Homicide: Chicago, New York City and Global Urban Policy" (Paper presented at the University of Illinois at Chicago Great Cities Institute, Chicago, June 2004).

7. See, for example, Yvonne Rafferty and Marybeth Shinn, "The Impact of Homelessness on Children," *American Psychologist* 46, no. 11 (November 1991): 1170–1179, or Ellen Hart-Shegos, "Homelessness and Its Effects on Children" (Minneapolis: Family Housing Fund, 1999).

8. The actual value of 200 *zuzim* in the Mishnaic period is not known. Talmudic commentators and codifiers of Jewish law disagree about the purchasing power of this sum. Moshe ben Simeon Margoliot (P'nai Moshe) explains that 200 *zuzim* is the value of food and clothing for an entire year (on *Yerushalmi, Pe'ah* 8:7 [20d]). Rabbi Yitzchak ben Rabbi Moshe of Vienna (Or Zarua) suggests that this amount also includes food for a man's wife, dishes, shoes, and other necessities (*Hilkhot Tzedakah* 14; cf. *Teshuvot haRashba* I: 572). For more on the question of a poverty line, see Jill Jacobs, "Toward a Halakhic Definition of Poverty," *Conservative Judaism* 57:1 (Fall 2004): 3–20. See also Daniel Sperber, *Roman Palestine 200–400: Money and Prices* (Ramat-Gen, Israel: Bar-Ilan, 1974).

9. See, for example Talmud, *Bava Batra* 110a, in which at least one opinion argues that it is better to earn money from work involving idol worship than to take *tzedakah*, or *Tur* and *Shulchan Arukh, Yoreh De'ah* 155:1, which recommend accepting unpleasant work (this may also be a reference to idol worship) rather than depend on *tzedakah*.

10. *Midrash Aggadah* to Deuteronomy 15.

11. See, for example, David Novak, *Covenantal Rights: A Study in Jewish Political Theory* (Princeton, NJ: Princeton University, 2000).

12. Joint Center for Housing Studies of Harvard University, *The State of the Nation's Housing* (Cambridge, MA: Harvard, 2007).

13. Christine Hauser, "Brooklyn Boy, 5, Falls 10 Stories to His Death after Public Housing Elevator Stalls," *New York Times*, August 19, 2008.

14. Deuteronomy 6:4–9, 11:13–21; Numbers 15:37–41.

15. Mishnah, *Sukkah* 1:1 records a disagreement between two academies, Beit Hillel and Beit Shammai, about the validity of an "old *sukkah*," defined as one built more than thirty days before Sukkot. Beit Hillel permits this *sukkah*, while Beit Shammai disqualifies it. After reporting this disagreement, the Mishnah comments that "if it was built for the purpose of Sukkot, even if it was built at the beginning of the year, it is acceptable." Commentators disagree about whether to interpret this final statement only as a qualification on Beit Shammai's restriction (Rashi on Talmud, *Sukkah* 9a) or as also referring to the situation under which, according to Beit Hillel, a person would not have to "do something new" to the *sukkah* in order to make it suitable for use on Sukkot (Tosefot, *loc. cit.*). The Ritba reads this *mishnah* as saying, "What is an old *sukkah* such that even Beit Hillel would agree with Beit Shammai that it is invalid? One made more than thirty days before Sukkot and not for the purpose of Sukkot" (*Chiddushei HaRitba* 2a). According to the Ritba, Beit Hillel and Beit Shammai disagree only about whether someone who builds a *sukkah* within thirty days before Sukkot must specify that the *sukkah* is being built for the holiday. All of these readings, but particularly the interpretations that apply the final line of the *mishnah* to the opinions of both Beit Hillel and Beit Shammai, assume the importance of intentionality in determining the appropriate use of a dwelling.

16. Talmud, *Shabbat* 6a. There are also two other types of space: the *karmalit* and *makom patur*, both of which exhibit some characteristics of public space and some characteristics of private space. These two secondary categories are not essential to our discussion.

17. Ibid., and *Shulchan Arukh, Orach Chayim* 345.

18. *Tur, Orach Chayim* 345, and *Mishneh B'rurah* 345:22.

19. Rashi on Talmud, *Eruvin* 59a; cf. *Chidushei HaRamban* on *Shabbat* 57a. The text refers to *shishim ribo*, or sixty ten-thousands. This number is presumably not intended literally.

20. It is interesting to note the extent to which public space, in contemporary America, is becoming increasingly less public. The prevalence of gated communities, the creation of locked public parks, and the detentions of people who seem out of place in a particular neighborhood all point to a growing desire, among some people, to claim their entire sphere of activity as private space and thus to seclude themselves from "intrusions" by people who do not look like them.

21. Robert F. Worth, "Landlord Is Found Guilty in Tenant's Murder," *New York Times*, March 9, 2002, http://query.nytimes.com/gst/fullpage. html?res=9400E7D61130F93AA35750C0A9649C8B63.

22. Jane H. Li, "Landlord Denies Wrongdoing in Disappearance of Tenants," *New York Times*, December 20, 1997, http://query.nytimes.com/ gst/fullpage.html?res=9D07E2DE163EF933A15751C1A961958260.

23. Rambam, *Mishneh Torah, Hilkhot S'khirut* 6:3; cf. Talmud, *Bava Metzia* 101b–102a.

24. See, for example, the Rosh, *Bava Metzia* 8:27.

25. See, for example, R. Aharon ben R. Jacob ha-Cohen, *Orchot Chayyim, Hilkhot Ma'akeh*, and Rabbenu Yerucham, *Tol'dot Adam v'Chavah* 21:5 179b.

26. Rabbi Meir ben Rabbi Yekutiel HaKohen, *Hagahot Maimoniyot, Hilkhot Rotzeah* 11:1.

27. *She'elot u'Teshuvot Benyamin Ze'ev* 301, *Dibbur haMatchil, "V'hineni chozer."*

28. Hillel Levine and Lawrence Harmon, *The Death of an American Jewish Community: A Tragedy of Good Intentions* (New York: Simon and Schuster, 1992), 184–193.

29. *Mishneh Torah, Hilkhot S'khirut* 6:7.

30. Susan Saulny, "At Housing Project Both Fear and Renewal," *New York Times*, March 18, 2007.

31. *Shulchan Arukh, Choshen Mishpat* 312:7.

32. Ibid., 312:1.

33. Talmud, *Bava Metzia* 101b, and *Shulchan Arukh, Choshen Mishpat* 312:11–12.

34. *Piskei Din—Yerushalayim, Dinei Mamonot u'Virurei Yahadut* 3, p. 144.

35. Homelessness in the United States and the Human Right to Housing" (Washington, DC: National Law Center on Homelessness and Poverty, 2004).

36. Danilo Pelletiere et al., *Out of Reach 2007–2008*, http://nlihc.org/oor/ oor2008/.

37. Kenneth Jackson, *Crabgrass Frontier* (New York: Oxford, 1985), 206.

38. *American Metropolis*, 4, quoted in Peter Dreier, John Mullenkupf, and Todd Swanstrom, *Place Matters: Metropolitics for the Twenty-first Century* (Lawrence: University of Kansas, 2001), 109. Robert Fishman, "The American Metropolis at Century's End: Past and Future Influences," *Housing Policy Debate*, no. 1 (2000):199-213.

39. Wright, *Building the Dream*, 232–234.

40. Herbert Gans, *The Urban Villagers: Group and Class in the Life of Italian-Americans* (New York: Free Press of Glencoe, 1962), 21.

41. Raymond A. Mohl, "Planned Destruction: The Interstates and Central City Housing," in Bauman et al., *From Tenements to the Taylor Homes*, 227–229.

42. Dreier, *Place Matters*, 119.

43. Jackson, *Crabgrass Frontier*, 197.

44. Wright, *Building the Dream*, 247.

45. Cushing Dolbeare, *Changing Priorities* (Washington, DC: National Low Income Housing Coalition, 2004), 4.

46. Ibid., 5–8. See also Thomas Hanchett, "The Other 'Subsidized Housing': Federal Aid to Suburbanization, 1940s to 1960s," in Bauman et al., *From Tenements to the Taylor Homes*, 171. The second wealthiest fifth of the population, with average incomes of $69,384, receives 24.1 percent of housing subsidies; the middle fifth, with average incomes of $44,111, receives 11.8 percent of subsidies; and the second poorest fifth, with average incomes of $26,177, receives 7.1 percent of subsidies.

47. Arnold Hirsch, *Making the Second Ghetto: Race and Housing in Chicago 1940–1960* (Chicago: University of Chicago, 1998), 212–275.

48. E. Jay Howenstine, "The New Housing Shortage: The Problem of Housing Affordability in the United States," in *The New Housing Shortage: Housing Affordability in Europe and the USA*, Graham Hallett, ed. (New York: Van Nostrand Reinhold, 1993), 8.

49. *Vayikra Rabbah* 27:1; cf. *Pesikta d'Rav Kahana* 9:1.

7. I Will Remove Illness from Within Your Midst: The Provision of Health Care

1. For discussions of competing priorities, see Laurie Zoloth, *Health Care and the Ethics of Encounter: A Jewish Discussion of Social Justice* (Chapel Hill: University of North Carolina, 1999).

2. For the most comprehensive discussion of this issue, see Yair Lorberbaum, *Tzelem Elohim* (Jerusalem: Schocken, 2004).

3. Mishnah, *Sanhedrin* 6:5. Most printed editions of the Mishnah insert the word *kiv'y'khol* (as if) before God's words here. This addition may be an attempt to soften the seemingly radical notion that God physically suffers when human beings do.

4. Max Kadushin, *The Rabbinic Mind* (New York: Bloch, 1952).

5. Comment to Mishnah, *N'darim* 4.

6. See, for example, Talmud, *Taanit* 2a, and *B'reishit Rabbah* 73:4.

7. Comment to Exodus 21:19.

8. *Treatise on Asthma*, Fred Rosner, trans. (Haifa, Israel: Rambam Research Institute, 1994), 118.

9. *Hilkhot Rotzeach Ush'mirat Hanefesh* ch. 11.

10. *Igg'rot Mosheh Even ha'Ezer* 4:10.

11. Comment to Leviticus 26:11.

12. *Shakh* on *Yoreh De'ah* 336:1

13. Ramban, *Kitvei Ha'adam* in *Kitvei Rabbenu Moshe ben Nachman* (Jerusalem, Mossad haRav Kook, 1964), 44–45.

14. Comment to *B'khorot* 29a.

15. Yitzchak Zilberstein, "S'khar haRofeh b'halakhah," *Assia* 21 (1978): 29.

16. Rosh on *Bava Kamma* 85, *Siman* 1.

17. Ran, *She'elot uteshuvot* 1, *Dibbur hamatchil* "V'haben hayoresh."

18. Arthur Aufses Jr. and Barbara Niss, *The House of Noble Deeds: The Mount Sinai Hospital 1882–2002* (New York: NYU, 2002), 1 and 20.

19. Quoted in Dorothy Levenson, *Montefiore: The Hospital as Social Instrument 1884–1984* (New York: Farrar, Straus & Giroux, 1984), 20.

20. Ibid.

21. Alan M. Kraut and Deborah A. Kraut, *Covenant of Care: Newark Beth Israel and the Jewish Hospital in America* (New Brunswick, NJ: Rutgers, 2007), 5.

22. See, for example, B. D. Smedley, A. Y. Stith, and A. R. Nelson, eds., *Unequal Treatment: Confronting Racial and Ethnic Disparities in Health Care* (Washington, DC: National Academies Press, 2003).

23. Ibid., 119.

24. Aufses Jr. and Niss, *This House of Noble Deeds*, 19.

25. Rabbi Shlomo Goren, "Sh'vitat haRofeh L'or Ha'halakhah," *Assia* 21 (1978): 40.

26. *Chaim David Halevy, Aseh L'cha Rav* 7:70.

27. Jack Hadley and John Holahan, *The Cost of Care for the Uninsured: What Do We Spend, Who Pays, and What Would Full Coverage Add to Medical Spending* (Menlo Park, CA: Kaiser Commission on Medicaid and the Uninsured, 2004); see also Institute of Medicine, *Hidden Costs, Value Lost: Uninsurance in America* (Washington, DC: National Academies Press, 2003).

28. Jonah Gerondi, *Sefer haYirah Dibbur haMatchil, "Hishamer Mil'tzaer."*

8. The City and the Garden: Environmental Sustainability for the Twenty-first Century

1. See, for example, Julian Agyeman, Robert D. Bullard, and Bob Evans, eds., *Just Sustainabilities: Development in an Unequal World* (Cambridge, MA: MIT, 2003); Agyeman, *Sustainable Communities and the Challenge of Environmental Justice* (New York: NYU, 2005); and Michael Jacobs, "Sustainable Development as a Contested Concept," in Andrew Dobson, ed., *Fairness and Futurity: Essays on Environmental Sustainability and Social Justice* (Oxford: Oxford University Press, 1999), 21–46.

2. The classic statement of this position is Lynn White's essay, "The Historical Roots of Our Ecological Crisis," in which White writes: "In antiquity every tree, every spring, every stream, every hill had its own *genius loci*, its guardian spirit. These spirits were accessible to men, but were very unlike men; centaurs, fauns, and mermaids show their ambivalence. Before one cut a tree, mined a mountain, or dammed a brook, it was important to placate the spirit in charge of that particular situation, and to keep it placated. By destroying pagan animism, Christianity made it possible to exploit nature in a mood of indifference to the feelings of natural objects" (*Science* 155:3767 [1967]: 1203–1207).

3. See, for example Neal Loevinger, "(Mis)Reading Genesis: A Response to Environmental Critiques of Judaism," in *Ecology and the Jewish Spirit*, Ellen Bernstein, ed. (Woodstock, VT: Jewish Lights, 1998), 32–40; Tikva Frymer-Kensky, "Ecology in a Biblical Perspective," in *Torah of the Earth*, Arthur Waskow, ed. (Woodstock, VT: Jewish Lights, 2000), 55–69; and Calvin DeWitt, "Christian Environmental Stewardship: Preparing the Way for Action," in *Perspectives on Science and Christian Faith* 46 (1994): 80–89.

4. Rambam, *Mishneh Torah, Hilkhot Sh'khenim* 6:12.

5. *Bava Batra* 25a, and Rashi on *Bava Batra* 25a.

6. There is also a category of actions considered *p'sik reisha d'lo nicha lei*—activities whose consequences are not desirable, and that are therefore generally not permitted on Shabbat. In general, the issues that we are considering here are ones in which the consequence of a person's action are desirable to him or her—for example, letting your waste water drip onto a neighbor's yard means that this water is not dripping onto your own yard; placing an oven such that the smoke will seep into a neighbor's apartment results in a reduction in the amount of smoke in your own apartment.

7. Talmud, *Bava Batra* 8a; Rambam, *Mishneh Torah, Hilkhot Sh'khenim* 6:1.

8. See, for example, Joni Adamson and Rachel Stein, *The Environmental Justice Reader* (Tucson: University of Arizona, 2002) for descriptions of environmental justice battles in Memphis, Alaska, and elsewhere.

9. Deuteronomy 23:13–14, and Rambam, *Mishneh Torah, Hilkhot Melakhim* 6:14–15.

10. For a history of New York City's waste disposal policies, see Benjamin Miller, *Fat of the Land* (New York: Four Walls Eight Windows, 2000).

9. When Your Brother Is Flogged: Crime, Punishment, and Rehabilitation

1. Pew Center on the States, *One in 100: Behind Bars in America, 2008* (Washington, DC: Pew Charitable Trust, 2008). The Pew report also shows that state spending on prisons tops $49 billion, with five states spending more on prisons than on higher education. In contrast, the twenty-six European nations with the highest rates of incarceration have a total population of 802.4 million people (compared to the total American population of 299.4 million), but a collective prison population of just over 1.8 million.

2. Bruce Western, *Punishment and Inequality in America* (New York: Russell Sage Foundation, 2006), 34–51.

3. Marie Gottschalk, *The Prison and the Gallows: The Politics of Mass Incarceration in America* (New York: Cambridge University Press, 2006), 25.

4. Western, *Punishment and Equality*, 3451, and Gottschalk, *The Prison and the Gallows*, 18–76.

5. Jamie Fellner, *Targeting Blacks: Drug Law Enforcement and Race in the United States* (New York: Human Rights Watch, May 2008).

6. Bureau of Justice Statistics, www.ojp.usdoj.gov/bjs/cp.htm.

7. See Beth Berkowitz, *Execution and Invention: Death Penalty Discourse in Early Rabbinic and Christian Cultures* (New York: Oxford University Press, 2006) for a comprehensive overview of capital punishment in the Talmud, as well as of the contemporary debate about the Jewish view of capital punishment.

8. Jonathan P. Caulkins and Sara Chandler, "Long-Run Trends in Incarceration of Drug Offenders in the United States," *Crime & Delinquency* 52:4 (2006): 619–641.

9. Ryan S. King and Marc Mauer, *Distorted Priorities: Drug Offenders in State Prisons* (Washington, DC: The Sentencing Project, September 2002), 2–7.

10. According to Jeremy Travis, about three-quarters of state prisoners report significant alcohol or drug abuse. At least 16 percent have mental illness, about 3 percent carry the HIV virus, 18 percent are infected with hepatitis C, and 7 percent are infected with tuberculosis. Travis, *But They All Come Back: Facing the Challenges of Prisoner Reentry* (Washington, DC: Urban Institute, 2005), 185–217.

11. See, for example, the National Institute of Health's pages at www.drugabuse.gov.

12. See, for example, Todd R. Clear, *Imprisoning Communities: How Mass Incarceration Makes Disadvantaged Neighborhoods Worse* (New York: Oxford, 2007).

13. See Berkowitz, *Execution and Invention*, ch. 2, "Reading Execution: A Century of Scholarship on the Ancient Jewish Death Penalty" for an overview of the contemporary discourse on capital punishment.

14. *Mishneh Torah, Hilkhot Sanhedrin* 2:3.

15. See, for example, Sasha Abramsky, *American Furies: Crime, Punishment, and Vengeance in the Age of Mass Imprisonment* (Boston: Beacon Press, 2007) for a glimpse into the conditions of some U.S. prisons.

16. The biblical punishment of "an eye for an eye; a tooth for a tooth" seems clear in the Torah: a person who takes another person's eye loses his or her own eye, and so forth. The Rabbis, however, take this text much less literally, and interpret the biblical text as mandating monetary compensation for injury. See, for example, Talmud, *Bava Kamma* 83b.

17. Jeremiah 37:11–21; I Kings 22:27; 2 Chronicles 16:10.

18. Genesis 39–41; Judges 16:21.

19. Talmud, *Sanhedrin* 81b. The word *kippah* literally means "dome"; elsewhere in the Talmud, it also refers to the small hat worn by the high priest in the Temple (*Chullin* 138a). Today, it has come to mean the skullcap that some Jews wear either throughout daily life or just in the synagogue and other ritual spaces.

20. See, for example, Rabbi Shmuel Eliezer Edels (Maharasha) on *Sanhedrin* 81b, and Rambam, *Mishneh Torah, Hilkhot Sanhedrin* 18:5.

21. *Mishneh Torah, Hilkhot Rotzea'ch v'Shmirat Hanefesh* 2:5.

22. See, for example, *Mishneh Torah, Hilkhot Sanhedrin* 14:13.

23. Menachem Elon, "*HaMa'aser b'Mishpat ha'Ivri*" in *Sefer Yovel l'Finchas Rozen*, Chaim Cohen, ed. (Jerusalem: Hebrew University Student Union, 1962), 171–201, and Simcha Assaf, *Ha'Onashim Acharei Chatimat haTalmud* (Jerusalem: Sifriyah Mishpatit, 1922).

24. See, for example, Isaac ben Sheshet Perfet (Rivash), *She'elot u'Teshuvot* 251, and Judah ben Asher *Zichron Yehudah* 79.

25. Isaac Jacob Weiss, *Minchat Yitzchak* 2:82.

26. *Piskei Uziel b'She'elot Hazman, Siman* 30.

27. Meshulam Rath, *Kol Mevaser* 1:83.

28. U.S. Department of Justice, Bureau of Justice Statistics 2007, http://www.ojp.usdoj.gov/bjs/prisons.htm.

29. Judah ben Asher, *Zichron Yehudah, Siman* 79.

30. Western, *Punishment and Inequality*, 172–174, and Abramsky, *American Furies*, 43–49.

31. *Mishneh Torah, Hilkhot Teshuvah* 5:1–4.

32. *Pesikta d'Rav Kahana* 24:2.

33. *Bava Metzia* 84a.

34. *B'rakhot* 10a.

35. Talmud, *Avodah Zarah* 18a.

36. Talmud, *Bava Kamma* 94b.

37. *She'elot v'teshuvot haRitba* 159.

38. *She'elot v'teshuvot haRashba* 5:138.

39. *Rambam, Hilkhot Teshuvah* 2:4.

40. *Machzor Vitry* 125. Traditionally, the *kohanim* perform this ritual of lifting the hands to bless the people (often called *"duchening"*) on Passover, Shavuot, Sukkot, Rosh Hashanah, and Yom Kippur in the Diaspora; every Shabbat in Israel; and every day in Jerusalem. This ceremony is meant as a reminder of the blessings that the

kohanim would give to the people when the Temple stood in Jerusalem.

41. *Sanhedrin* 19b.

42. For a full discussion of punishment and rehabilitation in Jewish law, see Nachum Rackover, *Rehabilitation of Criminals in Jewish Law* (Jerusalem: Ministry of Justice 2007) (Hebrew); Aharon Shemesh, *Punishments and Sins* (Jerusalem: Magnes, 2003) (Hebrew); Mordechai Frishtik, *Punishment and Rehabilitation in Judaism* (Jerusalem: Sanhedrin Institute, 1986) (Hebrew).

43. The Sentencing Project, "Felony Disenfranchisement in the United States," March 2008. (www.sentencingproject.org).

44. Travis, chapter 745. Legal Action Center, "After Prison: Roadblocks to Re-entry," 2004. (www.lac.org).

Conclusion: Judaism in the Public Sphere

1. Abraham Joshua Heschel, "What We Might Do Together," in *Moral Grandeur and Spiritual Audacity*, Susannah Heschel, ed. (Farrar, Straus and Giroux: 1996), 298. Emphasis Heschel's.

2. Judah Leib Gordon, "Awake my People," quoted in Michael Stanislawski, *For Whom Do I Toil: Judah Leib Gordon and the Crisis of Russian Jewry* (New York: Oxford, 1988), 50.

GLOSSARY

aggadah. Stories, narrative. Generally refers to the nonlegal portions of Jewish text. The stories and aphorisms of the Talmud are considered to be *aggadah*, as is *midrash* that is primarily narrative.

bal tashchit. Prohibition against wanton destruction, based in the biblical command not to destroy trees when going to war against a city (Deut. 20:19).

beit din. Court of law composed of at least three members.

beit midrash. Study hall.

Caro, Joseph (Spain/Tzfat, 1488–1575). Legal scholar and mystic, best known as the author of the *Shulchan Arukh*, a major code of Jewish law.

Fair Labor Standards Act. A 1938 law that established the federal minimum wage, set the workweek at forty hours, prohibited "oppressive child labor," and instituted overtime pay for those who work more than forty hours a week.

fair market rent. Estimate of the cost of rent in individual metropolitan areas, determined each year by the U.S. Department of Housing and Urban Development (HUD).

Federal Housing Administration. U.S. department created through the National Housing Act of 1934; intended to create a home financing system and to improve housing standards. FHA has now been absorbed into the U.S. Department of Housing and Urban Development (HUD).

Feinstein, Moshe (Lithuania/United States, 1885–1986). One of the most important legal authorities of the twentieth century. Feinstein is especially known for tackling topics such as labor and medical ethics.

Gemara. The second layer of the Talmud. (The first layer is the Mishnah.) The Gemara consists of interpretations of and debates about the text of the Mishnah, as well as stories, aphorisms, and folk wisdom.

get. A writ of divorce that a husband delivers to his wife, either in person or through an emissary.

halakhah. The body of Jewish law. The term comes from the Hebrew verb meaning "to go" or "to walk," and therefore connotes "the way to go."

HaLevy, Chaim David (1924–1998). The Sephardic chief rabbi of Tel Aviv from 1973 until his death. He wrote extensively on Jewish law

247

and issued many legal decisions, many of which dealt with issues specific to the modern world and to the state of Israel.

housing wage. The amount of money a person needs to earn per hour in order to keep housing costs at one-third of his or her income.

just sustainability. The attempt to distribute natural resources and environmental burdens equitably, while also creating an ecosystem that will be sustainable for the long term.

ketubah. Wedding contract that spells out what each party brings into the marriage. The traditional *ketubah* guarantees that the woman will receive a certain amount of money in the case of divorce or death. In modern times, many couples have created more personal and egalitarian *ketubot* that address issues in addition to money, and that stipulate obligations in either direction.

Kohen. A descendent of the priestly class. In the times of the Temple, the *kohanim* performed most ritual functions there.

kupah. Fund for the poor.

leket. Grain that falls to the ground as it is picked. The Torah mandates leaving this grain for the poor to collect.

Levi. Member of a tribe entrusted with special duties in the Temple.

ma'akeh. A guardrail built around the roof of a house to prevent accidental falls.

mezuzah. A scroll containing passages from Deuteronomy, that is hung on each door of a home in accordance with the command "to inscribe these words on your doorposts (*mezuzot*)" (Deut. 6:9).

midrash. Rabbinic interpretations and expansions on the biblical text. There are many volumes of *midrash*, which are broadly divided into two categories: *midrash aggadah* (primarily narrative material) and *midrash halakhah* (primarily legal material).

minhag. Custom. In some cases, *minhag* can affect or even overturn a legal principle.

minimum wage. The federal or state minimum that an employer must pay most classes of workers. The federal minimum wage is set by Congress.

Mishnah. The first layer of the Talmud. The Mishnah was codified around 200 CE, and consists primarily of case law and short statements of law with little discussion.

Mishneh Torah. An influential code of Jewish law composed by Moses Maimonides (Rambam) in the twelfth century. The *Mishneh Torah* distills talmudic law into an easy-to-follow and easy-to-read format aimed at making *halakhah* accessible to the layperson.

mitzvah. Commandment.

Mussar. A nineteenth-century Jewish movement focused on ethics, morality, and self-improvement. The word *mussar* can also simply mean "ethics."

pe'ah. The corners of the field, which are to be left for the poor.

Rabbi Moshe ben Maimon (Maimonides; Spain/Egypt, 1135–1204). One of the most important philosophers and legal thinkers of Jewish history. His most influential works were the *Mishneh Torah,* a code of Jewish law; and *Moreh Nevukhim* (*Guide of the Perplexed*), an attempt to reconcile Aristotelian philosophy with Judaism; and his commentary on the Mishnah. Rambam was also a physician who wrote a number of medical manuals.

Ramban (Rabbi Moshe ben Nachman; Spain, 1194–1270). An influential Jewish thinker best known for his biblical commentary, which incorporates mysticism as well as reference to *midrash* and to grammatical issues.

Rashi (Rabbi Shlomo Yitzchaki; France, 1040–1105). Perhaps the best-known commentator on the Bible and Talmud. In both commentaries, he focuses on the basic meaning of the text, while also bringing significant midrashic material into his biblical commentary.

Rema (Moshe Isserles; Poland, 1520–1572). Isserles composed two major commentaries on Jewish law: the *Mapah,* a gloss on the *Shulchan Arukh* in which he notes Ashkenazi (Eastern European) traditions, and the *Darkhei Moshe,* a commentary on the *Tur.*

shikh'cha. Grain forgotten in the field during the harvest. The Torah mandates leaving this grain for the poor to collect.

sh'mitah. The seventh year, during which debts are forgiven and land is allowed to be left fallow. The laws of *sh'mitah* apply only in the land of Israel.

Shulchan Arukh. A sixteenth-century code of law written by Joseph Caro. The *Shulchan Arukh* is widely considered the most authoritative Jewish law code.

sukkah. A temporary structure in which Jews traditionally eat and sleep during the fall holiday of Sukkot. This structure represents both the huts in which farmers would live during the harvest and the temporary dwellings in which the Israelites are said to have lived on their journey from slavery to freedom.

Talmud. The basic document of Jewish oral law. The Talmud consists of the Mishnah, a basic statement of case law; and the Gemara, discussions and expansions on the Mishnah. In general, the term "Talmud" refers to the Babylonian Talmud (*Talmud Bavli*), codified in Babylonia sometime between 500 and 700 CE. There is also a second version of the Talmud, known as the Palestinian or Jerusalem Talmud (*Talmud Yerushalmi*), which was codified in the land of Israel in the fourth or fifth century CE. The two Talmuds rely on the same Mishnah; in general, the *Yerushalmi* is shorter and less complete than the *Bavli*, and the *Bavli* is considered more authoritative.

tamchui. Early type of soup kitchen where the poor could receive food each day.

Tanakh. The Bible. Consists of Torah, *N'vi'im* (Prophets), and *K'tuvim* (Writings).

teshuvah. Literally "return" or "answer." This term can refer either to repentance (a return of your self) or to a legal opinion (an answer).

tikkun olam. Repairing or fixing the world. See Chapter 2 for a discussion of the development and various meanings of this term.

Torah. The first five books of the Bible (Genesis, Exodus, Leviticus, Numbers, Deuteronomy). More generally, "Torah" is often used to refer to the whole body of Jewish learning.

Tosefta. Early rabbinic text, possibly written down around the second century CE; it has a close relationship with the Mishnah.

Tur. Popular name for *Arba'ah Turim*, a legal code written by Rabbi Jacob ben Asher in the fourteenth century.

tzedakah. Gifts to the poor; derived from the word *tzedek* (justice).

tzedek. Justice. See Chapter 2 for a discussion of the development and various meanings of this term.

Uziel, Ben-Tzion Meir Chai (Israel, 1880–1953). Served as the Sephardic chief rabbi of Palestine, then Israel, from 1939 to 1954. His legal writings, most of which are collected in a work called *Mishpetei Uziel*, often pay attention to issues relating to modern life in the state of Israel.

yovel. Jubilee year, mandated by the Torah to be observed every fifty years. During this year, land returns to its original owner, slaves go free, and debts are forgiven.

Waldenberg, Eliezer (Israel, 1915–2006). A leader of the Supreme Rabbinical Court in Jerusalem and the rabbi of Shaare Zedek Hospital. He is best known for his legal writings on medical issues, as well as for his controversial positions on issues such as transsexuality and unions. He is often called the Tzitz Eliezer after the name of his collection of legal opinions.

SUGGESTIONS FOR FURTHER READING

Bauman, John F., Roger Biles, and Kristin M. Szylvian, eds. *From Tenements to the Taylor Homes: In Search of an Urban Housing Policy in Twentieth-Century America*. University Park, PA: Pennsylvania State University Press, 2000.

Dorff, Elliot N. *The Way Into Tikkun Olam (Repairing the World)*. Woodstock, VT: Jewish Lights, 2007.

Dreier, Peter, John Mollenkopf, and Todd Swanstrom. *Place Matters: Metropolitics for the Twenty-first Century*, Second Edition. Lawrence, KS: University Press of Kansas, 2005.

Heschel, Abraham Joshua. Susannah Heschel, ed. *Moral Grandeur and Spiritual Audacity*. New York: Farrar, Straus and Giroux, 1997.

Heschel, Abraham Joshua. *The Prophets*. New York: Harper Perennial Modern Classics, 2001.

Jones, Robert P. *Progressive & Religious: How Christian, Jewish, Muslim, and Buddhist Leaders are Moving Beyond the Culture Wars and Transforming American Public Life*. New York: Rowman & Littlefield Publishers, 2008.

Nussbaum, Martha C. *Poetic Justice: The Literary Imagination and Public Life*. Boston, MA: Beacon Press, 1997.

Pollin, Robert, Mark Brenner, Jeannette Wicks-Lim, and Stephanie Luce. *A Measure of Fairness: The Economics of Living Wages and Minimum Wages in the United States*. Ithaca, NY: ILR Press, 2008.

Rose, Or N., Jo Ellen Green Kaiser, and Margie Klein, eds. *Righteous Indignation: A Jewish Call for Justice*. Woodstock, VT: Jewish Lights, 2007.

Sacks, Jonathan. *To Heal a Fractured World: The Ethics of Responsibility*. New York: Schocken, 2007.

Schwarz, Sidney. *Judaism and Justice: The Jewish Passion to Repair the World*. Woodstock, VT: Jewish Lights, 2006.

Toulouse, Mark G. *God in Public: Four Ways American Christianity and Public Life Relate*. Louisville, KY: Westminster John Knox Press, 2006.

Walzer, Michael. *Exodus and Revolution*. New York: Basic Books, 1986.

Zoloth, Laurie. *Health Care and the Ethics of Encounter: A Jewish Discussion of Social Justice*. Chapel Hill, NC: University of North Carolina Press, 1999.

INDEX

Inspiration

Happiness and the Human Spirit: The Spirituality of Becoming the Best You Can Be *By Abraham J. Twerski, MD*
Shows you that true happiness is attainable once you stop looking outside yourself for the source.
6 x 9, 176 pp, Quality PB, 978-1-58023-404-7 **$16.99**; HC, 978-1-58023-343-9 **$19.99**

The Bridge to Forgiveness: Stories and Prayers for Finding God and Restoring Wholeness *By Rabbi Karyn D. Kedar*
Examines how forgiveness can be the bridge that connects us to wholeness and peace.
6 x 9, 176 pp, HC, 978-1-58023-324-8 **$19.99**

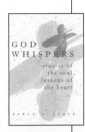

God's To-Do List: 103 Ways to Be an Angel and Do God's Work on Earth
By Dr. Ron Wolfson 6 x 9, 150 pp, Quality PB, 978-1-58023-301-9 **$16.99**

God in All Moments: Mystical & Practical Spiritual Wisdom from Hasidic Masters
Edited and translated by Or N. Rose with Ebn D. Leader
5½ x 8½, 192 pp, Quality PB, 978-1-58023-186-2 **$16.95**

Our Dance with God: Finding Prayer, Perspective and Meaning in the Stories of Our Lives *By Karyn D. Kedar* 6 x 9, 176 pp, Quality PB, 978-1-58023-202-9 **$16.99**
Also Available: **The Dance of the Dolphin** (HC edition of *Our Dance with God*)
6 x 9, 176 pp, HC, 978-1-58023-154-1 **$19.95**

The Empty Chair: Finding Hope and Joy—Timeless Wisdom from a Hasidic Master, Rebbe Nachman of Breslov *Adapted by Moshe Mykoff and the Breslov Research Institute*
4 x 6, 128 pp, 2-color text, Deluxe PB w/flaps, 978-1-879045-67-5 **$9.99**

The Gentle Weapon: Prayers for Everyday and Not-So-Everyday Moments—Timeless Wisdom from the Teachings of the Hasidic Master, Rebbe Nachman of Breslov *Adapted by Moshe Mykoff and S. C. Mizrahi, together with the Breslov Research Institute*
4 x 6, 144 pp, 2-color text, Deluxe PB w/flaps, 978-1-58023-022-3 **$9.99**

God Whispers: Stories of the Soul, Lessons of the Heart *By Karyn D. Kedar*
6 x 9, 176 pp, Quality PB, 978-1-58023-088-9 **$15.95**

Restful Reflections: Nighttime Inspiration to Calm the Soul, Based on Jewish Wisdom
By Rabbi Kerry M. Olitzky & Rabbi Lori Forman 4½ x 6½, 448 pp, Quality PB, 978-1-58023-091-9 **$15.95**

Sacred Intentions: Daily Inspiration to Strengthen the Spirit, Based on Jewish Wisdom
By Rabbi Kerry M. Olitzky and Rabbi Lori Forman 4½ x 6½, 448 pp, Quality PB, 978-1-58023-061-2 **$15.95**

Kabbalah/Mysticism

Awakening to Kabbalah: The Guiding Light of Spiritual Fulfillment
By Rav Michael Laitman, PhD 6 x 9, 192 pp, HC, 978-1-58023-264-7 **$21.99**

Seek My Face: A Jewish Mystical Theology *By Arthur Green*
6 x 9, 304 pp, Quality PB, 978-1-58023-130-5 **$19.95**

Zohar: Annotated & Explained *Translation and annotation by Daniel C. Matt; Foreword by Andrew Harvey* 5½ x 8½, 176 pp, Quality PB, 978-1-893361-51-5 **$15.99**
(A book from SkyLight Paths, Jewish Lights' sister imprint)

Ehyeh: A Kabbalah for Tomorrow
By Arthur Green 6 x 9, 224 pp, Quality PB, 978-1-58023-213-5 **$16.99**

The Flame of the Heart: Prayers of a Chasidic Mystic *By Reb Noson of Breslov. Translated by David Sears with the Breslov Research Institute* 5 x 7¼, 160 pp, Quality PB, 978-1-58023-246-3 **$15.99**

The Gift of Kabbalah: Discovering the Secrets of Heaven, Renewing Your Life on Earth
By Tamar Frankiel, PhD 6 x 9, 256 pp, Quality PB, 978-1-58023-141-1 **$16.95**
HC, 978-1-58023-108-4 **$21.95**

Kabbalah: A Brief Introduction for Christians
By Tamar Frankiel, PhD 5½ x 8½, 208 pp, Quality PB, 978-1-58023-303-3 **$16.99**

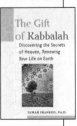

The Lost Princess and Other Kabbalistic Tales of Rebbe Nachman of Breslov
The Seven Beggars and Other Kabbalistic Tales of Rebbe Nachman of Breslov
Translated by Rabbi Aryeh Kaplan; Preface by Rabbi Chaim Kramer
Lost Princess: 6 x 9, 400 pp, Quality PB, 978-1-58023-217-3 **$18.99**
Seven Beggars: 6 x 9, 192 pp, Quality PB, 978-1-58023-250-0 **$16.99**

See also *The Way Into Jewish Mystical Tradition* in Spirituality / The Way Into... Series

Holidays/Holy Days

Rosh Hashanah Readings: Inspiration, Information and Contemplation
Yom Kippur Readings: Inspiration, Information and Contemplation
Edited by Rabbi Dov Peretz Elkins with Section Introductions from Arthur Green's These Are the Words
An extraordinary collection of readings, prayers and insights that enable the modern worshiper to enter into the spirit of the High Holy Days in a personal and powerful way, permitting the meaning of the Jewish New Year to enter the heart.
RHR: 6 x 9, 400 pp, HC, 978-1-58023-239-5 **$24.99**
YKR: 6 x 9, 368 pp, HC, 978-1-58023-271-5 **$24.99**

Jewish Holidays: A Brief Introduction for Christians
By Rabbi Kerry M. Olitzky and Rabbi Daniel Judson
5½ x 8½, 144 pp, Quality PB, 978-1-58023-302-6 **$16.99**

Reclaiming Judaism as a Spiritual Practice: Holy Days and Shabbat
By Rabbi Goldie Milgram
7 x 9, 272 pp, Quality PB, 978-1-58023-205-0 **$19.99**

7th Heaven: Celebrating Shabbat with Rebbe Nachman of Breslov
By Moshe Mykoff with the Breslov Research Institute
5⅛ x 8¼, 224 pp, Deluxe PB w/flaps, 978-1-58023-175-6 **$18.95**

Shabbat, 2nd Edition: The Family Guide to Preparing for and Celebrating the Sabbath
By Dr. Ron Wolfson 7 x 9, 320 pp, illus., Quality PB, 978-1-58023-164-0 **$19.99**

Hanukkah, 2nd Edition: The Family Guide to Spiritual Celebration
By Dr. Ron Wolfson. Edited by Joel Lurie Grishaver.
7 x 9, 240 pp, illus., Quality PB, 978-1-58023-122-0 **$18.95**

The Jewish Family Fun Book, 2nd Edition: Holiday Projects, Everyday Activities, and Travel Ideas with Jewish Themes *By Danielle Dardashti and Roni Sarig. Illus. by Avi Katz.*
6 x 9, 304 pp, 70+ b/w illus. & diagrams, Quality PB, 978-1-58023-333-0 **$18.99**

The Jewish Lights Book of Fun Classroom Activities: Simple and Seasonal Projects for Teachers and Students *By Danielle Dardashti and Roni Sarig*
6 x 9, 240 pp, Quality PB, 978-1-58023-206-7 **$19.99**

Passover

My People's Passover Haggadah
Traditional Texts, Modern Commentaries
Edited by Rabbi Lawrence A. Hoffman, PhD, and David Arnow, PhD
A diverse and exciting collection of commentaries on the traditional Passover Haggadah—in two volumes!
Vol. 1: 7 x 10, 304 pp, HC, 978-1-58023-354-5 **$24.99**
Vol. 2: 7 x 10, 320 pp, HC, 978-1-58023-346-0 **$24.99**

Leading the Passover Journey
The Seder's Meaning Revealed, the Haggadah's Story Retold
By Rabbi Nathan Laufer
Uncovers the hidden meaning of the Seder's rituals and customs.
6 x 9, 224 pp, Quality PB, 978-1-58023-399-6 **$18.99**; HC, 978-1-58023-211-1 **$24.99**

The Women's Passover Companion: Women's Reflections on the Festival of Freedom
Edited by Rabbi Sharon Cohen Anisfeld, Tara Mohr, and Catherine Spector
6 x 9, 352 pp, Quality PB, 978-1-58023-231-9 **$19.99**

The Women's Seder Sourcebook: Rituals & Readings for Use at the Passover Seder
Edited by Rabbi Sharon Cohen Anisfeld, Tara Mohr, and Catherine Spector
6 x 9, 384 pp, Quality PB, 978-1-58023-232-6 **$19.99**

Creating Lively Passover Seders: A Sourcebook of Engaging Tales, Texts & Activities
By David Arnow, PhD 7 x 9, 416 pp, Quality PB, 978-1-58023-184-8 **$24.99**

Passover, 2nd Edition: The Family Guide to Spiritual Celebration
By Dr. Ron Wolfson with Joel Lurie Grishaver 7 x 9, 352 pp, Quality PB, 978-1-58023-174-9 **$19.95**

Life Cycle
Marriage / Parenting / Family / Aging

The New Jewish Baby Album: Creating and Celebrating the Beginning of a Spiritual Life—A Jewish Lights Companion
By the Editors at Jewish Lights. Foreword by Anita Diamant. Preface by Rabbi Sandy Eisenberg Sasso.
A spiritual keepsake that will be treasured for generations. More than just a memory book, *shows you how—and why it's important*—to create a Jewish home and a Jewish life. 8 x 10, 64 pp, Deluxe Padded HC, Full-color illus., 978-1-58023-138-1 **$19.95**

The Jewish Pregnancy Book: A Resource for the Soul, Body & Mind during Pregnancy, Birth & the First Three Months
By Sandy Falk, MD, and Rabbi Daniel Judson, with Steven A. Rapp
Includes medical information, prayers and rituals for each stage of pregnancy, from a liberal Jewish perspective. 7 x 10, 208 pp, Quality PB, b/w photos, 978-1-58023-178-7 **$16.95**

Celebrating Your New Jewish Daughter: Creating Jewish Ways to Welcome Baby Girls into the Covenant—New and Traditional Ceremonies *By Debra Nussbaum Cohen; Foreword by Rabbi Sandy Eisenberg Sasso* 6 x 9, 272 pp, Quality PB, 978-1-58023-090-2 **$18.95**

The New Jewish Baby Book, 2nd Edition: Names, Ceremonies & Customs—A Guide for Today's Families *By Anita Diamant* 6 x 9, 336 pp, Quality PB, 978-1-58023-251-7 **$19.99**

Parenting as a Spiritual Journey: Deepening Ordinary and Extraordinary Events into Sacred Occasions *By Rabbi Nancy Fuchs-Kreimer* 6 x 9, 224 pp, Quality PB, 978-1-58023-016-2 **$16.95**

Parenting Jewish Teens: A Guide for the Perplexed
By Joanne Doades
Explores the questions and issues that shape the world in which today's Jewish teenagers live. 6 x 9, 200 pp, Quality PB, 978-1-58023-305-7 **$16.99**

Judaism for Two: A Spiritual Guide for Strengthening and Celebrating Your Loving Relationship *By Rabbi Nancy Fuchs-Kreimer and Rabbi Nancy H. Wiener; Foreword by Rabbi Elliot N. Dorff* Addresses the ways Jewish teachings can enhance and strengthen committed relationships. 6 x 9, 224 pp, Quality PB, 978-1-58023-254-8 **$16.99**

Embracing the Covenant: Converts to Judaism Talk About Why & How
By Rabbi Allan Berkowitz and Patti Moskovitz 6 x 9, 192 pp, Quality PB, 978-1-879045-50-7 **$16.95**

The Guide to Jewish Interfaith Family Life: An InterfaithFamily.com Handbook
Edited by Ronnie Friedland and Edmund Case 6 x 9, 384 pp, Quality PB, 978-1-58023-153-4 **$18.95**

Introducing My Faith and My Community
The Jewish Outreach Institute Guide for the Christian in a Jewish Interfaith Relationship
By Rabbi Kerry M. Olitzky 6 x 9, 176 pp, Quality PB, 978-1-58023-192-3 **$16.99**

Making a Successful Jewish Interfaith Marriage: The Jewish Outreach Institute Guide to Opportunities, Challenges and Resources *By Rabbi Kerry M. Olitzky with Joan Peterson Littman* 6 x 9, 176 pp, Quality PB, 978-1-58023-170-1 **$16.95**

The Creative Jewish Wedding Book, 2nd Edition: A Hands-On Guide to New & Old Traditions, Ceremonies & Celebrations *By Gabrielle Kaplan-Mayer* 9 x 9, 288 pp, b/w photos, Quality PB, 978-1-58023-398-9 **$19.99**

Divorce Is a Mitzvah: A Practical Guide to Finding Wholeness and Holiness When Your Marriage Dies *By Rabbi Perry Netter; Afterword by Rabbi Laura Geller.* 6 x 9, 224 pp, Quality PB, 978-1-58023-172-5 **$16.95**

A Heart of Wisdom: Making the Jewish Journey from Midlife through the Elder Years
Edited by Susan Berrin; Foreword by Harold Kushner 6 x 9, 384 pp, Quality PB, 978-1-58023-051-3 **$18.95**

So That Your Values Live On: Ethical Wills and How to Prepare Them
Edited by Jack Riemer and Nathaniel Stampfer 6 x 9, 272 pp, Quality PB, 978-1-879045-34-7 **$18.99**

Theology/Philosophy/The Way Into... Series

The Way Into... series offers an accessible and highly usable "guided tour" of the Jewish faith, people, history and beliefs—in total, an introduction to Judaism that will enable you to understand and interact with the sacred texts of the Jewish tradition. Each volume is written by a leading contemporary scholar and teacher, and explores one key aspect of Judaism. The Way Into... series enables all readers to achieve a real sense of Jewish cultural literacy through guided study.

The Way Into Encountering God in Judaism
By Rabbi Neil Gillman, PhD
For everyone who wants to understand how Jews have encountered God throughout history and today.
6 x 9, 240 pp, Quality PB, 978-1-58023-199-2 **$18.99**; HC, 978-1-58023-025-4 **$21.95**
Also Available: **The Jewish Approach to God:** A Brief Introduction for Christians
By Rabbi Neil Gillman, PhD
5½ x 8½, 192 pp, Quality PB, 978-1-58023-190-9 **$16.95**

The Way Into Jewish Mystical Tradition
By Rabbi Lawrence Kushner
Allows readers to interact directly with the sacred mystical text of the Jewish tradition. An accessible introduction to the concepts of Jewish mysticism, their religious and spiritual significance and how they relate to life today.
6 x 9, 224 pp, Quality PB, 978-1-58023-200-5 **$18.99**; HC, 978-1-58023-029-2 **$21.95**

The Way Into Jewish Prayer
By Rabbi Lawrence A. Hoffman, PhD
Opens the door to 3,000 years of Jewish prayer, making available all anyone needs to feel at home in the Jewish way of communicating with God.
6 x 9, 208 pp, Quality PB, 978-1-58023-201-2 **$18.99**

Also Available: **The Way Into Jewish Prayer Teacher's Guide**
By Rabbi Jennifer Ossakow Goldsmith
8½ x 11, 42 pp, Quality PB, 978-1-58023-345-3 **$8.99**
Visit our website to download a free copy.

The Way Into Judaism and the Environment
By Jeremy Benstein, PhD
Explores the ways in which Judaism contributes to contemporary social-environmental issues, the extent to which Judaism is part of the problem and how it can be part of the solution.
6 x 9, 288 pp, Quality PB, 978-1-58023-368-2 **$18.99**; HC, 978-1-58023-268-5 **$24.99**

The Way Into *Tikkun Olam* (Repairing the World)
By Rabbi Elliot N. Dorff, PhD
An accessible introduction to the Jewish concept of the individual's responsibility to care for others and repair the world.
6 x 9, 304 pp, Quality PB, 978-1-58023-328-6 **$18.99**; 320 pp, HC, 978-1-58023-269-2 **$24.99**

The Way Into Torah
By Rabbi Norman J. Cohen, PhD
Helps guide in the exploration of the origins and development of Torah, explains why it should be studied and how to do it.
6 x 9, 176 pp, Quality PB, 978-1-58023-198-5 **$16.99**

The Way Into the Varieties of Jewishness
By Sylvia Barack Fishman, PhD
Explores the religious and historical understanding of what it has meant to be Jewish from ancient times to the present controversy over "Who is a Jew?"
6 x 9, 288 pp, Quality PB, 978-1-58023-367-5 **$18.99**; HC, 978-1-58023-030-8 **$24.99**

Theology/Philosophy

A Touch of the Sacred: A Theologian's Informal Guide to Jewish Belief
By Dr. Eugene B. Borowitz and Frances W. Schwartz Explores the musings from the
leading theologian of liberal Judaism. 6 x 9, 256 pp, HC, 978-1-58023-337-8 **$21.99**

Talking about God: Exploring the Meaning of Religious Life with
Kierkegaard, Buber, Tillich and Heschel *By Daniel F. Polish, PhD*
Examines the meaning of the human religious experience with the greatest theolo-
gians of modern times. 6 x 9, 160 pp, HC, 978-1-59473-230-0 **$21.99**
(A book from SkyLight Paths, Jewish Lights' sister imprint)

Jews & Judaism in the 21st Century: Human Responsibility, the
Presence of God, and the Future of the Covenant *Edited by Rabbi Edward Feinstein;
Foreword by Paula E. Hyman* Five celebrated leaders in Judaism examine contemporary
Jewish life. 6 x 9, 192 pp, Quality PB, 978-1-58023-374-3 **$19.99**; HC, 978-1-58023-315-6 **$24.99**

Christians and Jews in Dialogue: Learning in the Presence of the Other
By Mary C. Boys and Sara S. Lee; Foreword by Dr. Dorothy Bass
6 x 9, 240 pp, Quality PB, 978-1-59473-254-6 **$18.99**; HC, 978-1-59473-144-0 **$21.99**
(A book from SkyLight Paths, Jewish Lights' sister imprint)

The Death of Death: Resurrection and Immortality in Jewish Thought
By Neil Gillman 6 x 9, 336 pp, Quality PB, 978-1-58023-081-0 **$18.95**

Ethics of the Sages: Pirke Avot—Annotated & Explained
Translation & Annotation by Rabbi Rami Shapiro
5½ x 8¼, 208 pp, Quality PB, 978-1-59473-207-2 **$16.99** *(A book from SkyLight Paths, Jewish Lights' sister imprint)*

Hasidic Tales: Annotated & Explained *By Rabbi Rami Shapiro; Foreword by Andrew Harvey*
5½ x 8½, 240 pp, Quality PB, 978-1-893361-86-7 **$16.95**
(A book from SkyLight Paths, Jewish Lights' sister imprint)

A Heart of Many Rooms: Celebrating the Many Voices within Judaism
By David Hartman 6 x 9, 352 pp, Quality PB, 978-1-58023-156-5 **$19.95**

The Hebrew Prophets: Selections Annotated & Explained
Translation & Annotation by Rabbi Rami Shapiro; Foreword by Zalman M. Schachter-Shalomi
5½ x 8¼, 224 pp, Quality PB, 978-1-59473-037-5 **$16.99** *(A book from SkyLight Paths, Jewish Lights' sister imprint)*

A Jewish Understanding of the New Testament
By Rabbi Samuel Sandmel; Preface by Rabbi David Sandmel
5½ x 8¼, 368 pp, Quality PB, 978-1-59473-048-1 **$19.99** *(A book from SkyLight Paths, Jewish Lights' sister imprint)*

Keeping Faith with the Psalms: Deepen Your Relationship with God Using the Book
of Psalms *By Daniel F. Polish* 6 x 9, 320 pp, Quality PB, 978-1-58023-300-2 **$18.99**

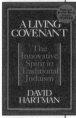

A Living Covenant: The Innovative Spirit in Traditional Judaism
By David Hartman 6 x 9, 368 pp, Quality PB, 978-1-58023-011-7 **$20.00**

Love and Terror in the God Encounter: The Theological Legacy of Rabbi Joseph
B. Soloveitchik *By David Hartman* 6 x 9, 240 pp, Quality PB, 978-1-58023-176-3 **$19.95**

The Personhood of God: Biblical Theology, Human Faith and the Divine Image
By Dr. Yochanan Muffs; Foreword by Dr. David Hartman
6 x 9, 240 pp, Quality PB, 978-1-58023-338-5 **$18.99**; HC, 978-1-58023-265-4 **$24.99**

Traces of God: Seeing God in Torah, History and Everyday Life *By Neil Gillman*
6 x 9, 240 pp, Quality PB, 978-1-58023-369-9 **$16.99**; HC, 978-1-58023-249-4 **$21.99**

We Jews and Jesus: Exploring Theological Differences for Mutual Understanding
By Rabbi Samuel Sandmel; Preface by Rabbi David Sandmel
6 x 9, 176 pp, Quality PB, 978-1-59473-208-9 **$16.99** *(A book from SkyLight Paths, Jewish Lights' sister imprint)*

Your Word Is Fire: The Hasidic Masters on Contemplative Prayer
Edited and translated by Arthur Green and Barry W. Holtz
6 x 9, 160 pp, Quality PB, 978-1-879045-25-5 **$15.95**

I Am Jewish
Personal Reflections Inspired by the Last Words of Daniel Pearl
Almost 150 Jews—both famous and not—from all walks of life, from all around
the world, write about many aspects of their Judaism.
Edited by Judea and Ruth Pearl 6 x 9, 304 pp, Deluxe PB w/flaps, 978-1-58023-259-3 **$18.99**
Download a free copy of the *I Am Jewish Teacher's Guide* at our website:
www.jewishlights.com

Spirituality

Journeys to a Jewish Life: Inspiring Stories from the Spiritual Journeys of American Jews *By Paula Amann*
Examines the soul treks of Jews lost and found. 6 x 9, 208 pp, HC, 978-1-58023-317-0 **$19.99**

The Adventures of Rabbi Harvey: A Graphic Novel of Jewish Wisdom and Wit in the Wild West *By Steve Sheinkin*
Jewish and American folktales combine in this witty and original graphic novel collection. Creatively retold and set on the western frontier of the 1870s.
6 x 9, 144 pp, Full-color illus., Quality PB, 978-1-58023-310-1 **$16.99**

Rabbi Harvey Rides Again
A Graphic Novel of Jewish Folktales Let Loose in the Wild West *By Steve Sheinkin*
6 x 9, 144 pp, Quality PB Original, Full-color illus., 978-1-58023-347-7 **$16.99**

Ethics of the Sages: *Pirke Avot*—Annotated & Explained
Translation and Annotation by Rabbi Rami Shapiro 5½ x 8½, 192 pp, Quality PB, 978-1-59473-207-2
$16.99 *(A book from SkyLight Paths, Jewish Lights' sister imprint)*

A Book of Life: Embracing Judaism as a Spiritual Practice
By Michael Strassfeld 6 x 9, 528 pp, Quality PB, 978-1-58023-247-0 **$19.99**

Meaning and Mitzvah: Daily Practices for Reclaiming Judaism through Prayer, God, Torah, Hebrew, Mitzvot and Peoplehood *By Rabbi Goldie Milgram*
7 x 9, 336 pp, Quality PB, 978-1-58023-256-2 **$19.99**

The Soul of the Story: Meetings with Remarkable People
By Rabbi David Zeller 6 x 9, 288 pp, HC, 978-1-58023-272-2 **$21.99**

Aleph-Bet Yoga: Embodying the Hebrew Letters for Physical and Spiritual Well-Being
By Steven A. Rapp. Foreword by Tamar Frankiel, PhD and Judy Greenfeld. Preface by Hart Lazer.
7 x 10, 128 pp, b/w photos, Quality PB, Layflat binding, 978-1-58023-162-6 **$16.95**

Does the Soul Survive? A Jewish Journey to Belief in Afterlife, Past Lives & Living with Purpose *By Rabbi Elie Kaplan Spitz; Foreword by Brian L. Weiss, MD*
6 x 9, 288 pp, Quality PB, 978-1-58023-165-7 **$16.99**

First Steps to a New Jewish Spirit: Reb Zalman's Guide to Recapturing the Intimacy & Ecstasy in Your Relationship with God *By Rabbi Zalman M. Schachter-Shalomi with Donald Gropman* 6 x 9, 144 pp, Quality PB, 978-1-58023-182-4 **$16.95**

God in Our Relationships: Spirituality between People from the Teachings of Martin Buber *By Rabbi Dennis S. Ross* 5½ x 8½, 160 pp, Quality PB, 978-1-58023-147-3 **$16.95**

Judaism, Physics and God: Searching for Sacred Metaphors in a Post-Einstein World
By Rabbi David W. Nelson 6 x 9, 368 pp, Quality PB, inc. reader's discussion guide, 978-1-58023-306-4 **$18.99**;
HC, 352 pp, 978-1-58023-252-4 **$24.99**

The Jewish Lights Spirituality Handbook: A Guide to Understanding, Exploring & Living a Spiritual Life *Edited by Stuart M. Matlins*
What exactly is "Jewish" about spirituality? How do I make it a part of my life? Fifty of today's foremost spiritual leaders share their ideas and experience with us.
6 x 9, 456 pp, Quality PB, 978-1-58023-093-3 **$19.99**

Bringing the Psalms to Life: How to Understand and Use the Book of Psalms
By Daniel F. Polish 6 x 9, 208 pp, Quality PB, 978-1-58023-157-2 **$16.95**;
HC, 978-1-58023-077-3 **$21.95**

God & the Big Bang: Discovering Harmony between Science & Spirituality
By Daniel C. Matt 6 x 9, 216 pp, Quality PB, 978-1-879045-89-7 **$16.99**

Minding the Temple of the Soul: Balancing Body, Mind, and Spirit through Traditional Jewish Prayer, Movement, and Meditation *By Tamar Frankiel, PhD, and Judy Greenfeld*
7 x 10, 184 pp, illus., Quality PB, 978-1-879045-64-4 **$16.95**

One God Clapping: The Spiritual Path of a Zen Rabbi *By Alan Lew with Sherril Jaffe*
5½ x 8½, 336 pp, Quality PB, 978-1-58023-115-2 **$16.95**

There Is No Messiah ... and You're It: The Stunning Transformation of Judaism's Most Provocative Idea *By Rabbi Robert N. Levine, DD*
6 x 9, 192 pp, Quality PB, 978-1-58023-255-5 **$16.99**

These Are the Words: A Vocabulary of Jewish Spiritual Life
By Arthur Green 6 x 9, 304 pp, Quality PB, 978-1-58023-107-7 **$18.95**

Spirituality/Lawrence Kushner

Filling Words with Light: Hasidic and Mystical Reflections on Jewish Prayer
By Lawrence Kushner and Nehemia Polen
5½ x 8½, 176 pp, Quality PB, 978-1-58023-238-8 **$16.99**; HC, 978-1-58023-216-6 **$21.99**

The Book of Letters: A Mystical Hebrew Alphabet
Popular HC Edition, 6 x 9, 80 pp, 2-color text, 978-1-879045-00-2 **$24.95**
Collector's Limited Edition, 9 x 12, 80 pp, gold foil embossed pages, w/limited edition silkscreened
print, 978-1-879045-04-0 **$349.00**

The Book of Miracles: A Young Person's Guide to Jewish Spiritual Awareness
6 x 9, 96 pp, 2-color illus., HC, 978-1-879045-78-1 **$16.95** *For ages 9 and up*

The Book of Words: Talking Spiritual Life, Living Spiritual Talk
6 x 9, 160 pp, Quality PB, 978-1-58023-020-9 **$16.95**

Eyes Remade for Wonder: A Lawrence Kushner Reader   *Introduction by Thomas Moore*
6 x 9, 240 pp, Quality PB, 978-1-58023-042-1 **$18.95**

God Was in This Place & I, i Did Not Know: Finding Self, Spirituality and
Ultimate Meaning   6 x 9, 192 pp, Quality PB, 978-1-879045-33-0 **$16.95**

Honey from the Rock: An Introduction to Jewish Mysticism
6 x 9, 176 pp, Quality PB, 978-1-58023-073-5 **$16.95**

Invisible Lines of Connection: Sacred Stories of the Ordinary
5½ x 8½, 160 pp, Quality PB, 978-1-879045-98-9 **$15.95**

Jewish Spirituality—A Brief Introduction for Christians
5½ x 8½, 112 pp, Quality PB, 978-1-58023-150-3 **$12.95**

The River of Light: Jewish Mystical Awareness
6 x 9, 192 pp, Quality PB, 978-1-58023-096-4 **$16.95**

The Way Into Jewish Mystical Tradition
6 x 9, 224 pp, Quality PB, 978-1-58023-200-5 **$18.99**; HC, 978-1-58023-029-2 **$21.95**

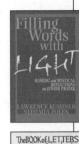

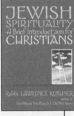

Spirituality/Prayer

My People's Passover Haggadah: Traditional Texts, Modern Commentaries
Edited by Rabbi Lawrence A. Hoffman, PhD, and David Arnow, PhD   Diverse commentaries
on the traditional Passover Haggadah—in two volumes!   Vol. 1: 7 x 10, 304 pp, HC
978-1-58023-354-5 **$24.99** Vol. 2: 7 x 10, 320 pp, HC, 978-1-58023-346-0 **$24.99**

Witnesses to the One: The Spiritual History of the Sh'ma   By Rabbi Joseph B. Meszler;
Foreword by Rabbi Elyse Goldstein   6 x 9, 176 pp, HC, 978-1-58023-309-5 **$19.99**

My People's Prayer Book Series

Traditional Prayers, Modern Commentaries   *Edited by Rabbi Lawrence A. Hoffman*
Provides diverse and exciting commentary to the traditional liturgy, helping modern
men and women find new wisdom in Jewish prayer, and bring liturgy into their lives.
Each book includes Hebrew text, modern translation, and commentaries from all
perspectives of the Jewish world.

Vol. 1—The *Sh'ma* and Its Blessings
 7 x 10, 168 pp, HC, 978-1-879045-79-8 **$24.99**

Vol. 2—The *Amidah*
 7 x 10, 240 pp, HC, 978-1-879045-80-4 **$24.95**

Vol. 3—*P'sukei D'zimrah* (Morning Psalms)
 7 x 10, 240 pp, HC, 978-1-879045-81-1 **$24.95**

Vol. 4—*Seder K'riat Hatorah* (The Torah Service)
 7 x 10, 264 pp, HC, 978-1-879045-82-8 **$23.95**

Vol. 5—*Birkhot Hashachar* (Morning Blessings)
 7 x 10, 240 pp, HC, 978-1-879045-83-5 **$24.95**

Vol. 6—*Tachanun* and Concluding Prayers
 7 x 10, 240 pp, HC, 978-1-879045-84-2 **$24.95**

Vol. 7—Shabbat at Home
 7 x 10, 240 pp, HC, 978-1-879045-85-9 **$24.95**

Vol. 8—*Kabbalat Shabbat* (Welcoming Shabbat in the Synagogue)
 7 x 10, 240 pp, HC, 978-1-58023-121-3 **$24.99**

Vol. 9—Welcoming the Night: *Minchah* and *Ma'ariv* (Afternoon and
 Evening Prayer) 7 x 10, 272 pp, HC, 978-1-58023-262-3 **$24.99**

Vol. 10—Shabbat Morning: *Shacharit* and *Musaf* (Morning and
 Additional Services) 7 x 10, 240 pp, HC, 978-1-58023-240-1 **$24.99**

Congregation Resources

Inspired Jewish Leadership: Practical Approaches to Building Strong Communities
By Dr. Erica Brown 6 x 9, 256 pp, HC, 978-1-58023-361-3 **$24.99**

Becoming a Congregation of Learners: Learning as a Key to Revitalizing
Congregational Life By Isa Aron, PhD; Foreword by Rabbi Lawrence A. Hoffman
6 x 9, 304 pp, Quality PB, 978-1-58023-089-6 **$19.95**

Finding a Spiritual Home: How a New Generation of Jews Can Transform the
American Synagogue By Rabbi Sidney Schwarz
6 x 9, 352 pp, Quality PB, 978-1-58023-185-5 **$19.95**

Jewish Pastoral Care, 2nd Edition: A Practical Handbook from Traditional &
Contemporary Sources Edited by Rabbi Dayle A. Friedman, MSW, MAJCS, BCC
6 x 9, 528 pp, HC, 978-1-58023-221-0 **$40.00**

Jewish Spiritual Direction: An Innovative Guide from Traditional and Contemporary
Sources Edited by Rabbi Howard A. Addison and Barbara Eve Breitman
6 x 9, 368 pp, HC, 978-1-58023-230-2 **$30.00**

The Self-Renewing Congregation: Organizational Strategies for Revitalizing
Congregational Life By Isa Aron, PhD; Foreword by Dr. Ron Wolfson
6 x 9, 304 pp, Quality PB, 978-1-58023-166-4 **$19.95**

Spiritual Community: The Power to Restore Hope, Commitment and Joy
By Rabbi David A. Teutsch, PhD 5½ x 8½, 144 pp, HC, 978-1-58023-270-8 **$19.99**

The Spirituality of Welcoming: How to Transform Your Congregation into a
Sacred Community By Dr. Ron Wolfson 6 x 9, 224 pp, Quality PB, 978-1-58023-244-9 **$19.99**

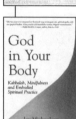

Rethinking Synagogues: A New Vocabulary for Congregational Life
By Rabbi Lawrence A. Hoffman 6 x 9, 240 pp, Quality PB, 978-1-58023-248-7 **$19.99**

Meditation

The Handbook of Jewish Meditation Practices
A Guide for Enriching the Sabbath and Other Days of Your Life
By Rabbi David A. Cooper Easy-to-learn meditation techniques.
6 x 9, 208 pp, Quality PB, 978-1-58023-102-2 **$16.95**

Discovering Jewish Meditation: Instruction & Guidance for Learning an Ancient
Spiritual Practice By Nan Fink Gefen 6 x 9, 208 pp, Quality PB, 978-1-58023-067-4 **$16.95**

Meditation from the Heart of Judaism: Today's Teachers Share Their Practices,
Techniques, and Faith Edited by Avram Davis
6 x 9, 256 pp, Quality PB, 978-1-58023-049-0 **$16.95**

Ritual/Sacred Practice

The Jewish Dream Book: The Key to Opening the Inner Meaning of
Your Dreams By Vanessa L. Ochs with Elizabeth Ochs; Full-color illus. by Kristina Swarner
Instructions for how modern people can perform ancient Jewish dream practices
and dream interpretations drawn from the Jewish wisdom tradition.
8 x 8, 128 pp, Full-color illus., Deluxe PB w/flaps, 978-1-58023-132-9 **$16.95**

God in Your Body: Kabbalah, Mindfulness and Embodied Spiritual Practice
By Jay Michaelson
The first comprehensive treatment of the body in Jewish spiritual practice and an
essential guide to the sacred. 6 x 9, 288 pp, Quality PB, 978-1-58023-304-0 **$18.99**

The Book of Jewish Sacred Practices: CLAL's Guide to Everyday & Holiday
Rituals & Blessings Edited by Rabbi Irwin Kula and Vanessa L. Ochs, PhD
6 x 9, 368 pp, Quality PB, 978-1-58023-152-7 **$18.95**

Jewish Ritual: A Brief Introduction for Christians
By Rabbi Kerry M. Olitzky and Rabbi Daniel Judson
5½ x 8½, 144 pp, Quality PB, 978-1-58023-210-4 **$14.99**

The Rituals & Practices of a Jewish Life: A Handbook for Personal Spiritual
Renewal Edited by Rabbi Kerry M. Olitzky and Rabbi Daniel Judson
6 x 9, 272 pp, illus., Quality PB, 978-1-58023-169-5 **$18.95**

The Sacred Art of Lovingkindness: Preparing to Practice
By Rabbi Rami Shapiro 5½ x 8½, 176 pp, Quality PB, 978-1-59473-151-8 **$16.99**
(A book from SkyLight Paths, Jewish Lights' sister imprint)

Social Justice

Conscience: The Duty to Obey and the Duty to Disobey
By Rabbi Harold M. Schulweis
This clarion call to rethink our moral and political behavior examines the idea of conscience and the role conscience plays in our relationships to governments, law, ethics, religion, human nature, God—and to each other.
6 x 9, 160 pp, HC, 978-1-58023-375-0 **$19.99**

Judaism and Justice: The Jewish Passion to Repair the World
By Rabbi Sidney Schwarz; Foreword by Ruth Messinger
Explores the relationship between Judaism, social justice and the Jewish identity of American Jews, offering new ways to understand these important aspects of Jewish life.
6 x 9, 352 pp, Quality PB, 978-1-58023-353-8 **$19.99**; HC, 978-1-58023-312-5 **$24.99**

Shared Dreams: Martin Luther King, Jr. & the Jewish Community
By Rabbi Marc Schneier; Preface by Martin Luther King III
6 x 9, 240 pp, Quality PB, 978-1-58023-273-9 **$18.99**

Spiritual Activism: A Jewish Guide to Leadership and Repairing the World
By Rabbi Avraham Weiss; Foreword by Alan M. Dershowitz
6 x 9, 224 pp, HC, 978-1-58023-355-2 **$24.99**

Righteous Indignation: A Jewish Call for Justice
Edited by Rabbi Or N. Rose, Jo Ellen Green Kaiser and Margie Klein; Foreword by Rabbi David Ellenson
Leading progressive Jewish activists are gathered together in one groundbreaking volume as they explore meaningful intellectual and spiritual foundations for their social justice work.
6 x 9, 384 pp, HC, 978-1-58023-336-1 **$24.99**

Spirituality/Women's Interest

The Quotable Jewish Woman: Wisdom, Inspiration & Humor from the Mind & Heart
Edited and compiled by Elaine Bernstein Partnow
6 x 9, 496 pp, Quality PB, 978-1-58023-236-4 **$19.99**; HC, 978-1-58023-193-0 **$29.99**

The Divine Feminine in Biblical Wisdom Literature
Selections Annotated & Explained
Translated and Annotated by Rabbi Rami Shapiro
5½ x 8½, 240 pp, Quality PB, 978-1-59473-109-9 **$16.99**
(A book from SkyLight Paths, Jewish Lights' sister imprint)

The Women's Haftarah Commentary: New Insights from Women Rabbis on the 54 Weekly Haftarah Portions, the 5 Megillot & Special Shabbatot
Edited by Rabbi Elyse Goldstein
In this groundbreaking book, more than fifty women rabbis come together to offer us inspiring insights on the Torah, in a week-by-week format.
6 x 9, 560 pp, Quality PB, 978-1-58023-371-2 **$19.99**; HC, 978-1-58023-133-6 **$39.99**

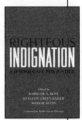

The Women's Torah Commentary: New Insights from Women Rabbis on the 54 Weekly Torah Portions
Edited by Rabbi Elyse Goldstein
This compendium will challenge—and possibly change—the way you experience Judaism as it illuminates the historical significance of female portrayals in the Haftarah and the Five Megillot.
6 x 9, 496 pp, Quality PB, 978-1-58023-370-5 **$19.99**; HC, 978-1-58023-076-6 **$34.95**

The Year Mom Got Religion: One Woman's Midlife Journey into Judaism
By Lee Meyerhoff Hendler
6 x 9, 208 pp, Quality PB, 978-1-58023-070-4 **$15.95**

See Holidays for *The Women's Passover Companion: Women's Reflections on the Festival of Freedom* and *The Women's Seder Sourcebook: Rituals & Readings for Use at the Passover Seder.*

About Jewish Lights

People of all faiths and backgrounds yearn for books that attract, engage, educate, and spiritually inspire.

Our principal goal is to stimulate thought and help all people learn about who the Jewish People are, where they come from, and what the future can be made to hold. While people of our diverse Jewish heritage are the primary audience, our books speak to people in the Christian world as well and will broaden their understanding of Judaism and the roots of their own faith.

We bring to you authors who are at the forefront of spiritual thought and experience. While each has something different to say, they all say it in a voice that you can hear.

Our books are designed to welcome you and then to engage, stimulate, and inspire. We judge our success not only by whether or not our books are beautiful and commercially successful, but by whether or not they make a difference in your life.

For your information and convenience, at the back of this book we have provided a list of other Jewish Lights books you might find interesting and useful. They cover all the categories of your life:

Bar/Bat Mitzvah	Life Cycle
Bible Study / Midrash	Meditation
Children's Books	Parenting
Congregation Resources	Prayer
Current Events / History	Ritual / Sacred Practice
Ecology / Environment	Spirituality
Fiction: Mystery, Science Fiction	Theology / Philosophy
Grief / Healing	Travel
Holidays / Holy Days	12-Step
Inspiration	Women's Interest
Kabbalah / Mysticism / Enneagram	

Stuart M. Matlins, Publisher

Or phone, fax, mail or e-mail to: **JEWISH LIGHTS Publishing**
Sunset Farm Offices, Route 4 • P.O. Box 237 • Woodstock, Vermont 05091
Tel: (802) 457-4000 • Fax: (802) 457-4004 • www.jewishlights.com
Credit card orders: (800) 962-4544 (8:30AM–5:30PM ET Monday–Friday)
Generous discounts on quantity orders. SATISFACTION GUARANTEED. Prices subject to change.

For more information about each book, visit our website at www.jewishlights.com